*Revealed at last my theological, scientific, systematic and methodical approach to financial increase, prosperity and eventually wealthy. I introduce to you Finanatomy, the economic plan for financial success.*

D1431734

# Money Answers All Things

*To: Jimmy Bryant*

*God wants you to prosper.*

*"A feast is made for laughter, and wine maketh merry: but money answereth all things." Ecclesiastes 10:19*

# Dexter L Jones

**UWriteIt Publishing Company**
**Goldsboro, NC USA**
http://www.moneyanswersallthings.org

Money Answers All Things by Dexter Jones
Copyright © 2013 Dexter Jones

**ISBN-13: 978-0615788043 (UWriteIt Publishing Company)**
**ISBN-10: 0615788041**

First Printing – April 2013

This publication is designed to provide information in regard to the subject matter covered. It is published with the understanding that the authors are not engaged in rendering legal counsel or other professional services. If legal advice or other professional advice is required, the services of a professional person should be sought.

Printed in the U.S.A.

## Dedication

I dedicate this book to my Heavenly Father God, my Lord and Savior Jesus Christ and the Person of the Holy Spirit. I praise Almighty God for giving me the gift of writing, with the ability to be able to reach multitudes of people with the written word. I thank you Father for the opportunity to write this book "MONEY ANSWERS ALL THINGS", for multitudes of individuals are having problems understanding how money works and how to make it work for them. If this is you I dedicate this book to you also.

I dedicate this book to my most precious wife **Princess Petula**, honey I Love You and thank God for bringing you into my life, you are one in a billion.

As I do in all my books I dedicate this book to my beautiful and precious daughter **Jasmine,** a daughter that I am so proud of that brings me constant happiness. Jasmine I love you and thank God that you are a focused young lady even in your teen years.

Also, to my son **Brandon**, a young man that is focused and one that I am proud to say, in this day and time you really know how to take care of your own. Keep up the GREAT work!

## Table of Contents

## Introduction

## Money in the Fishes Mouth

*"And when they were come to Capernaum, they that received tribute money came to Peter, and said, Doth not your master pay tribute? He saith, Yes. And when he was come into the house, Jesus prevented him, saying, What thinkest thou, Simon? Of whom do the kings of the earth take custom or tribute? Of their own children, or of strangers? Peter saith unto him, Of strangers. Jesus saith unto him, Then are the children free. Notwithstanding, lest we should offend them, go thou to the sea, and cast an hook, and take up the fish that first cometh up; and when thou hast opened his mouth, thou shalt find **a piece of money**: that take, and give unto them for me and thee."*
*Matthew 17:24-27*

## The Widow's Oil and Meal Increased

*"And the word of the LORD came unto him, saying, Arise, get thee to Zarephath, which belongeth to Zidon, and dwell there: behold, I have commanded a widow woman there to sustain thee. So he arose and went to Zarephath. And when he came to the gate of the city, behold, the widow woman was there gathering of sticks: and he called to her, and said, Fetch me, I pray thee, a little water in a vessel, that I may drink. And as she was going to fetch it, he called to her, and said, Bring me, I pray thee, a morsel of bread in thine hand. And she said, As the LORD thy God liveth, I have not a cake, but a handful of meal in a barrel, and a little oil in a cruse: and, behold, I am gathering two sticks, that I may go in and dress it for me and my son, that we may eat it, and die. And Elijah said unto her, Fear not; go and do as thou hast said: but make me thereof a little cake first, and bring it unto me, and after make for thee and for thy son. For thus saith the LORD God of Israel, The barrel of meal shall not waste, neither shall the cruse of oil fail, until the day that the LORD sendeth rain upon the earth. And she went and did according to the saying of Elijah: and she, and he, and her house, did eat many days. **And the barrel of meal wasted not, neither did the cruse of oil fail,** according to the word of the LORD, which he spake by Elijah." 1 Kings 17:8-16*

## The Water Made Wine

*"And the third day there was a marriage in Cana of Galilee; and the mother of Jesus was there: And both Jesus was called, and his disciples, to the marriage. And when they wanted wine, the mother of Jesus saith unto him, They have no wine. Jesus saith unto her, Woman, what have I to do with thee? Mine hour is not yet come. His mother saith unto the servants, Whatsoever he saith unto you, do it. And there was set there six waterpots of stone, after the manner of the purifying of the Jews, containing two or three firkins apiece. Jesus saith unto them, Fill the waterpots with water. And they filled them up to the brim. And he saith unto them, Draw out now, and bear unto the governor of the feast. And they bare it. When the ruler of the feast had tasted the water that was made wine, and knew not whence it was: (but the servants which drew the water knew;) the governor of the feast called the bridegroom, And saith unto him, Every man at the beginning doth set forth good wine; and when men have well drunk, then that which is worse: but thou hast kept the good wine until now. **This beginning of miracles did Jesus in Cana of Galilee, and manifested forth his glory; and his disciples believed on him.**" St. John 2:1-11*

## The Five Thousand Fed

*"And Jesus, when he came out, saw much people, and was moved with compassion toward them, because they were as sheep not having a shepherd: and he began to teach them many things. And when the day was now far spent, his disciples came unto him, and said, This is a desert place, and now the time is far passed: Send them away, that they may go into the country round about, and into the villages, and buy themselves bread: for they have nothing to eat. He answered and said unto them, Give ye them to eat. And they say unto him, Shall we go and buy two hundred pennyworth of bread, and give them to eat? He saith unto them, How many loaves have ye? Go and see And when they knew, they say, Five, and two fishes. And he commanded them to make all sit down by companies upon the green grass. And they sat down in ranks, by hundreds, and by fifties. And when he had taken the five loaves and the two fishes, he looked up to heaven, and blessed, and brake the loaves, and gave them to his disciples to set before them; and the two fishes divided he among them all. And they did all eat, and were filled. **And they took up twelve baskets full of the fragments, and of the fishes. And they that did eat of the loaves were about five thousand men.**" St. Mark 6:34-44*

## The Net Full of Fishes

*"And it came to pass, that, as the people pressed upon him to hear the word of God, he stood by the lake of Gennesaret, And saw two ships standing by the lake: but the fishermen were gone out of them, and were washing their nets. And he entered into one of the ships, which was Simon's, and prayed him that he would thrust out a little from the land. And he sat down, and taught the people out of the ship. Now when he had left speaking, he said unto Simon, Launch out into the deep, and let down your nets for a draught. And he answering said unto him, Master, we have toiled all the night, and have taken nothing: nevertheless at thy word I will let down the net. And when they had this done, they inclosed a great multitude of fishes: and their net brake. And they beckoned unto their partners, which were in the other ship, that they should come and help them. And they came, and filled both the ships, so that they began to sink. When Simon Peter saw it, he fell down at Jesus knees, saying, Depart from me; for I am a sinful man, O, Lord.* **For he was astonished, and all that were with him, at the draught of the fishes which they had taken."** *St. Luke 5:1-9*

## TESTIMONY

This book is the truth the whole truth and nothing but the truth so help me God. The things that you are about to read in this book WORKS! If you have a money matter or a financial situation you are just knowledge away from your deliverance. I am here to tell you as a living witness that truly Money Answers All Things and that God has made it so that money is the answer to your financial dilemma. Whatever monies you need for your situation(s) know that God is ready, willing and able to bring you out of your financially sick situation.

I know because I have been in a financial situation that was most pressing and urgent. I needed money to come out of my situation and it was a dire situation. I needed it yesterday and I was already in today and if I did not get it there would be great loss. I needed it badly!

Well, I am here to tell you that the Word still works and the God of Jehoshaphat in 2 Chronicles 20 is still fighting battles and allowing his people to walk away with abundance that they did not work for but God freely gave. God blessed me to receive $3,000 in my bank account and I don't know where it came from, so that we could go forth and fulfill an obligation. Just as the battle was already won and the victory was already wrought for me, God is no respecter of person and he will do the same for you. No matter what you may be facing do not focus on the bigness of your financial situation but focus on the bigness of your God. For he is well *"able to do exceeding abundantly above all that we ask or think, according to the power that worketh in us." Ephesians* 3:20 Hallelujah!!! **Today is your day of victory,** *lift your head up and let the King of Glory come in. Who is the King of glory? The LORD strong and mighty, the LORD mighty in battle. Lift up your heads, O ye gates; even lift them up, ye everlasting doors; and the King of glory shall come in. Who is the King of glory? The LORD of host, he is the King of glory. Selah Psalms 24:7-10*

## Introduction

This isn't just another book on money I guarantee you. However, money belongs to you just as much as it belongs to anyone else and in this book I will show you the kingdom secrets for acquiring money. In this book I will give you truths that you may have never heard of before. We will not focus on the many things that other money books focus on; much of this book will be based on what I term THE LAW OF ABSOLUTES. When you properly conform to the law of absolute it will never let you down.

However, if you violate the law of absolutes two things will manifest in the area of life you are focusing upon. Either you will experience from minor injury to death occurring. Also, the thing about the law of absolute is that it is inviolable and self-enforcing, it has a mind of its own and when it is violated it moves into action. However, when it is obeyed it likewise moves into action to bring forth success and happiness. In the area of money this law works with absolute certainty and infallibility. There is not a person on the face of the earth which the law of Absolutes will not work for in the area of money. Also, in this book you will learn about truth verses lies, hypothesis and even half-truths. When you come into the revelation of what truth can and will do for you, never again will you have any financial problems, no more money matters.

For *"ye shall know the truth, and the truth shall make*

*you free. If the Son therefore shall make you free, ye shall be free indeed." John 8:32,36* As a citizen of the kingdom you have been given dominion and authority over the earth and money is a part of the earth, it comes from the earth and I will show you how to attract money to you like iron to a magnet. Jesus our King was the truth and he lived and walked in the truth and it was no problem for him to get money out of the mouth of a fish or get money and things whenever he needed it.

The scripture says, *"And when they were come to Capernaum, they that received tribute money came to Peter, and said, Doth not your master pay tribute? He saith, Yes. And when he was come into the house, Jesus prevented him, saying, What thinkest thou, Simon? Of whom do the kings of the earth take custom or tribute? Of their own children, or of strangers? Peter saith unto him, Of strangers. Jesus saith unto him, Then are the children free. Notwithstanding, lest we should offend them, go thou to the sea, and cast an hook, and take up the fish that first cometh up; and when thou hast opened his mouth, thou shalt find **a piece of money**: that take, and give unto them for me and thee."* Matthew 17:24-27

Likewise you will learn how to know the truth and operate in the truth and allow that truth to manifest in your life in the area of money. Money, what a subject to write about, it's a subject that every person alive is confronted with, a subject that daily touches every person life. Many individuals try to avoid the subject of money as if it's some type of plague or disease. My objective in writing this book is to bring you face to face with money and help clean up your mind about this subject, so that you can stop fooling yourself and thinking of money as a dirty word. Through this book you will learn spiritual, mental and natural principles about how to attract money to you, also a scientific, systematic and methodical approach to financial increase, prosperity and eventually wealth. However, the mental and natural will be backed with the word of God exemplifying principles that He has instituted in the earth that will work for all. The Scripture stipulates this truth saying, *"Moreover the profit of the earth is for all: the king himself is served by the field." Ecclesiastes 5:9*

I want to get you on God's side and get your thinking in direct line with the word of God concerning money and money matters. When your thoughts about money are contrary to God's thoughts about money then you have been bamboozled and hoodwinked out of money that could now be in your possession. God's thoughts about money are, ***"money answereth all things** and **money is a defence." Ecclesiastes 10:19, 7:12*** If you don't see money as God sees it then the two of you don't agree on the topic of money. As a result, God will not walk with you in relations to this topic. When the topic of money comes up God will not give you wisdom or empower you to get it because you have no faith for it and no agreement with Him concerning money. For the Scripture says, *"Can two walk together, except they be agreed?" Amos 3:3*

My desire is that this book will bring about a change in your life about the wonderful and marvelous topic of money. Such a change that it will evoke you to go forth and acquire the financial increase, prosperity and wealth that God has for your life. God wants you to be successful and financially blessed, for your own life, the work of God and so that you can be a blessing to others. God told Abraham, *"And I will bless thee, and make thy name great; and thou shalt be a blessing." Genesis 12:2* Money is needed in this world and God wants you to have an abundance of it, now my question is do you want an abundance of it or do you just want to make ends meet? The choice is up to you why settle for little when God has so much to give? St. John 10:10

Also in this book you will learn about the awesome and amazing concept of FINANATOMY. Finanatomy is the science of the shape and structure of financial increase, financial prosperity and wealth. This book is not written to the Capitalist, the Rich and the Super Rich; to them such an economic plan is ludicrous and useless as far as financial advancement. However, to the 85-95% of the financial downtrodden it will be a ray of hope, a beacon on a hill and a financial compass to steer them out of financial disaster into financial freedom. Finanatomy is a problem solving approach to helping ordinary people get out of the rat race of living paycheck to paycheck, poverty and barely making ends meet. We will unfold in this book an economic plan that will take you from where you are to financial increase, from there to prosperity and then ultimately to wealth. I will break this concept down to a science, so that if you can read the words in this book, you can understand the simplicity of the finanatomy concept and apply it to your life. In order to break free there must be a combination of spiritual, mental and natural principles designed to work with absolute certainty. Principals that is just as sure as God Himself. Our focus will be concentrated upon the concept of **finanatomy**, which is defined as *the science of the shape and structure of financial increase, prosperity and wealth.*

We will focus on real issues, not pie in the sky theories or hypothesis. We will prove that the ordinary person can indeed experience and enjoy the American dream. Mankind was not destined to just be in the pursuit of happiness all of his life without being able to manifest his dream, right here, right now. And it's going to take money to be able to partake of the American dream. We will take a step-by-step approach to show the 85-95%, from the working couple, to the single man, the single woman, the single parent, the underclass, the working poor, the working class, the lower middle class, the upper middle class and all the 85-95% that struggles in their finances daily, how to apply finanatomy in their everyday life.

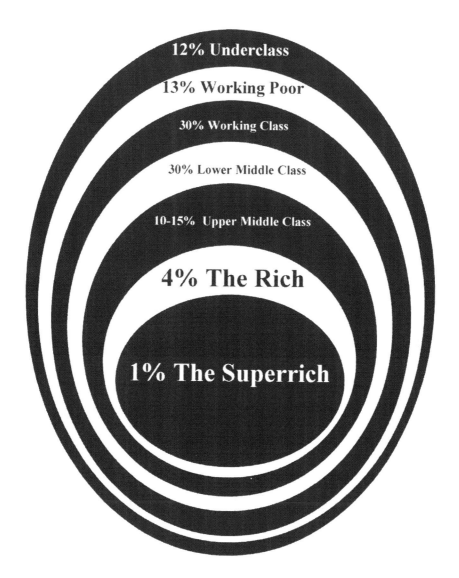

The statistics of America's financial situation is terrifying and it doesn't have to be that way. You have the haves and the have-nots and the gap between the two groups is immense. As we observe the financial debt which America at the writing of this book is in its truly unbelievable and downright catastrophic?

- America is at an almost 17 trillion dollar deficit.

- American's have over 900 billion dollars in credit card debt.

- A child is born into poverty every 1.2 seconds throughout the world.

- Over 60% of Americans live paycheck to paycheck part or all of the time.

- Nearly 95%of Americans 65 and older retire or die broke.

- The official poverty line for a family of 2 Adults and 1 child is $18,106.

- Over 1.46 million Americans filed bankruptcy in 2012.

- Taxpayers spend 220 billion dollars per year paying off interest on the national debt.

- Nearly 1 in 2 people have fallen into poverty or scraping by.

- Over 4 million Americans lost their home to foreclosure last year.

- Over 50% of marriages end in divorce due to money problems.

- When America had a time of productive gains the workers didn't share in those economic gains.

12% Underclass

13% Working Poor

30% Working Class

30% Lower Middle Class

10-15% Upper Middle Class

4% The Rich

1% The SuperRich
$1,000,000,000 or More

$1,000,000 or More

$100,000 - $200,000

$35,000 -$75,000

$16,000 - $30,000

Extreme Poverty

Government Reliance

Finanatomy is the economic plan that will break the back of poverty and lack, and get your finances back on track. Here is your practical guide, your step-by-step approach to financial increase, prosperity and ultimately wealth. It's time for a change; we can't keep doing business the same old way and expect different results. That change will come through the concept of finanatomy.

As a citizen of the kingdom you are called to live by your faith and operate in the realm of the spirit. Either you're living your life in faith and attracting the finances that you desire or you're living your life in fear and living a life of barely making ends meet. Most people are living in fear and the thoughts which are deposited deep in their spirit are thoughts such as:

- It's hard to get ahead financially in life.
- Maybe I am destined for financial failure.
- Sinners and unbelievers can prosper easily.
- Blah, Blah, Blah, etc...

When you live in fear it creates a magnetic field that pulls to you the thing that you feared. Job said, *"For the thing which I greatly feared is come upon me and that which I was afraid of is come unto me." Job 3:25* You must stop operating in fear, fear is of the devil and it causes uncertainty and a feeling of doubt about what you're asking. You must get rid of the spirit of fear, that spirit that causes you to be afraid, anxiety, panic, trepidation, uncertainty and distrust. The word of God says, *"For God hath not given us the spirit of fear, but of power, love and a sound mind." 2 Timothy 1:7*

As a citizen of the Kingdom it's time to learn how to move in the spirit realm for your finances and live by the faith which never fails. When you move in the spirit realm you call those things that do not exist in the natural realm but does exist in the spirit realm to become a material reality in your life. The word of God says, *"Even God (you must begin to act just like God), who quickeneth the dead, and calleth those things which be not as though they were." Romans 4:17* It is time to cast aside the doubt and fear and begin to live in belief and faith where there is unlimited blessings and liberty in the spirit.

No matter what you may have believed or witness in your life in the past as far as your finances is concerned I want you to know that you don't have to live the present reality you're living; you can create a new reality by the Spirit of God. As a citizen of the kingdom God has a better plan and method for you to get your finances in order so that you can begin to prosper. It's time for you to create your realities and in order to do that we will present to you Kingdom Principles. Get ready to go on a spiritual journey of adventure and intrigue into the realm of the spirit where things are continually revealed and there is life more abundantly.

*Get ready to say good-by to your financial failures and economic woes as you learn what kingdom principles and finanatomy can do for you to bring about a change in your life, starting today.*

## Where Are You Today?

1. *How much money did you save last year?*_____
2. *How much money did you save the year before?*_____
3. *How much money did you save the year before that?*_____
4. *How much money did you save the year before that?*_____
5. *How much money do you have in your savings now?*_____
6. *Would you like to have $1000 in your savings Yes___ No___?*

Well, I can show you how to make that happen GUARANTEED. Then from there I can show you financial prosperity and then ultimately we will discover the keys to obtain wealth.

This book can and will bring you out. Within this book is the greatest financial increase, prosperity and wealth creation strategy you will ever come across. What I want you to commit to from this day forward and before you even go to the next page is to pay the price in application to do what this book tells you, so that you can get from where you are to where you desire to be. The greatest principles in the world will not work unless they are applied. You are about to learn infallible and time honored principles that will give you financial increase, prosperity and eventually wealth, as sure as the night follows the day and these principles belong to you just as much as they belongs to anyone else.

*"I _____, commit to applying these time honored and tested principles in my life. I will give my all to the application of these strategies so that I can start my journey to financial increase, prosperity and eventually wealth. If it's to be, it's up to me"*

*Date:_____ Signature:_____*

## *GET READY, GET SET, RECEIVE*

This is the book that you always wanted in your possession and just to show you that this book is unlike any book on money that you've ever purchased, get ready to receive a blessing.

This book is ordained of God and it is anointed to destroy the yoke of poverty over your life. Purchasing this book is one of the greatest investments that you will ever make in a financial book. God wants you to know that the day of miracles has not ceased because the God of miracles still lives.

Individuals that have read this book have suddenly found amazing and miraculous things happening for them in the financial and material realm of life. We're not talking about in a year's time but within days and weeks. So get ready to receive not only what you paid for this book back in either the financial or material realm but above that several times over within days or weeks.

The Lord wants you to know that this is not just another book on money but it is a book ordained of God to instruct you about how to come out of poverty and lack and come into financial increase, prosperity and eventually wealth. We look forward to hearing your testimony about what the Lord has done for you. **GET READY, GET SET, RECEIVE!!!**

# 1
# The King and the Kingdom

*"Now after that John was put in prison, Jesus came into Galilee, preaching the gospel of the kingdom of God." Mark 1:14*

In order to understand kingdom principles we must first delve into the idea of who is King and what does the kingdom consist of. In the book of Matthew 2:2, we first hear of Jesus being called King in the scripture stating, *"Where is he that is born King of the Jews? for we have seen his star in the east, and are come to worship him."*

(Another instance we hear Jesus claiming himself as King saying, *"Then Pilate entered into the judgment hall again, and called Jesus, and said unto him, Art thou the King of the Jews? Jesus answered him, Sayest thou this thing of thyself, or did others tell it thee of me? Pilate answered, Am I a Jew? Thine own nation and the chief priest have delivered thee unto me: what hast thou done? Jesus answered, My kingdom is not of this world: if my kingdom were of this world, then would my servants fight, that I should not be delivered to the Jews: but now is my kingdom not from thence. Pilate therefore said unto him, Art thou a king then? Jesus answered, Thou sayest that I am a king. **To this end was I born, and for this cause came I into the world, that I should bear witness unto the truth.** Every one that is of the truth heareth my voice." John 18:33-37*

Here we see Jesus proclaiming himself as King and he has come forth to preach the gospel or good news of the kingdom. In his first message about the kingdom it says, *"From that time Jesus began to preach, and to say, Repent: for the kingdom of heaven is at hand."* *Matthew 4:17* Jesus message was a proclamation to turn individuals from their ways and turn them to the ways of the kingdom. As a King he has come forth to proclaim his kingdom and invite all that will to come and partake of the kingdom.

His kingdom is not an earthly kingdom that you can see with the natural eye. It is not a visible kingdom that you can touch with your hands but it is a spiritual kingdom and you enter into it by faith through salvation. You cannot join it nor buy your way into it you must be born into it by way of the Spirit. You have already been born once by the birth of your parents but now you must be born from above.

Jesus told Nicodemus, *"Verily, verily, I say unto thee, Except a man be born again, he cannot see the kingdom of God. Nicodemus saith unto him, How can a man be born when he is old? can he enter the second time into his mother's womb, and be born? Jesus answered, Verily, verily, I say unto thee, Except a man be born of water and of the Spirit, he cannot enter into the kingdom of God. That which is born of the flesh is flesh; and that which is born of the Spirit is spirit. Marvel not that I said unto thee, Ye must be born again."* John 3:3-7

The message of the King is plain and simple, you must be born again, and you must repent and turn from your ways and obey the ways of the kingdom.

Except you be born again you cannot see, believe nor know the things of the kingdom because they are revealed to you by the Spirit of God. He that does not have the Spirit of God does not belong to God and cannot know the things of God. *"For what man knoweth the things of a man, save the spirit of man which is in him? even so the things of God knoweth no man, but the Spirit of God. Now we have received, not the spirit of the world, but the spirit which is of God; that we might know the things that are freely given to us of God. Which things also we speak, not in the words which man's wisdom teacheth, but which the Holy Ghost teacheth; comparing spiritual things with spiritual. But the natural man receiveth not the things of the Spirit of God: for they are foolishness unto him: neither can he know them, because they are spiritually discerned."* 1 Corinthians 2:11-14

As citizens of the kingdom you must know what the kingdom of God is and what it isn't. Another definition of the kingdom according to the Kings manual (the Bible) is that the kingdom is, *"righteousness, peace and joy in the Holy Ghost."* Romans 14:17 In other words righteousness is the right standing that citizens has with the King that comes by acceptance of the King. Peace and joy in the Holy Ghost are the fruit of the Spirit that is given to all citizens of the kingdom. Those that are foreigners and aliens which are not a part of the kingdom desires these things but until they accept the King they will never have them. This is why a citizen must obey the principles of the kingdom in order to partake of the things that belong to all citizens.

In this book you will learn things that concern the kingdom about finances that will seem foolish to the natural man. All of your financial ideas that do not come from the Kings' manual (**the Bible**) are foolish in the eyes of the King. When your ideas are contrary to the ideas of the King and his kingdom you are a rebel and a disobedient person to the King.

The King has one main concern and that is his kingdom and the manual by which his kingdom is ran. The most important thing in the kingdom is the manual which consist of the words of the King. The kingdom is the sphere of God's sovereign rule and domain. Because the kingdom is not an earthly kingdom that can be seen naturally it is still as real as any earthly kingdom. However, it is revealed to those that accept the teaching of the King and obey his words. The kingdom is spiritual and cannot be seen by sight but by faith and if you can receive it by faith you will have no need of an observation of the kingdom.

The Pharisees in doubt asked Jesus about the kingdom saying, *"And when he was demanded of the Pharisees, when the kingdom of God should come, he answered them and said, The kingdom of God cometh not with observation (by sight and what you can see naturally): Neither shall they say, Lo here! or, lo there! for, behold, the kingdom of God is within you." Luke 17:20-21* When you accept the King you also have the kingdom for the King and his kingdom are one. When it says the kingdom of God is within you it means the King is in your midst and now that the King is your Lord and abides in you his rule and reign and all that he is and has is dwelling in your spirit man.

As a citizen of the kingdom you come under the rule of the King and follow the laws of the kingdom. Every citizen of the kingdom favors the King and his laws and daily abides by them. As citizens, *"Now therefore ye are no more strangers and foreigners, but fellow citizens with the saints, and of the household of God." Ephesians 2:19*

Your mission as a citizen is to learn the commandments and words from the manual of the King, *"And thou shalt love the LORD thy God (the King) with all thy heart, and with all thy soul, and with all thy mind, and with all thy strength: this is the first commandment. And the second is like, namely this, Thou shalt love thy neighbor as thyself. There is none other commandments greater than these. Mark 12:30-31*

As a citizen of the kingdom here are some of the things that you must do and know:

*"But seek ye first the kingdom of God, and his righteousness; and all these things shall be added unto you." Matthew 6:33*

*"For the kingdom of God is not meat and drink; but*

righteousness, and peace, and joy in the Holy Ghost." Romans 14:17

"For the kingdom of God is not in word, but in power." 1 Corinthians 4:20

"Know ye not that the unrighteous shall not inherit the kingdom of God? Be not deceived: neither fornicators, nor idolaters, nor adulterers, nor effeminate, nor abusers of themselves with mankind, Nor thieves, nor covetous, nor drunkards, nor revilers, nor extortioners, shall inherit the kingdom of God." 1 Corinthians 6:9-10

"Who hath delivered us from the power of darkness, and hath translated us into the kingdom of his dear Son." Colossians 1:13

"And I will give unto thee the keys of the kingdom of heaven: and whatsoever thou shalt bind on earth, shall be bound in heaven: and whatsoever thou shalt loose on earth shall be loosed in heaven." Matthew 16:19

Herein is the message in its simplicity, if you obey the words of the King you are a child of the King and a citizen of the kingdom, "And if children, then heirs; heirs of God, and joint heirs with Christ." Romans 8:17 "Fear not, little flock; for it is your Father's good pleasure to give you the kingdom."Luke 12:32 Now let's go learn the things that essential for citizens of the kingdom to know so that you can go forth and possess the financial life that is equivalent for a King's Kid.

# 2
# Faith

*"Through faith we understand that the worlds were framed by the word of God, so that things which are seen were not made of things which do appear." Hebrews 11:3*

Faith is the opposite of fear. Either you're living your life from faith or you're living it from fear. In order to attract finances into your life you must begin to live a life of faith. Faith is of the spirit and it operates in the unseen realm because the things which are seen were not made of things which do appear. Because you cannot mix fear and faith together either fear or faith is having the preeminence in your financial life at this very moment and our objective through this book is to help you get rid of fear so you can live by faith.

- Faith is belief in the unseen.
- Faith is belief in the spiritual.
- Faith is belief in the positive.
- Faith will cause you to operate in the unseen realm.
- Faith is unlimited and liberty.

Faith creates a magnetic field that pulls to you the things you believe for. In the book of Hebrew we have a list of the heroes of faith that obtained a good report as a result of their faith. It says, *"For by* it the elders obtained a good report. Through faith we understand that the worlds were framed by the word of God, so that things which are seen were not made of things which do appear. By faith Abel offered unto God a more excellent sacrifice than Cain, by which he obtained witness that he was righteous, God testifying of his gifts: and by it he being dead yet speaketh. By faith Enoch was translated that he should not see death; and was not found, because God had translated him: for before his translation he had this testimony, that he pleased God. But without faith it is impossible to please him: for he that cometh to God must believe that he is, and that he is a rewarder of them that diligently seek him.

By faith Noah, being warned of God of things not seen as yet, moved with fear, prepared an ark to the saving of his house; by the which he condemned the world, and became heir of the righteousness which is by faith. By faith Abraham, when he was called to go out into a place which he should after receive for an inheritance, obeyed; and he went out, not knowing whither he went. By faith he sojourned in the land of promise, as in a strange country, dwelling in tabernacles with Isaac and Jacob, the heirs with him of the same promise: For he looked for a city which hath foundations, whose builder and maker is God. Through faith also Sara herself received strength to conceive seed, and was delivered of a child when she was past age, because she judged him faithful who had promised. By faith Abraham, when he was tried, offered up Isaac: and he that had received the promises offered up his only begotten son, Of whom it was said, That in Isaac shall thy seed be called: Accounting that God was able to raise him up, even from the dead; from whence also he received him in a figure. By faith Isaac blessed Jacob and Esau concerning things to come. By faith Jacob, when he was a dying, blessed both the sons of Joseph; and worshipped, leaning upon the top of his staff. By faith Joseph, when he died, made mention of the departing of the children of Israel; and gave commandment concerning his bones.

By faith Moses, when he was born, was hid three months of his parents, because they saw he was a proper child; and they were not afraid of the king's commandment. By faith Moses, when he was come to years, refused to be called the son of Pharaoh's daughter; Choosing rather to suffer affliction with the people of God, than to enjoy the pleasures of sin for a season; Esteeming the reproach of Christ greater riches than the treasures in Egypt: for he had respect unto the recompence of the reward. By faith he forsook Egypt, not fearing the wrath of the king: for he endured, as seeing him who is invisible. Through faith he kept the passover, and the sprinkling of blood, lest he that destroyed the firstborn should touch them. By faith they passed through the Red sea as by dry land: which the Egyptians assaying to do were drowned. By faith the walls of Jericho fell down, after they were compassed about seven days. By faith the harlot Rahab perished not with them that believed not, when she had received the spies with peace. And what shall I more say? for the time would fail me to tell of Gedeon, and of Barak, and of Samson, and of Jephthae; of David also, and Samuel, and of the prophets: Who through faith subdued kingdoms, wrought righteousness, obtained promises, *stopped the mouths of lions. Quenched the violence of fire, escaped the edge of the sword, out of weakness were made strong, waxed valiant in fight, turned to flight the armies of the aliens. Women received their dead raised to life again:" Hebrews 11:2-9, 17-35a*

As a citizen of the kingdom that desire to be financially free you must get rid of fear and replace it with faith. When you say such things as:

- It's hard to get ahead financially in life.
- I am destined to struggle all my life.
- I am doomed to living a life of barely making ends meet.
- The devil is keeping me in financial bondage?
- It seems like God is not hearing me.

When you say such things you are living in fear and are being overtaken by a spirit that causes you to be uncertain about your future. A spirit that causes anxiety in your life and distrust in your Creator who says, *"But seek ye first the kingdom of God and his righteousness and all these things shall be added unto you." Matthew 6:33*

Also when fear has the preeminence in your life it shows that you're not walking in perfect love for *"There is no fear in love; but perfect love casteth out fear: because fear hath torment. He that feareth is not made perfect in love." 1 John 4:18* The definition of torment means to have extreme pain, anguish, torture, misery, vexation and distress. How are you going to attract finances in your life with all these emotions going on in your heart and mind? The answer is you're not going to attract finances but just more paycheck to paycheck living and barely making ends meet. When God created Adam he put Adam in the Garden of Eden which was a place of plenty.

Likewise God has financial prosperity for you so that you can begin to live life more abundantly, but you must get rid of fear and learn to move in the realm of the spirit where the miraculous and the supernatural flows. For *"He is able to do exceeding abundantly above all we ask or think according to the power that worketh in us." Ephesians 3:20*

# 3
# The Law of Absolutes

*"So God created man in his own image, in the image of God created he him; male and female created he them." Genesis 1:27*

When God created man he gave him dominion and authority over all things. *"And God said, Let us make man in our image, after our likeness: and let them have dominion over the fish of the sea, and over the fowl of the air, and over the cattle, and over all the earth, and over every creeping thing that creepeth upon the earth." Genesis 1:26* When God created man some of the law of absolutes was already in effect others came into effect later. Adam experienced many of these Absolutes and obeyed them promptly and as long as he obeyed them, he prospered in everything he did. When he failed many of the Absolutes begin to work against him instead of for him. God has instituted many laws and principles in the earth that will work for you or against you, but his desire is that they work for you.

The law of absolutes is an infallible law. They are instituted to work for everyone regardless of race, religion, sex, personality or circumstance. When the law of absolutes is conformed with and followed it will never fail to work. In my research I have come across 12 Absolutes, there is no doubt more but these are the twelve majors that I will focus on in this writing.

These Absolutes are as following:

- God
- Gravity
- Time
- Seasons
- Aging
- Faith
- Sowing & Reaping
- Math
- Cause & Effect
- The Bible (Truth)
- We become what we think about
- Prayer

Most of these absolutes we engage in on a daily basis and they are enforced without any effort on our part. Anything that is absolute is something that is conceived or exists independently and not in relation to other things. The law of Absolutes does not depend upon anything outside of itself. It is beyond human control and it is not relative. Absolutes are not generally influenced by mortal beings and are mostly complete and self-existing. These Absolutes are self-sufficient and non-dependent; they are constant in their execution and can continue without intermission. Absolutes don't operate in the realm of conditions or control; they are free from limitations or control and are unrestricted by the will of man.

In regard to the 12 absolutes that we have stated above *(God is included because truly God is an Absolute of himself, and no one can say unto him, what does thou, or influence him in any way. God will do what he wants to do because he is a Supreme Being and is omniscience, omnipotent and omnipresence. Also God can suspend any of the Absolutes at any time he desires. Ephesians 1:11)*, I have come to the conclusion that 7 of the 12 Absolutes cannot be influenced or altered by mankind in any way unless God desires man to alter them or man come into the knowledge of who he truly is and learn that he himself is a god. Such is the case when Jesus suspended the absolute law of gravity and walked on water and also called Peter forth and he walked on the water. Matthew 14:25-31 Otherwise, these Absolutes are uncontrolled and unrestricted. These seven are as follow:

- God
- Gravity
- Time
- Seasons
- Aging
- The Bible (Truth)
- Math

However, God bless me to discover a loophole in 5 of the absolutes that can indeed be influenced and altered by mankind even without him realizing that he is a god. The thing about these 5 is that they are truly Absolutes and they will run their course unhindered if they are allowed to continue without intermission or interruption. But God in his infinite wisdom has given to mankind the ability to alter these 5 Absolutes to influence his/her course by using the God-given privilege of choice and thought. God made man in his image and gave him these two awesome traits that make him different from all of His creations. These two traits alone give us power and dominion not only over God's creation but also over these remaining 5 Absolutes of:

- Sowing & Reaping
- Cause & Effect
- Faith
- Prayer
- We become what we think about.

The power of choice gives us the right to choose what we want to sow and therefore what we will reap.

The power of choice gives us the right to choose the right cause so that we can get the right effect.

The power of thought gives us the ability to think in the realm of faith and not doubt for doubt is actually faith working in reverse.

The power of choice gives us the ability to choose the power of prayer that never fails if *"when we pray, we believe that we receive our desire, we shall have them."* Mark 11:24

However, most individuals pray in unbelief which is still prayer, but it's not what they want and it doesn't give them the petition which they truly desired. *"But let him ask in faith, nothing wavering. For he that wavereth is like a wave of the sea driven with the wind and tossed. For let not that man think that he shall receive any thing of the Lord. A double minded man is unstable in all his way." James 1:6-8* So this Absolute is still working but not constructively for the person that prays.

The power of thought gives us the ability to decide what thoughts we want to think and therefore what we want to become. If you choose to allow these 5 Absolutes to go on without choosing to intervene or alter their course then you will end up like the majority of society who has chosen to let these Absolutes run their course. At this writing over 60% of American households is one paycheck away from bankruptcy. The remaining 30% is barely making ends meet, 1-5% is living well and the other 5% are living in abundance, wealth, luxury and total financial freedom. Our chart displays a breakdown of America's poverty and wealth.

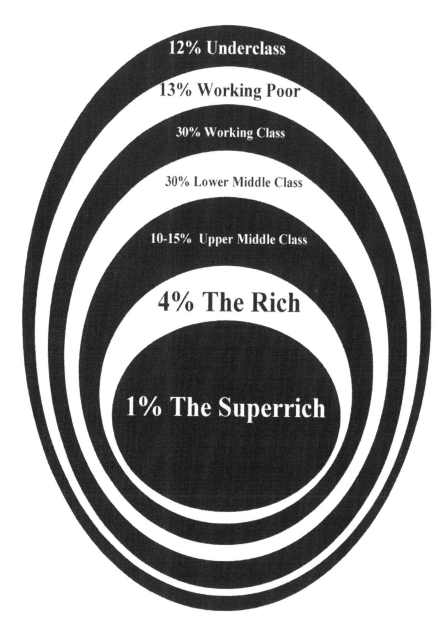

12% Underclass

13% Working Poor

30% Working Class

30% Lower Middle Class

10-15% Upper Middle Class

4% The Rich

1% The Superrich

These 5 Absolutes will work for you with 100% accuracy in your financial life. They can do for you everything that you need them to do, because God is at the helm and backing everyone of these 5 Absolutes and they are as certain to fulfill their objective as the night follows the day. They will not fail you in the realm of finances; you can have financial increase, prosperity and eventually wealth if you apply these 5 Absolutes to work in your favor even if you live in the remote desert.

- *Alter the course by sowing the right financial principles and laws and you will reap the benefits of financial success.*

- *Alter the course by producing the right causes for financial success and you will receive the right financial effects.*

- *Alter the course by having the faith of God and every money mountain that stands in your way you will be able to say to it "be thou removed, and be thou cast into the sea: and you shall have whatsoever you saith." Mark 11:23*

- *Alter the course by praying the prayers that believes that it receives and you will attract money to you for "nothing shall be impossible unto you." Matthew 17:20*

- *Alter the course by having dominating thoughts that work for you instead of against you. "For as he (mankind) thinketh in his heart, so is he." Proverbs 23:7*

The law of Absolutes works regardless of whether or not you intervene to enable them to work for you or continue to allow them to work against you. You can alter the course of your financial destiny by simply altering the course of these Absolutes, for in each financial success there is an adequate and definite cause, so if you desire to know the kingdom money secrets and crack the success and money code, then you must seek the condition, which will attain the result. Understanding that these absolutes exist and how they work are the beginning stages on the road to financial increase and accumulation.

# 4
# The Truth

*"And ye shall know the truth, and the truth shall make you free."* St. John 8:32

Either you are financially free or you are financially in bondage. How do you classify an individual and label them as being financially free? According to statistics and the chart that we have included in several sections of this book, 4% of individuals are considered Rich and 1% is considered the Super Rich. So that leaves 90-95% of individuals are in financial bondage or living paycheck to paycheck.

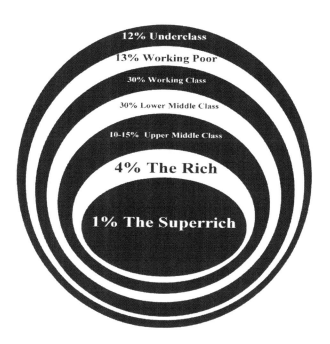

Some of the individuals in the top 5% became Rich and Super Rich as a result of truth that they have either stumbled upon or consciously and knowingly applied. The thing about truth is that it will work for whosoever will learn the truth and apply it. Now there are spiritual truths, mental truths and natural truths. Spiritual truths deal with things in the spirit realm. Mental truths deal with things in the mental realm. Natural truths deal with things in the natural realm. Also these truths can overlap one another because of the simple truth that God is at the helm of them all.

**Spiritual Truths =** This type of truth is revealed by God to those that have the spirit of God and that are in contact with him and obey his word. The scripture says, *"But as it is written, Eye hath not seen, nor ear heard, neither have entered into the heart of man, the things which God hath prepared for them that love him. But God hath revealed them unto us by his Spirit: for the Spirit searcheth all things, yea, the deep things of God. For what man knoweth the things of a man, save the spirit of man which is in him? even so the things of God knoweth no man, but the Spirit of God. Now we have received, not the spirit of the world, but the spirit which is of God; that we might know the things that are freely given to us of God. Which things also we speak, not in the words which man's wisdom teacheth, but which the Holy Ghost teacheth; comparing spiritual things with spiritual. But the natural man receiveth not the things of the Spirit of*

God: *for they are foolish unto him: neither can he know them, because they are spiritually discerned. But he that is spiritual judgeth all things, yet he himself is judged of no man. For who hath known the mind of the Lord, that he may instruct him? But we have the mind of Christ. 1 Corinthians 2:9-16*

Spiritual things come as a result of revealed truth by God not by man. Mankind apart from God cannot **know** spiritual things, he can have mental assent and have a slight understanding of them but he cannot **know** spiritual things *"because they are spiritually discerned."* When Jesus asked the disciples *"Whom do men say that I the Son of man am? But whom say ye that I am? Matthew 16:13-15* They begin to give him many answers but Peter spoke up and said *"Thou are the Christ, the Son of the living God. And Jesus answered and said unto him, Blessed art thou, Simon Bar-jona: for flesh and blood (man) hath not revealed it unto thee, but my Father which is in heaven." Matthew 16:16-17* If I were to write this chapter with nothing but scriptures throughout the entire chapter that deals with truth no natural man will be able to know what I am saying because *"the natural man receiveth not the things of the Spirit of God: for they are foolishness unto him."*

Another reason that natural man cannot know spiritual truths is because the word of God is unlike any other written word or book in the world. Jesus said *"It is the spirit that quickeneth; the flesh (the natural) profiteth nothing: the words that I speak unto you, they are spirit, and they are life." John 6:63* The word of God which is the only word of truth is full of spirit and life and the natural minded-man cannot know what is really being said and what is really being discerned. With spiritual truths if you were to take two fishes and five loaves of bread you can feed *"five thousand men, beside women and children."* Matthew 14:21 Read the full story in Matthew 14:14-21 yet, to the natural minded-man this is foolishness and absurd.

**Mental Truths =** This type of truth is also revealed by God but it's not truth that is saturated and full of spirit and life. It can be known and understood by natural man. Nevertheless it is truth and it can stand the test of time as long as it does not conflict with spiritual truth. Mental truth can accomplish some of the most amazing things but it cannot accomplish all things and all things are not possible with mental truth. For an example *"In the fourth watch of the night Jesus went unto them, walking on the sea. And told Peter to Come, And when Peter was come down out of the ship, he walked on the water, to go to Jesus."* Matthew 14:25-29 Now no amount of mental assent and belief apart from spiritual knowing and discernment can cause a natural man to walk on water.

Mental truths are focused and saturated with things pertaining to the mind. It is according to man's mental state of belief and focus. When the mind of man is full of belief and focus he can accomplish seemingly impossible things but in reality they are not impossible things they are possible things that can be done by natural man in the realm of the mind. Do you remember the story of the tower of Babel and what these individuals were setting out to accomplish using mental truths saturated with things pertaining to the mind with a mental state of belief and focus? These individuals were doing a work so awesome that God himself had to behold what they were doing and had to put a stop to it.

So the story goes, *"And the whole earth was of one language, and of one speech. And it came to pass, as they journey from the east, that they found a plain in the land of Shinar; and they dwelt there. And they said one to another, Go to, let us make brick, and burn them thoroughly. And they had brick for stone, and slime had they for mortar. And they said, Go to, let us build us a city and a tower, whose top may reach unto heaven; and let us make us a name, lest we be scattered abroad upon the face of the whole earth. And the LORD came down to see the city and the tower, which the children of men builded. And the LORD said, Behold, the people is one, and they have all one language; and this they begin to do: and now* **nothing will be restrained from them, which they have imagined to do.** *Go to, let us go down, and there confound their language, that they may not understand one another's speech. So the LORD scattered them abroad from thence upon the face of all the earth: and they left off to build the city. Therefore is the name of it called Babel; because the LORD did there confound the language of all the earth:*

*and from thence did the LORD scatter them abroad upon the face of all the earth." Genesis 11:1-9*

**When mental truth is in full force with belief and focus and operating at an optimum:**

- It can cause one to become extremely successful in life.
- It can cause one to become a multi-billionaire in the financial realm.
- It can cause one to conquer nations in battle.
- It can build great companies.
- It can cause one to accomplish great things in the earth.
- It can cause one to accumulate many material things in the earth.
- It can cause one to tap into the principles and laws of the universe and bring forth great discoveries etc.

Likewise mental truth can help you break the cycle of failure, financial bondage and lack and get your finances back on the right track. If natural man can become a billionaire using mental truths surely you can make .001% of what he has made in life or $1,000,000 (one million dollars). This is not even 1% of what he has made and everyone has the potential to do this when they understand how mental truths works and follow the principles laid out in this book.

**Natural Truths =** This type of truth is also revealed by God but likewise it is not truth that is saturated and full of spirit and life. It can also be known and understood by natural man. Likewise it's truth that can stand the test of time as long as it does not conflict with spiritual truth. Most natural truths are set truths that have been established by God and will flow with continuity unless they are interrupted by God or by a spiritual truth exemplified by mankind that is full of the Spirit and operating by the Spirit of God.

Natural truths are truths that have been set in the earth by God to enable mankind to live in harmony and blessedness while here upon the earth. The scripture says, *"Through faith we understand that the worlds were framed by the word of God, so that things which are seen were not made of things which do appear. And God said, Let there be light: and there was light. And God saw that the light, was good: and God divided the light from the darkness. And God called the light Day, and the darkness he called Night. And God said, Let there be lights in the firmament of the heaven to divide the day from the night; and let them be for signs and for seasons, and for days, and years: And let them be for lights in the firmament of the heaven to give light upon the earth: and it was so. And God made two great lights; the greater light to rule the day, and the lesser light to rule the night: he made the stars also." Hebrews Genesis 1:3-5, 14-16*

Natural truths can be powerful factors in the earth when known and understood by mankind, they can work for you and cause your life to be fruitful and productive. The scripture says, *"While the earth remaineth, seedtime and harvest, and cold and heat, and summer and winter, and day and night shall not cease."* Genesis 8:22 If you can learn how to use these natural truths for your benefit they can prosper you financially and cause you to:

- Prosper and succeed financially.
- Increase when others fail to increase.
- Operate with an insight that is foreign to other.
- Produce when others can't get things to work for them.
- Soar to great heights while others can barely get off the ground.

With an understanding of natural truths you can begin to turn your success and finances around within the next 30 days and begin to reap the benefits that belong to you as a child of God.

## HOW TRUTHS WORK

The thing about truth is that truth will set you free of whatever circumstance or situation that holds you in bondage. Jesus said, *"And ye shall **know** the truth, and the truth shall make you free."* John 8:32 The reason that individuals are not set free and not successful in life or in their finances is because they do not **know** the truth that can set them free in the realm of success and money. And the ones that do know the truth are not applying the truth that they know.

**Here's how it works with spiritual truth.** One word from God can set you free financially for the rest of your life. When you **know** that word not by mental assent but by that word conceived and birthed in your spirit, success and finances will be your last concern upon the earth. The key word here is **KNOW.** The mind understands but the spirit knows. Now you can take the written word or logos and extract a scripture that deals with finances or supply and confess that scripture and meditate upon that scripture until it gets in your spirit and become real to you and when that happens all things are possible. The word of God says, *"Death and life are in the power of the tongue: and they that love it shall eat the fruit thereof." "This book of the law shall not depart out of thy mouth; but thou shalt meditate therein day and night, that thou mayest observe to do according to all that is written therein: for then thou shalt make thy way prosperous, and then thou shalt have good success." Proverbs 18:21 Joshua 1:8:* You will learn more about both of these methods of use in the following chapters.

Second, you can also ask God to allow the Holy Spirit to quicken a word from the word to you that will produce life in your finances. The scriptures say, *"But the Comforter, which is the Holy Ghost, whom the Father will send in my name, he shall teach you all things, and bring all things to your remembrance, whatsoever I have said unto you. Howbeit when he, the Spirit of truth is come, he will guide you into all truth: for he shall not speak of himself; but whatsoever he shall hear, that shall he speak: and he will show you things to come. He shall glorify me: for he shall receive of mine, and shall show it unto you." St. John 14:26, 16:13-14*

When the Holy Spirit quickens a word from the word to you this is called a rhema word, it is a living word and it makes everything in accordance to that word alive. A rhema word is also a specific word for a specific person at a specific time. In the book of Hebrews it says, *"For the word of God (that rhema word) is quick, (it's living, active and alive) and powerful, and sharper than any twoedged sword, piercing even to the dividing asunder of soul and spirit, and of the joints and marrow, and is a discerner of the thoughts and intents of the heart." Hebrews 4:12* When this happens you can then:

- Turn water into wine. St. John 2:1-11
- Take two fishes and five loaves and feed thousands. Matthew 14:14-21
- Extract money from a fish mouth. Matthew 17:24-27
- Catch huge nets of fishes and multiply in whatever your business is. Luke 5:4-11
- Cause the fig tree to wither or cause your finances to prosper. Mark 11:12-14, 20-25
- And a thousand other things……..

Here is the missing truth in relations to success and money in spiritual understanding. If you get this truth and apply this truth you will be set free. The scripture says, *"This then is the message which we have heard of him, and declare unto you, that God is light, and in him is no darkness at all."1 John 1:5* In order to understand light and darkness we need to understand what light and darkness in the spirit realm consist of. Darkness consists of:

1. **Hatred**
2. **Poverty & Lack**
3. **Sickness**
4. **Confusion**
5. **Ignorance**
6. **Death**
7. **Lust**
8. **Powerlessness**
9. **Liar**
10. **Fear**

- *"He that saith he is in the light, and **hateth** his brother, is in darkness even until now. In this the children of God are manifest and the children of **the devil**: whosoever doeth not righteousness is not of God, neither he that **loveth not** his brother."* 1 John 2:9

- *"**The thief** cometh not, but for to **steal, and to kill, and to destroy.**" John 10:10a*

- *"How God anointed Jesus of Nazareth with the Holy Ghost and with power: who went about doing good, and **healing all** that were oppressed of **the devil**; for God was with him."* Acts 10:38

- *"This wisdom descendeth not from above, but is earthly, sensual, **devilish**. But where envying and strife is, there **is confusion** and every evil work."* James 3:15-16

- *"Why do ye not **understand my speech (ignorance)**? Even because ye cannot hear my word. Ye are of your father **the devil**, and the lust of your father ye will do."* John 8:43-44a

- *"**The thief** cometh not for to steal, and **to kill**, and to destroy."* John 10:10a

- *"Let no man say when he is tempted, I am tempted of God: for God cannot be tempted with **evil (the devil is the author of evil)**, neither tempteth he any man. But every man is tempted, when he is drawn away of his **own lust,** and enticed."* James 1:13-14

- *"Thou couldest **have no power (powerlessness)** at all against me, except it were given thee from above."* John 19:11a

- *"**He was a murderer (the devil)** from the beginn-*

*ing, and abode not in the truth, because there is no truth in him. When he speaketh a lie, he speaketh of his own: for he is a **liar**, and the father of it." John 8:44b*

- *"Because **fear (the devil is the author)** hath torment." 1 John 4:18b*

All those things are characteristics of darkness which is derived from the devil. All of these are the works of the devil and the fruits and power of evil. Any of these things that are exemplified in your life are not the works of God or the fruits of righteousness but of evil. As you see in each scripture I highlighted the words devil, evil and the associated word in that scripture according to the list of the works of darkness. Light consist of:

1. **Love**
2. **Success, Prosperity and Abundance**
3. **Health**
4. **Peace**
5. **Knowledge, Wisdom and Understanding**
6. **Life**
7. **Desire**
8. **Power**
9. **Truth**

- *"He that **loveth** his brother abideth in the **light**, and there is none occasion of stumbling in him.*

- *"**I am** come that they might have life, and that they might have it more **abundantly.**"* John 10:10b

- *"Beloved, I wish above all things that thou mayest prosper and be in **health**, even as thy soul prospereth."* 3 John 2

- *"Thou wilt keep him in **perfect peace**, whose mind is **stayed on thee**: because he trusteth **in thee.**"* Isaiah 26:3

- *"For **the LORD** giveth **wisdom**: out of his mouth cometh **knowledge** and **understanding**."* Proverbs 2:6

- *"**Jesus** saith unto him, I am the way, the truth, and **the life**."* John 14:6

- *"The **desire** of the **righteous** is only good."*

- *"And **Jesus** came and spake unto them saying, **All power** is given unto me in heaven and in earth. Behold, **I give unto you power** to tread on serpents and scorpions, and **over all the power of the enemy**: and nothing shall by any means hurt you."* Matthew 28:18, Luke10:19

- *"And ye shall know the **truth**, and the **truth** shall make you free. If the **Son** therefore shall make you free, ye shall be free indeed."* John 8:32, 36

- *"For **God** hath not given us **the spirit of fear; but of power, and of love, and of a sound mind.**" 2 Timothy 1:7*

All those things are characteristics of light which is derived from God. All of these are the works of God and the fruits and power of good. Any of these things that are exemplified in your life are the works of God and the fruits of righteousness and you're walking in the light. As you see in each scripture I highlighted the words God, Jesus, Son, righteous, in thee and the associated word in that scripture according to the list of the works of light. If you say that you are in the light yet the work(s) of darkness are exemplified in your life then you don't have an understanding of spiritual truth in that area and you're living as a slave, walking in darkness, and have the fruits of darkness displayed in your life while you're a child of light. *"If therefore the light that is in thee be darkness, how great is that darkness!" Matthew 6:23b* You cannot serve light and darkness: for one will have the dominance in your life and basically it will be the darkness. These things should not be. Remember, *"God is light, and in him is no **darkness at all**." 1 John 1:5b* So if God is light and he is in you how can you have the power and works of darkness manifested in your life? The answer is because you have accepted the power and the works of darkness as being a part of your Christian life instead of rejecting and denying them access into your life.

Jesus never accepted anything from the power and works of darkness. He said, *"For the prince of this world cometh, and hath nothing in me (no power in or over me)."* John 14:30b Jesus did not walk in any darkness at all for he realized that God is light, and in him is no darkness at all. Jesus never displayed any of the works of darkness in his own life even though they were all around him, and neither should you. Therefore, in order to get rid of the evil and the works of darkness you must come into spiritual truth and that spiritual truth must become personal to you.

1. **There is no evil for you. You must refuse to believe that it exists within your life. You must believe for you there is only good for God is good and Jesus has defeated all evil and therefore you are free.**

2. **You must deny all the works of darkness as lies in your life. Forget about the appearances of darkness that you now see, you must learn and understand that** *"We walk by faith, not by sight (or what you see)."* 2 Corinthians 5:7 **And you must begin to live in this manner for** *"The just shall live by his faith."* Habakkuk 2:4 **You will find that as you live your life in this manner** *"Thy faith hath made thee whole." "Thy faith hath saved thee."* Matthew 9:22b, Luke 7:50

3. In your life God is Omnipotence, Omniscience and Omnipresence. Therefore there can be nothing but the works and fruits of light manifest in your life. God is all and all, all-powerful, all-wise and all-present therefore the works and fruits of darkness have no power anywhere at any time over you.

4. Failure, Poverty, or Lack has no dominion in your life for *"you reign in life by one, Jesus Christ." Romans 5:17b*

5. You no longer have to fear failure, poverty or lack nor any kind of fear *"For God hath not given us the spirit of fear; but of power, and of love, and of a sound mind." 2 Timothy 1:7*

6. Refuse to walk by sight. Refuse to see these works of darkness as existing in your life. Refuse to receive them. Deny them and they will lose their power over you for you will no longer be a person that walks by sight giving power to the works of darkness, you will be a person that has the faith of God and walks by faith and *"nothing shall be impossible unto you." Matthew 17:20b*

7. You must have the same mind as Christ, a mind that says, *"I and my Father are one." John 10:30* Understand that God and you are not

**two but one for he is in you and you are in him. Jesus said,** *"At that day ye shall know that I am in my Father, and ye in me, and I in you."* **Therefore,** *"Let this mind be in you, which was also in Christ Jesus: Who, being in the form of God, thought it not robbery to be equal with God."* *Philippians 2:5-6* **When you do this you will no longer see God as outside of you but within you as the two of you are one and at that moment you have learned the truth that will set you free and would have cracked the first code to success and money.**

So let's hear the conclusion of the whole matter of spiritual truths, *"The words I speak unto you they are spirit and they are life. God is light, and in him is no darkness at all. For we walk by faith, not by sight"* St. John 6:63b

**Here's how it works with mental truths.** If you can grasp and imagine a truth in your mind and can believe it to the exclusion of all else and stay focused on that belief with absolute certainty you can achieve that thing. The key words here are **imagine** and **believe.** You remember the story of the tower of Babel when God said, *"and now nothing will be restrained from them, which they have imagined to do."* *Genesis 11:6b*

Next to your spirit the most powerful thing you possess is your mind. Most individuals are being defeated in the realm of their mind in reference to the thoughts that dominates their thinking. Your thoughts are the dominating factor in the realm of your mind. If your thoughts about your finances aren't right then your finances will not be right either. You cannot wish, hope and desire financial increase and then have thoughts of poverty and lack dominating your thought life. Either one thought pattern or the other will dominate your mind and produce results in accordance with the dominating thoughts you're thinking.

- **"For as he (mankind) thinketh in his heart, so is he." Proverbs 23:7**
- **You cannot think one way and expect another way to come forth. You will become what you think and there's no way around it.**
- **Your thoughts are what you will become and those dominating thoughts have a direct correlation and connection with the things that you are currently experiencing in your life.**

There is a universal law in the realm of the mind that works the same for all mankind, that law is **"like attracts like, cause and effect and everything produces after its kind."** The thoughts that dominate your thinking about your finances are the life or death of your financial life. Man is not a creature of conditions but instead creates his conditions by his dominating thoughts. All mankind will eventually become that which they secretly think about. The dominating thoughts of their mind that's hidden from others attract to them the environment and circumstances which their thoughts secretly long for, whether good or bad, prosperity or poverty, luxury or lack, abundance or barely making ends meet. In essence, what you think you will soon become, riches or rags are the direct result of continual thinking in one way or the other. Those dominating thoughts over time will form a picture or image as a way of life for you. This image and picture over time in return will create your circumstance.

- Did you know that imagery has a direct effect on your circumstance? Before I show you how it affects your circumstance I want to show you how images work.

- Do you know that you do not think in words, you think in images or pictures?

- The words that you hear or say produces a thought and that thought produces an image or picture.

- The image that you consistently hold in your mind will produce for you according to the image held.

- If you hold an image or picture of financial increase, prosperity and wealth, God will use that image to bring you financial increase, prosperity and wealth.

Your future is in your hands and it will be made according to the mental truth that dominates your thinking. It has been estimated that the average man uses only 10% of his mental power; the other 90% is just lying dormant and unused. It remains with you to arouse this untapped mental power and put it to use.

1. You can have what you want to have if you will only believe it.
2. You can possess what you desire to have if you can only imagine it.
3. Your financial destiny awaits your beckoning call if you can only accept it.
4. You are only 30 days away to seeing a change in your life if you can only receive it.

It rests with you to take action and make it happen through the power of thought and the power of choice.

So let's hear the conclusion of the whole matter of mental truths, *"And be not conformed to this world (**this world's way of negative thinking and doing**): but be ye transformed by the **renewing of your mind,** that ye* *may prove what is that good, and acceptable, and perfect will of God." Romans 12:2*

**Here's how it works with natural truths.** Natural truths are truths that are set in the earth and they are absolutes as we have stated in the above chapter. Natural truths will work with continuity without any interference from mankind. A great natural truth that we all encounter or consent to is the truth of *"sowing and reaping."* This is a truth that is evident in the natural world such as seedtime and harvest time. When we plant a seed in the ground for something to grow we expect to reap a harvest. But every day we are sowing negative seeds that we don't want to reap as a harvest. In order to reap the right harvest then we must sow the right seeds, this principle works just as well in your life as it does in the natural world of seedtime and harvest time.

Money is a natural thing therefore it is the answer to all natural things. You and money come from the same place, meaning from the earth. Money is not made out of thin air nor is it made from the clouds or any heavenly body of things. Money comes from the earth; it is earthy and is a commodity that only has value here on earth. Money has no clout in heaven nor in hell, it only has value right here on the earth. As a son of the living God you have been given dominion and authority over the earth and money is a part of the earth, it comes from the earth and you and I should be able to attract money to us just as a result of the dominion and authority that has been given us as mankind. The scripture says, *"And God said, Let us make man in our image, after our likeness: and let them have dominion over the fish of the sea, and over the fowl of the air, and over the cattle, and over all the earth, and over every creeping thing that creepeth upon the earth."Genesis 1:26*

Someone may say that when Adam sinned we lost that dominion and authority in the earth. But I say unto you, *"For as by one man's disobedience many were made sinners, so by the obedience of one shall many be made righteous. Moreover the law entered, that the offence might abound. But where sin abounded, grace did much more abound. That as sin hath reigned unto death, even so might grace reign through righteousness unto eternal life by Jesus Christ our Lord." Romans 5:19-21*

Also, because money is made from a natural thing you have the ability within you to call that natural thing forth to attract itself to you in abundance. According to the scriptures all of nature is waiting for you and me to become mature and full grown men and women of God, and when we do we can do and operate just like Jesus did in speaking to natural things to produce or die at our command. *"For the earnest expectation of the creature waiteth for the manifestation of the sons of God. For the creature was made subject to vanity, not willingly, but by reason of him who hath subjected the same in hope, Because the creature itself also shall be delivered from the bondage of corruption into the glorious liberty of the children of God. For we know that the whole creation groaneth and travaileth in pain together until now." Romans 8:19-22*

All of nature and natural things is waiting to be ruled once again by mankind as it was made to do in the original plan of God. When Jesus came he showed us how we should live and walk as man upon the earth, and he came down in the form of a man to show us how to do it. When he cursed the fig tree this was only one example of his power over the earth, *"And when he saw a fig tree in the way, he came to it, and found nothing thereon, but leaves only, and said unto it, Let no fruit grow on thee henceforward for ever. And presently the fig tree withered away." Matthew 21:19* Just as he cursed this fig tree he could have easily told a dead fig tree to live exemplifying his power over nature and natural things. Jesus then told us *"The works that I do shall you do also and greater works than these because I go back to the Father." You have the power and authority to sow the right seeds and therefore reap the right harvest. So let us hear the conclusion of the whole matter over natural truths. "Whatsoever a man soweth that shall he also reap." Galatians 6:7b*

## 5
## God's Definition of Success

*"I am come that they might have life, and that they might have it more abundantly." John 10:10b*

God's definition of success is different from man's definition of success. The hallmark of God's definition is obedience. In the book of Isaiah it says, *"If ye be willing and obedient, ye shall eat the good of the land: But if ye refuse and rebel, ye shall be devoured with the sword: for the mouth of the LORD hath spoken it." Isaiah 1:19-20* When you are obedient to the word of God this positions you to eat the good of the land. However, just because someone has wealth and riches and material accumulation this doesn't make them a success in the eyes of God if they are not rich toward God first. In the scriptures Jesus told the parable about the rich man saying, *"The ground of a certain rich man brought forth plentifully: And he thought within himself, saying, What shall I do, because I have no room where to bestow my fruits? And he said, This will I do: I will pull down my barns, and build greater; and there will I bestow all my fruits and my goods. And I will say to my soul, Soul, thou hast much goods laid up for many years; take thine ease, eat, drink, and be merry. But God said unto him, Thou fool, this night thy soul shall be required of thee: then whose shall those things be, which thou hast provided? So is he that layeth up treasure for himself, and is not rich toward God." Luke 12:16-21*

No man or woman is a success in God's eyes that does not accept his Son Jesus Christ into their life as their Lord and Savior no matter what they accomplish in this world. The reason is because God is more concerned with your soul than your success, however, when your soul is right with God then he wants you to be all you can be. Jesus said, *"I am come that they might have life, and that they might have it more abundantly." John 10:10b* The word life is *zoe* and it means the nature of God. He wants mankind to have his nature so that mankind can *"walk in his statures, and keep his judgments, and do them." Ezekiel 36:27b* No man is a success that hasn't been reconciled to God.

Mankind's old nature and ways are at enmity with God and nothing he does can reconcile him to God. He must become a new creature through Christ. *"Therefore if any man be in Christ, he is a new creature: old things are passed away; behold, all things are become new. And all things are of God who hath reconciled us to himself by Jesus Christ, and hath given to us the ministry of reconciliation; To wit, that God was in Christ, reconciling the world unto himself, not imputing their trespasses unto them; and hath committed unto us the word of reconciliation. Now then we are ambassadors for Christ, as though God did beseech you by us: we pray you in Christ's stead, be ye reconciled to God. For he made him to be sin for us, who knew no sin; that we might be made the righteousness of God in him." 2 Corinthians 5:17-21*

As the righteousness of God it positions you to partake of all the blessings of God and throughout this book you will learn what you need to do to not only position yourself but to possess the blessings of God in this life. Obedience is the key to unlock every door along with the proper knowledge and understanding. If you want to be a success in God's eyes you must learn to hearken to the voice of God and obey his word, when you do he has promised to bless you abundantly saying, *"AND IT shall come to pass, if thou shalt hearken diligently unot the voice of the LORD thy God, to observe and to do all his commandments which I command thee this day, that the LORD thy God will set thee on high above all nations of the earth: And all these blessings shall come on thee, and overtake thee, if thou shalt hearken unto the voice of the LORD thy God.*

1. *"God will set you on high above all nations of the earth." Success and Financial freedom.*

2. *"All these blessing shall come on thee, and overtake thee." Success and Financial freedom.*

3. *"Blessed shall thou be in the city, and blessed shalt thou be in field." Success and Financial freedom.*

4. *"Blessed shall be the fruit of thy body, and the fruit of thy ground, and the fruit of thy cattle, the increase of thy kine, and the flocks of thy sheep." Success and Financial freedom.*

5. *"Blessed shall be thy basket and thy store."* Success and Financial freedom.

6. *"Blessed shall thou be when thou comest in, and blessed shalt thou be when thou goest out."* Success and Financial freedom.

7. *"Your enemies shall be smitten before thy face and flee before thee seven ways"* (God will fight your battles for you). Success and Financial freedom.

8. *"The LORD shall command the blessing upon thee in thy storehouses, in that which you set your hand unto, and he shall bless your land."* Success and Financial freedom.

9. *"The LORD shall establish thee a holy people unto himself"* (God's people that understand God's way shall have). Success and Financial freedom.

10. *"And all the people of the earth shall see that thou art called by the name of the LORD; and they shall be afraid of thee"* (because the hand of God is prospering your life). Success and Financial freedom.

11. *"And the LORD shall make thee plenteous in goods."* Success and Financial freedom.

12. *"And the LORD shall open unto thee his good treasure, and bless all the work of thine hand, thou*

*shalt lend unto many nations, and thou shalt not borrow." Success and Financial freedom.*

13. *"And the LORD shall make thee the head, and not the tail; and thou shalt be above only and thou shalt not be beneath."* Success and Financial freedom.

14. *"And thou shalt not go aside from any of the words which I command thee this day, to the right hand, or to the left, to go after other gods to serve them"(if you keep God's word and serve him only then you shall have Success and  Financial freedom.)*

God only want the best for you and he wants you to experience good success not the success of the world. When you have the kind of success that comes from God only then your success will be noticed:

- By you first.
- By your family members.
- By your co-workers.
- By your friends.
- By your associates.
- By your neighbors.
- By your enemies.

The basis of making anything happen for you and turning things around in your life is your obedience and your belief.

- Belief will make you a success in life.
- Belief is enough to change any situation.
- Belief can get money in your pocket.
- Belief can turn bad into good.
- Belief is the answer to getting that job you want.
- Belief is the answer to making that business work or coming up with a business.
- Belief is the trampoline that can bounce you into the destiny that you were created to fulfill.
- Belief can get set you on the road to prosperity.
- Belief can do a thousand other things too numerous to mention.

You are where you are at this very moment because of your belief system about the success and financial aspect of your life. You can contribute the bad or good that you're experiencing to your belief about the thoughts that dominate your thinking in the success and financial aspect of your life. But beliefs can be changed from what it is to what you want it to be. You are a recipient of the strong beliefs that are currently dominant in your heart. Change your belief and you change your life. In the words of scriptures, *"For as he thinketh in his heart, so is he."* *Proverbs 23:7* If you've always had problems believing fear not, for there is power in the word and *"faith cometh by hearing and hearing by the word."* These simple scriptures on the power of belief once they get in your spirit can turn things around for you.

1. *"Therefore I say unto you, What things soever ye desire, when ye pray, believe that ye receive them, and ye shall have them." Mark 11:24*

2. *"For verily I say unto you, If ye have faith s a grain of mustard seed, ye shall say unto this mountain, Remove hence to yonder place; and it shall remove; and nothing shall be impossible unto you." Matthew 17:20*

3. *"For verily I say unto you, That whosoever shall say unto this mountain, Be thou removed, and be thou cast into the sea; and shall not doubt in his heart, but shall believe that those things he saith shall come to pass; he shall have whatsoever he saith." Mark 11:23*

Belief is one of the laws of Absolutes. When properly conformed to the law of absolutes will never let you down. If you are tired of:

- Losing in life.
- Being broke busted and disgusted.
- Not having enough money to do what you need/want to do.
- Being the borrower instead of the lender.
- Not fulfilling your destiny in life.
- Being the tail instead of the head.
- Unable to acquire the finer things of life.

- Being tormented in your mind about success and finances.
- Being beneath instead of above.
- Repelling success and money from you instead of attracting it to you.
- Not having money in your pocket and bank account.

This book can do for you whatever you want it to do. If you accept this idea your success and money troubles will be over and success and money will begin to attract itself to you like iron to a magnet. It doesn't matter what your condition is at the moment, you've done the greatest thing that you could do in investing in the price of this book. You will get the price of this book back many times over. Every person is entitled to prosper financially in life and you are included.

- Money wants to be in your possession.
- Money needs you and your ideas.
- Money wants you to circulate it in the earth.
- Money is waiting on you to get the right attitude.
- Money awaits your beckoning call.

No longer see yourself as you are but begin to see yourself, as you want to be. Keep your mind off what you don't want and on what you do want. I must repeat this again: keep your mind off what you don't want and on what you do want. What do you want?

- You want to win in life.
- You want money in your pocket and in your accounts.
- You want success in life.
- You want wealth and riches in your house.
- You want financial prosperity and abundance.
- You want to be able to afford the finer things of life.
- You want to be the head.
- You want to be the lender.
- You want to be above only.
- You want peace in your mind about your finances.
- You want to be a money magnet.

Then you must begin to see yourself as this right now. Not tomorrow, not next week or next year but right now. NOW, NOW, NOW, NOW, NOW, NOW, NOW! Forget the past it's gone and the present and future is what you make it. This is your day, it's your turn to prosper in life and you will. Forget the past, it's over. You can't go back and change it but you can change your future. Stop the madness of failure in life and living in lack, you have it within you to stop it now. You were not created to fail or live in lack but for success, abundance and plenty. Begin to focus your mind on the things that money will buy and what success will do for you. See yourself doing all these things.

- You can have a new car just as well as anyone else.
- You can have a nice home just as well as anyone else.
- You can wear fine clothes just as well as anyone else.
- You can eat at the best restaurants just as well as anyone else.
- You can contribute to charitable organizations just as well as anyone else.
- You can shop without the concern of money spent just as well as anyone else.
- You can be a financial blessing to others just as well as anyone else.
- You can take nice vacations just as well as anyone else.
- You can fulfill your life long desires just as well as anyone else.
- You can make money work for you just as well as anyone else.

You only have to believe that you can and when you are walking in obedience to God's word then all things are yours. In Joshua 1:8 it says, "*This book of the law shall not depart out of thy mouth; but thou shalt meditate therein day and night, that thou mayest observe to do according to all that is written therein: for then thou shalt make thy way prosperous, and then thou shalt have good success (or deal wisely in the affairs of life).* In Psalms 1:1-3 it states, *"BLESSED is the man that walketh not in the counsel of the ungodly, nor standeth in the way of sinners, nor sitteth in the seat of the scornful. But his delight is in the law of the LORD; and in his law doth he meditate day and night. And he shall be like a tree planted by the rivers of water, that bringeth forth his fruit in his season; his leaf also shall not wither; and whatsoever he doeth shall prosper."***It's Prosperity Time!**

# 6
# You Are Wired for Wealth

*"I will praise thee; for I am fearfully and wonderfully made: Marvelous are thy works: and that my soul knoweth right well." Psalms 139:14*

Mankind is God's greatest creation. God made man in His image and likeness. Man was made to be a representation and profile of God. God is the archetype man is the prototype. Mankind is an awesome creature endowed with awesome ability and potential. When man comes into the knowledge and understanding of who he is, how he is made and live according to the word of God he will realize that he is a god. Now before my Christian brothers and sisters get ready to stone me, please allow me to explain such a statement, as **"you are a god."** Neither have I converted over to new age, but allow me to amuse myself (and hopefully you) for a few minutes. In the scriptures there are three statements made by three different individuals making a confession that we are gods. The first statement we behold in the book of Genesis 3:5, where Satan speaking through a serpent told Eve *"For God doth know that in the day ye eat thereof, your eyes shall be opened, and ye shall be as gods, knowing good and evil."* The second statement was written by Asaph in the Psalms saying, *"I have said, Ye are gods." Psalms 82:6* The third statement was spoken by Jesus Christ himself saying, *"Is it not* *written in your law, I said, Ye are gods? If he called them gods; unto whom the word of God came, and the scripture cannot be broken." John 10:34-35*

In the first statement made by Satan his motive and objective was to get Adam and Eve to disobey God and commit treason against God. He told Eve that ye would be as gods, when in all actuality they were already created and made by God to be a god. You are a representation and image of that which you came from. A human being births another human being. A dog births a dog. A cat births a cat. An elephant births an elephant etc. A human does not birth a dog, nor does a cat birth an elephant. A tree produces another tree of its kind. An apple tree does not produce an orange, nor does a pear tree produce bananas etc... Everything produces after its kind. The scripture says, *"And God said, Let the earth bring forth grass, the herb yielding seed, and the fruit tree yielding fruit AFTER HIS KIND, whose seed is in itself, upon the earth: and it was so." And the earth brought forth grass, and herb yielding seed. AFTER HIS KIND, and the tree yielding fruit, WHOSE SEED WAS IN ITSELF, AFTER HIS KIND: and God saw that it was good." Genesis 1:11-12*

When God created and made Adam and Eve He was only creating and making more like Him, namely more gods. He was not making Almighty Gods but gods lower and subject to Him. If you have children they will never be your parents, howbeit they can become parents themselves, but they can never be your parents. It does not matter if the child becomes a billionaire and world famous and the parent was a bum on the street. The roles would not reverse; the parent would still be the parent and the child the child. Well, when God created mankind the scripture says, *"What is man, that thou art mindful of him? And the son of man, that thou visitest him? For thou hast made him a little lower than the angels, and hast crowned him with glory and honour. Thou madest him to have dominion over the works of thy hands; thou hast put all things under his feet." Psalms 8:4-6*

What an awesome position to be in. What a blessing it is to be a part of the human race. Mankind was given dominion and authority over all the works of thy hand, made a ruler, a leader, a provider and a god. Man that has intelligence and wisdom, endowed with the supernatural ability of God. Man that has the ability within him to speak several languages fluently and has the mind capacity to remember entire volumes of Encyclopedias and the potential to invent gadgets of all kind. But one of mankind's greatest blessings is the makeup of his body. The scripture says, *"And the LORD God formed man of the dust of the ground, and breathed into his nostrils the breath of life; and man became a living soul." Genesis 2:7* When God made man of the dust of the ground He formed and shaped man's body into the image we have today. Man's body is fearfully and wonderfully made, he is full of energy and full of life. If you could be seen as you really are you would be seen as an awesome, unbelievable creation full of potential and possibilities.

Now you can understand why the scripture says, *"you are fearfully and wonderfully made." Psalms 139:14* But it gets better; you are a creation endowed with intelligence and powers beyond your belief. The making of your body combined with the ability of your soul makes you a creation far above the animal kingdom. You have the God-given intelligence unlike any other creature. Out of all of God's creations, mankind has the most highly developed brains. Your brain is the master nucleus of the body. It consistently receives information from the senses both about the inside and outside of the body. It takes this information and quickly analyzes it, and then sends out messages that control the body actions and functions. The human brain consists of billions of interconnected cells which enable you to be creative, use language, plan and solve difficult problems.

You are a creation to be reckoned with, and the will of God for you is total life prosperity. You were made to be rich and wealthy. You were made for a life of abundance and plenty. When God made Adam He put him in the Garden of Eden, a place of plenty and voluptuous living. You were not made to be poor and broke and to live paycheck-to-paycheck barely making ends meet. You are too great for poverty; you are fearfully and wonderfully made.

You have God in you and you were created as a god and no god lives in lack and insufficiency. Wealth and abundance is your birth right as a child of God. From this day forward state your claim and make your claim. Come forth and be the god you were created to be. As a god you are full of life and energy. Open up the door of your heart and let all of you come forth.

- You are great.
- You are full of potential.
- You have awesome ability.
- You have intelligence.
- You are gifted.
- You are magnanimous.
- You are priceless.
- You are powerful.
- You have been given dominion and authority.
- You are a god.

It's time for you to come forth and possess what belongs to you. You need money in this life for money answers all natural things. How do I get the money I need you may ask? You will learn in this book how to get all the money you need. But first come to the realization that you are full of energy and according to how you channel that energy will determine how prosperous financially you will become in life. The best way to channel that energy is through your gifting and passion. Here are questions to ask you.

1. What is my gift?
2. What is my passion?
3. What do I love to do?
4. What would I be doing right now if money were no object?
5. What do I dream about doing in life?

If you're working on a job or in a business and you would rather be doing something other than what you're currently doing, then you should be working towards doing that thing. You should be doing what you're constantly thinking about doing and what consumes your thoughts on a daily basis. You have to come to the understanding that the thing you're doing that's contrary to your dominating thoughts is neither your passion nor your purpose, it's just a job and a means of survival no matter how much money you're making doing it. Therefore make it your business to do what consumes your thoughts (and we will talk more about this later) and the money will come in abundance. Everything else you're doing is a by-product of what you should be doing.

You were created for happiness and success, doing your passion will bring forth your happiness and create unlimited financial success (with the proper wisdom and understanding) for a lifetime. You are already wired for wealth you just don't know how to go about possessing that which is already yours. In this book we will take you step by step as promised to unveil to you the wisdom and understanding of how to get from where you are to where you desire to be. In this book I will not leave anything to chance I will guide you by the help of the Holy Ghost to the right way of thinking and planning. Many plans that are essential for financial success are known and used by the financially successful few. In this book I will help you to think, and lay out the plan for you of how to achieve your financial goals in life. You are one step away from financial increase!

## 7

# The Ability of God Within You

*"God has placed within you awesome ability and that ability has empowered you to know all things, that ability can attract to you money, gold and all things that pertain to life and godliness so that you might be partakers of the divine nature." 1 Peter 1:3-4*

*"In the beginning was the Word, and the Word was with God, and the Word was God. The same was in the beginning with God. All things were made by him; and without him was not anything made that was made. In him was life; and the life was the light of men. And the light shineth in darkness; and the darkness comprehended it not. There was a man sent from God, whose name was John. The same came for a witness, to bear witness of the Light, that all men through him might believe. He was not that Light, but was sent to bear witness of the Light. That was the true Light, which lighteth every man that cometh into the world. He was in the world, and the world was made by him, and the world knew him not. He came unto him own, and his own received him not. But as many as received him, to them gave he power (ability) to become the sons of God, even to them that believe on his name." St. John 1:1-12*

As a believer you have the ability of God in you, God's ability resides in your spirit man, *"The spirit of man is the candle of the LORD, searching all the inward parts of the belly." Proverbs 20:27* Man's makeup consist of a threefold nature; spirit, soul and body. Paul said *"And the very God of peace sanctify you* wholly; and I pray God your whole spirit and soul and body be preserved blameless unto the coming of our Lord Jesus Christ." 1 Thessalonian 5:23 The spirit of man consist of your inward man or innermost man the spirit man is the real you. Some call this your subconscious.

The soul of man consist of your will, emotions and intellect your conscious man. The body of man consists of your physical outward shell and casing this is the man that we see physically on a daily basis. The ability of God dwells not in your soul or body but in your spirit man. God has designed it so that the strongest part of man should be his spirit, his soul should be subject to his spirit and his body should be subject to his soul. The spirit of man is supposed to be the dominant one, the soul should take his orders from the spirit and the body is supposed to take his orders from the soul. People are arranged in three manners relevant to the threefold makeup of man, some are ruled by their body, some by their soul and very few by their spirit.

1. Body ruled individuals are led and focused more on *"the lust of the flesh, and the lust of the eyes, and the pride of life."* 1 John 2:16

2. Soul ruled individuals are led and focused more on "intellect, natural things, education and worldly wisdom.

3. Spirit ruled individuals are led and focused more on *"things which the Holy Ghost teacheth; comparing spiritual things with spiritual."* 1 Corinthians 2:14

## Money Answer All Things

If you want to know how to attract money, gold and all the things that pertain to life and godliness to you, you had better learn to be led and ruled by your spirit man instead of your soul or body. You may ask what does this have to do with money, what importance does my spirit; soul and body play in the acquiring of money. My answer to you is everything, because man was created to do all things by his spirit in control of his life not his soul or body being in control. You will never go further than the knowledge you possess in your spirit, only when something has gotten in your spirit has it really become real to you. Once something get in your spirit it's hard to shake whether it's negative or positive and the thing which gets in your spirit will come alive for you.

A child sleeping alone may believe that a monster is in their closest or under their bed when there is really nothing of the sort. Yet, the child has allowed this belief to get embedded in their spirit to the point that they're convinced of the monster's existence. The only way to convince them that no monster exist is to give them another belief greater than the belief they have that will supersede what's currently embedded in their spirit. Once the new belief has come alive in their spirit then they're free to let go of the old belief and their new belief now has the ascendancy over the old belief and has taken charge. If belief can be eradicated in the mind before it reaches the spirit it can be more easily resolved, for the mind only understand while the spirit knows. Belief in the spirit is a thousand times greater than belief in the mind and likewise is much harder to eliminate when something has gotten in. Since the spirit man is so strong, it behooves us to learn how to live and operate in life from our spirit. God never intended for man to operate by his soul or his body these were designed to be subject to the spirit.

The spirit of man knows many things that the soul and body does not know and is unable to produce. When man is strong in his spirit, he can even sustain his infirmity no matter what they are. The word of God says, "*The spirit of man will sustain his infirmity; but a wounded spirit who can bear? Proverbs 18:14* When a person is sick of cancer or some other major disease if they allow that sickness to influence their spirit man and once it gets into their spirit then all hope is gone and short of a miracle they want recover. Yet, the opposite should be true when sickness comes upon an individual, his spirit should be so strong that it can sustain and uphold him in the midst of the sickness until he get his deliverance or healing. However, when sickness come man's spirit because it's weak and not strong is wounded and his spirit is unable to help him because it's broken, out of order and defeated. God designed man's spirit so that it can help him solve his problems in life and direct him to answers and solutions that he need for any given subject.

The word of God is abounding with scriptures that accentuate what the spirit of man can do for him. If you need money, the spirit of man knows where to get it because God's Spirit dwells in your spirit and His Spirit knows all things. The scripture says *"But ye have an unction from the Holy One, and ye know all things. But the anointing which ye have received of him abideth in you, and ye need not that any man teach you: but as the same anointing teacheth you of all things, and is truth, and is no lie, and even as it hath taught you, ye shall abide in him." 1 John 2:20, 27*

God speaks to man's spirit to direct and instruct him in all things that pertains to life and godliness. The scriptures says *"But as it is written, Eye hath not seen, nor ear heard, neither have entered into the heart of man, the things which God hath prepared for them that love him. But God hath revealed them unto us by his Spirit: for the Spirit searcheth all things, yea, the deep things of God. For what man knoweth the things of a man, save the spirit of man which is in him? Even so the things of God knoweth no man, but the Spirit of God. Now we have received, not the spirit of the world, but the spirit which is of God; that we might know the things that are freely given to us of God. Which things also we speak, not* in the words which man's wisdom teacheth, but which the Holy Ghost teacheth; comparing spiritual things with spiritual. But the natural man receiveth not the things of the Spirit of God: for they are foolishness unto him: neither can he know them, because they are spiritually discerned." 1 Corinthians 2:9-14

All things belong to God and he knows where all things are for "The eyes of the LORD are in every place, God understandeth the way thereof, and he knoweth the place thereof. For he looketh to the ends of the earth, and seeth under the whole heaven." Proverbs 15:3, Job 28:23-24 God knows where the money is, all the lost treasures, the buried gold, hidden money and all the valuable jewels located throughout the whole earth. The scriptures said "Surely there is a vein for the silver, and a place for gold where they fine it. Iron is taken out of the earth, and brass is molten out of the stone. As for the earth, out of it cometh bread: and under it is turned as it were fire. The stones of it are the place of sapphires: and it hath dust of gold." Job 28:1-6

In the story of the money in the fish mouth, we have to ask ourselves how Jesus knew where to get that money to pay those taxes. So the story goes, "And when they were come to Capernaum, they that received tribute money came to Peter, and said, Doth not your master pay tribute? He saith, Yes. And when he was come into the house, Jesus prevented him, saying, What thinkest thou, Simon? Of whom do the kings of the earth take custom or tribute? Of their own children, or of strangers? Peter saith unto him, Of strangers. Jesus saith unto him, Then are the children free. Notwithstanding, lest we should offend them, go thou to the sea, and cast an hook, and take up the fish that first cometh up; and when thou hast opened his mouth, thou shalt find a piece of money: that take, and give unto them for me and thee." Matthew 17:24- 27 In order to understand and perceive this we have to look at this story from a spiritual standpoint because all reason and logic will tell us that such a thing is foolish and cannot happen. For the scriptures say "the natural man (unsaved, logical) man receiveth not the things of the Spirit of God: for they are foolishness unto him: neither can he know them, because they are spiritually discerned. But he that is spiritual judgeth all things." 1 Corinthians 2:14

Jesus did not say this simply as God because for him to operate as God would have disallowed us as men to do the things which he did when he said, "Verily, verily, I say unto you, He that believeth on me, the works that I do shall he do also; and greater works than these shall he do; because I go unto the Father." John 14:1 For now let's look at doing only what Jesus did the greater works would be another book, did Jesus locate money that was hidden from the natural eye and mind of man, the answer is obviously yes. So the least we should be able to do is operate in this ability to be able to attract and locate money that's needed to pay a bill for this is what Jesus needed money to do. On every occasion when money or things were needed Jesus knew how to attract what was needed or take what he had and cause it to increase and multiply to meet the need.

Jesus was able to do this as a result of God working in him and through him telling and showing him exactly what to do and where to go. In the book of John it says *"Verily, verily, I say unto you, The Son can do nothing of himself, but what he seeth the Father do: for what things soever he doeth, these also doeth the Son likewise. For the Father loveth the Son, and sheweth him all things that himself doeth: and he will shew him greater works than these, that ye may marvel. I can of mine own self do nothing: as I hear, I judge: and my judgment is just; because I seek not mine own will, but the will of the Father which hath sent me (we will talk more about this later).* God told Jesus about the money in the mouth of the fish and showed him where to go to get the money to pay the taxes, and Jesus told Peter saying, *"go thou to the sea, and cast an hook, and take up the fish that first cometh up;" Matthew 17:27* Now Peter had to do exactly what Jesus said, he had to go to the sea and the first fish not the second or third but the first fish is the one where the money is. Likewise, God is in you and you have the ability through God to do likewise. God is the creator of the universe and all things are exposed unto him *"heaven is his throne and the earth is his footstool."Isaiah 66:1* In order to operate as Jesus did you have to realize who dwells in you and the ability of the indwelling one that abides within you and the potential of his power. The word of God says:

- *"In the beginning God created the heavens and the earth." Genesis 1:1*

- *"The earth is the LORD's, and the fullness thereof; the world, and they that dwell therein. Psalms 24:1*

- *"Delight thyself also in the LORD; and he shall give thee the desires of thine heart." Psalms 37:4*

- *"God is our refuge and strength, a very present help in trouble." Psalms 46:1*

- *"Let the people praise thee, O God; let all the people praise thee. Then shall the earth yield her increase; and God, even our own God shall bless us. God shall bless us; and all the ends of the earth shall fear him." Psalms 67:5-7*

- *"Bless the LORD, O my soul. O LORD my God, thou art great; thou art clothed with honour and majesty. Who coverest thyself with light as with a garment: who stretchest out the heavens like a curtain: Who layeth the beams of his chambers in the waters: who maketh the clouds his chariot: who walketh upon the wings of the wind: Who maketh his angels spirits; his ministers a flaming fire: Who laid the foundations of the earth, that it should not be removed for ever." Psalms 104*

God is great and greatly to be praised and this same God which *"stretchest out the heavens like a curtain"* dwells in you and he *"is able to do exceeding abundantly above all that we ask or think, according to the power that worketh in us." Ephesians 3:20*

The greatness of God is without question what then hinders mankind from doing what Jesus did, the one thing that hinders mankind from doing what Jesus did is the faith that man lacks in God and the negative thoughts that dominate his thinking about God, himself and his ability to do the same. In other words the negative thoughts that dominate your thinking rule not only your thought life but your faith in God and persuade you that you can't do the same or anything close to it. These thoughts have the ascendancy in your mind and reign in your life and as a result it gets in your spirit and then your belief is not of possibility but of impossibility. When these satanic negative thoughts of doubt and unbelief get in your spirit it becomes a thousand times stronger than any thought in your mind and then all your mental assent of the word of God that you try to muster up means nothing because the true thoughts of your life is lodged in your spirit. What needs to lodge in your spirit and abide there is the greatness of God, who God is, how great he is, what he can do, where he dwells at (in you) and his ability to do what you ask him to do.

The power, wisdom and ability of God reside in you and what Jesus did he has given us the right and ability to do the same. On one occasion, Jesus saw a man that had infirmity for thirty eight years and Jesus spoke to the man, told him what to do and the man was made whole. So the story goes, *"And a* certain man was there, which had an infirmity thirty and eight years. When Jesus saw him lie, and knew that he had been now a long time in that case, he saith unto him, Wilt thou be made whole? The impotent man answered him, Sir, I have no man, when the water is troubled, to put me into the pool: but while I am coming, another steppeth down before me. Jesus said unto him, Rise, take up thy bed and walk. And immediately the man was made whole, and took up his bed, and walked." St. John 5:1-8

"And therefore did the Jews persecute Jesus, and sought to slay him, because he had done these things on the Sabbath day. But Jesus answered them, (what Jesus answered them is the apex of this chapter and therein is the foundation for which to build on) My Father worketh hitherto, and I work. "Verily, verily, I say unto you, The Son can do nothing of himself, but what he seeth the Father do: for what things soever he doeth, these also doeth the Son likewise. For the Father loveth the Son, and sheweth him all things that himself doeth: and he will shew him greater works than these, that ye may marvel. For as the Father raiseth up the dead, and quickeneth them; even so the Son quickeneth whom he will. For as the Father hath life in himself; so hath he given to the Son to have life in himself." St. John 5:16-26

Here Jesus was telling them just as my Father work I do the same work as he do, I can't do this of myself, but as I see the Father do I do just like the Father. The Father loves me and shows me all things that he does and he will show me greater works that will make you wonder. The Father has life in himself and he has given me the ability to have this same life in me.

Dear reader, Jesus realized that the ability of God resided in him and he was not operating as God but as man with the ability of God in him, and this ability caused him to be able to do as the Father. The thoughts of Jesus were not dominated by negative thinking at all but by the word and the knowledge of God that lodged in his spirit. In order for us to do as Jesus did you must *"Let this mind be in you, which was also in Christ Jesus: Who, being in the form of God, thought it not robbery to be equal with God."* Philippians 2:5-6

The reason Jesus thought it not robbery or sacrilege to be equal with God was because he realized that God was not just with him but in him and because God was in him he would do what God would do if God was there in person. He had all right to do what God would do because he had seen what God did and he knew that he was empowered with ability to do the same. The same life that God has in him he had given Jesus to have in himself and this life (zoe) represents the nature of God. This same zoe life abides in you and I, we have the same ability in us for that was the express purpose and reason for Jesus coming, he said *"I am come that they might have life (zoe), and that they might have it more abundantly."* St. John 10:10b

Jesus came to change our nature and give us the nature and ability of God so that we can work the works of God no matter what it is. Jesus said *"Verily, verily, I say unto you, He that believeth on me, the works that I do shall he do also; and greater works than these shall he do; because I go unto my Father. And whatsoever ye shall ask in my name, that will I do, that the Father may be glorified in the Son. If ye shall ask anything in my name, I will do it."* St. John 14:12-14 Believe on Jesus and you shall do as he did and greater works because he has gone back unto the father and he said *"my Father is greater than all"* and whatever you ask in his name he will do it that the Father may be glorified in the Son. From this day forward don't just think like a mere man for then you will only be able to do what a man can do, begin to think like God and think it not robbery for he is in you and desires to work through you to do as he did.

## 8

# Financial Prosperity is of the Spirit

*"But there is a spirit in man: and the inspiration of the Almighty giveth them understanding." Job 32:8*

In our society many individuals have failed to realize where wealth begins, in this chapter we shall explain the true source of wealth from the perspective of what you must know and apply in order to appropriate wealth. Many times individuals have a tendency to believe that wealth begin in ones bank account or in relation to ones status or position in life. These things do have some relevancy to accumulation but the truth is that individuals make their status and position their status and position doesn't make them. You will never see a bum working in the plush offices of Wall Street because of the simple fact that the position does not make the person but the person makes the position. According to the scriptures, you cannot entrust a fool with the responsibility of a wise man.

- *"Delight is not seemly for a fool; much less for a servant to have rule over princes." Proverbs 19:10*

- *"He that sendeth a message by the hand of a fool cutteth off the feet, and drinketh damage." Proverbs 26:6*

- *"Though thou shouldest bray a fool in a mortar among wheat with a pestle, yet will not his foolishness depart from him." Proverbs 27:22*

In order to understand how wealth comes we must search the scriptures for insight and revelation from the Holy Spirit who *"will guide us into all truth." St. John 16:13a* God is the true source of wealth, the scriptures accentuates this truth saying *"But thou shalt remember the LORD thy God: for it is he that giveth thee power to get wealth, that he may establish his covenant which he sware unto thy fathers, as it is this day." Deuteronomy 8:18* Here we see that God is the giver of wealth and it's his will that man has wealth and abundance rather than poverty, God desired that the children of Israel would obey him continuously and live a life of plenty and opulence.

The scriptures affirm this saying, *"Wherefore it shall come to pass, if ye hearken to these judgments, and keep and do them, that the LORD thy God shall keep unto thee the covenant and the mercy which he sware unto thy fathers: And he will love thee, and bless thee, and multiply thee: he will also bless the fruit of thy womb, and the fruit of thy land, thy corn, and thy wine, and thine oil, the increase of thy kine, and the flocks of thy sheep, in the land which he sware unto thy fathers to give thee. Thou shalt be bless above all people: there shall not be male or female barren among you, or among your cattle." Deuteronomy 7:12-14*

If God desired this for the children of Israel under the Old covenant how much more he desires for the church seeing we're under *"a better covenant, which was established upon better promises." Hebrews 8:6* As the church we not only have the Spirit of God with us but we have the awesome Spirit of God dwelling within us *"Even the Spirit of truth; whom the world cannot receive, because it seeth him not, neither knoweth him: but ye know him; for he dwelleth with you, and shall be in you." St John 14:17* The Spirit of God which dwells in your spirit carries the Omnipotent, Omniscience and Omnipresence God and this God dwells in your spirit man. *"Know ye not that ye are the temple of God, and that the Spirit of God dwelleth in you?" 1 Corinthians 3:16* If the Spirit of God dwells in your spirit and wealth comes from God then all the wealth you need resides in your spirit and when your spirit and your mind can work in complete harmony then wealth will be attracted to you like iron is to a magnet.

As a born again Christian you are walking around with all the answers to acquiring wealth in your spirit and when you realize it and know how to listen to and walk according to your spirit then you can possess all the wealth you need. The same God that dwells in you knows where all the wealth resides, have all the wisdom of how to get wealth and the understanding of how money works.

- *"The earth is the LORD's, and the fullness thereof;*

the world, and they that dwell therein." Psalms 24:1

- "For every beast of the forest is mine, and the cattle upon a thousand hills. If I were hungry, I would not tell thee: for the world is mine, and the fulness thereof." Psalms 50:10,12
- "The silver is mine, and the gold is mine, saith the LORD of hosts." Haggi 2:8
- "I wisdom dwell with prudence, and find out knowledge of witty inventions. By me kings reign, and princes decree justice. By me princes rule, and nobles, even all the judges of the earth. I love them that love me; and those that seek me early shall find me. Riches and honour are with me; yea, durable riches and righteousness. That I may cause those that love me to inherit substance; and I will fill their treasures." Proverbs 8:12, 15-18, 21

The answers to your questions about how to acquire wealth, where is it, how to make money work and how to get rich is within your spirit for it's in your spirit that the Spirit of God resides. Get along with your spirit and ask the Lord all your wealth questions, and ask him to give you the wisdom that you need to get the wealth that he promised to give to you to establish his covenant. For *"If any of you lack wisdom, let him ask of God, that giveth to all men liberally, and upbraideth not; and it shall be given him. But let him ask in faith, nothing wavering. For he that wavereth is like a wave of the sea driven with the wind and tossed. For let not that man think that he shall receive anything of the*

*Lord. A doubleminded man is unstable in all his ways."*
*James 1:5-8*

In order to get wealth and answers from God you must have faith for faith and wealth works in conjunction with each other, you cannot have one without the other. *"Now faith is the substance (**the inner knowing**) of things hoped for, the evidence (**conviction**) of things not seen." Hebrews 11:1* Wealth is nothing more than an inner knowing in your spirit that you have that which you desire and this inner knowing causes you to act just as if you have that which you desire even though presently it's not manifested outwardly. You act this inner knowing out in your imagination as you go through the total process of a fulfilled desire, as you see yourself having wealthy things, doing wealthy things or things which wealthy people do. In your imagination drive the car of your dreams, wear the fine expensive clothes, live in the new house, make the large deposits, give the large tithes and offerings, go on the vacation of your dreams and fulfill your life long desires. The feeling of acting as if you already have what you desire will soon trickle down into your spirit man and incite you into right action and cause right action to be magnetized to you. Ultimately and eventually bringing your desires into the external world of reality for all to see and it shall happen without fail as surely as the night follows the day.

God will use your faith to cause it to happen, your

belief is your most vital weapon for you will only receive what you believe nothing more, nothing less. *"Jesus answered and said unto them, Verily I say unto you, If ye have faith, and doubt not, ye shall not only do this which is done to the fig tree, but also if ye shall say unto this mountain, Be thou removed, and be thou cast into the sea; it shall be done. And all things, whatsoever ye shall ask in prayer, **believing**, ye shall receive."* Matthew 21:21-22

Wealth is of the spirit and when you can get both your spirit and mind working together in complete harmony you will never again dwell another day in lack, poverty, barely making ends meet or paycheck living. You will be a force to reckon with because you would have learned how to live and walk in the Spirit *"for the Spirit searcheth all things, yea, the deep things of God. For what man knoweth the things of a man, save the spirit of man which is in him? Even so the things of God knoweth no man, but the Spirit of God. Now we have received, not the spirit of the world, but the spirit which is of God; that we might know the things that are freely given to us of God. Which things also we speak, not in the words which man's wisdom teacheth; but which the Holy Ghost teacheth; comparing spiritual things with spiritual. But the natural man receiveth not the things of the Spirit of God: for they are foolishness unto him: neither can he know them, because they are spiritually discerned. But he that is spiritual judgeth all things, yet he himself is judged of no man. For who hath known the mind of the Lord, that he may instruct him? But we have the mind of Christ. If we live in the Spirit, let us also walk in the Spirit. For whatsoever a man soweth, that shall he also reap."* 1 Corinthians 2:10-16, Galatians 5:25, 6:7b

# 9
# Your Sleepless Spirit

*"I call to remembrance my song in the night: I commune with mine own heart: and my spirit made diligent search."* Psalms 77:6

Man is a tri-fold being consisting of spirit, soul and body. Each part of man has its particular function and operation, when all parts are working harmoniously and in totality then mankind is at their best. Yet, in the midst of his makeup we discover that two out of the three of his tri-fold being must eventually come to a halt and shut down in order to rest.

**The soul of man** which a part houses his mind from which derives his thoughts, emotions and intellect works in connection with his brain which is the master control nucleus of the body. The brain receives information from the senses both about the inside and outside of the body. It takes this information and quickly analyzes it, and then sends out messages that control the body actions and functions. The brain is also the information center that stores past experiences which makes learning and remembering possible. The human brain consist of billions of interconnected cells which enables people to be creative, use language, plan and solve difficult problems. A network of blood vessels supplies the brain with the vast quantities of oxygen and food that it requires. The brain of man is a most powerful thing yet it's not omnipotent and the brain must have a time of rest and sleep. When a person deprives themselves of sleep for an extended period of time, the brain becomes fuzzy and the person thinking began to deteriorate and becomes distorted. A person therefore must get a certain amount of sleep in order for the brain to function at its optimum so that it can be creative, make learning and remembering flow fluently and planning and solving problems possible. Sleep also stills the conscious part of man and quite his consciousness so that his subconscious can work without the interference of his conscious mind.

**The body of man**, which consists of his outward physical makeup, must also have a certain amount of rest and sleep, without it the body becomes deprived of its vitality and health. When the body does not get its proper rest and sleep it begins to feel sluggish and lethargy the once energetic person now feels drained and exhausted. The body is trying to tell you that it must get rest and sleep in order to be revived and energized, if one continue on its deprived course permanent damage can occur and serious consequences of health problems will be the result.

**The spirit of man** is that part of man that neither slumbers nor sleeps and houses the omnipotent and omniscience presence of God, that part of man is his spirit. Your spirit never sleeps day or night, the spirit can go nonstop without rest or sleep, Jesus said it best saying *"the spirit indeed is willing, but the flesh is weak, the spirit truly is ready, but the flesh is weak."* Matthew 26:41, Mark 14:38b

Because your spirit never slumbers nor sleep you have been endowed with an awesome power that can help chart your destiny in every phase of your life. You can influence your spirit for good, success, increase, prosperity and wealth by speaking to your spirit man at the time when he is most accessible and open to influence. Your spirit which never sleeps is more open to your prayers, suggestions, commands and affirmations just prior to sleep than any other time because your conscious mind has become quite and silent. During sleep your spirit, which never sleeps, is not challenged by your conscious mind. During sleep your spirit can more easily get you answers to prayers and even suggestions and commands that you make just prior to your dosing off. During sleep your spirit can even bring you solutions to problems that may have been hard to come by.

I am reminded of how one of my books in particular came into existence *the book hidden riches of secret places was given to me in a dream, in this dream I was riding on a bus and on the bus was another young man that I know and respect as a man of God, as I was sitting behind him he turned around and looked at me and made this one simple statement that changed the course of my life and thinking about finances. The statement was,* **"The human body and finances work the same. If you can understand the working of the human body finances work the same way."** *(See our book:* **Hidden Riches of Secret Places***)* This was obviously a message that God wanted my spirit to receive but my conscious mind may have been blocking it out from coming up so that I could perceive it yet on that particular night of sleep my conscious mind was still and God revealed it to my spirit which never sleeps and it came forth in a dream.

On many occasions, I have gotten answers that I needed in a dream or either during times of meditation when my conscious mind was still and God was able to speak in my spirit and bring it forth in a dream or in a still small voice in my spirit where I was able to perceive it clearly. 1 Kings 19:11-13 I remember on another occasion while I was traveling I had a problem with my vehicle while resting at a rest stop, not being mechanically inclined and not knowing what the problem was I begin to meditate. I asked God to speak to my spirit which never sleeps and reveal to me the answer to my vehicle dilemma, within less than five to ten minutes the answer came up and I obeyed the answer and my problem was solved immediately and I never experienced that problem again.

On many occasions throughout Scripture, we see God speaking to men in dreams and visions revealing to them answers in many areas present and future. Seeing that God dwells in our spirit this is where he communicates to us his plans, answers and purposes, he reveals many things in dreams and visions of the night. He revealed in a dream the vision of Jacob's ladder, so it goes *"And he (Jacob) dreamed, and behold a ladder set up on the earth, and the top of it reached to heaven: and behold the angels of God ascending and descending on it. And, behold, the LORD stood above it, and said, I am the LORD God of Abraham thy father, and the God of Isaac: the land whereon thou liest, to thee will I give it, and to thy seed; And thy seed shall be as the dust of the earth; and thou shalt spread abroad to the west, and to the east, and to the north, and to the south: and in thee and in thy seed shall all the families of the earth be blessed. And, behold, I am with thee, and will keep thee in all places whither thou goest, and will bring thee again into this land; for I will not leave thee, until I have done that which I have spoken to thee of. And Jacob awaked out of his sleep, and he said, Surely the LORD is in this place; and I knew it not." Genesis 28:12-16*

Also, we see in the book of Daniel the man of God that needed immediate answers concerning the king's dream, *"Then Daniel went in, and desired of the king that he would give him time, and that he would shew the king the interpretation. Then Daniel went to his house, and made the thing known to Hananiah, Mishael, and Azariah, his companions: That they would desire mercies of the God of heaven **concerning this secret**; that Daniel and his fellows should not perish with the rest of the wise men of Babylon. Then was the secret revealed unto Daniel* *in a night vision. Then Daniel blessed the God of heaven (saying).* **He revealeth the deep and secret things: he knoweth what is in the darkness, and the light dwelleth with him."** *Daniel 2:16-23* Here we see Daniel and his companions asking the God of heaven to reveal this secret, we do not know whether Daniel and his companions prayed right before they went to sleep but we do know that it was revealed in a night vision. Throughout the scriptures we see many things revealed in dreams and visions, many times this is God's great time to speak to man and confirm or answer man's request, prayers or affirmations. One of the reasons is because at this time man's consciousness is less active and his spirit or subconscious mind is more open and receptive to divine intervention, spiritual things and your own spirit's voice. Within your spirit lies an awesome ability to perform many things because of the simple fact that your spirit as a born again Christian is alive towards God and more tuned to the voice of God and the Spirit of God have freer access to lead and guide you. As a Christian, you have a divine connection and your spirit is the gauge that connects you to God.

- *"The spirit of man is the candle of the LORD, searching all the inward parts of the belly."* Proverbs 20:27

- *"The Spirit itself beareth witness with our spirit, that we are the children of God."* Romans 8:16

- *"That which is born of the flesh is flesh; and that which is born of the Spirit is spirit." John 3:6*

- *"But ye are not in the flesh, but in the Spirit, if so be that the Spirit of God dwell in you. Now if any man have not the Spirit of Christ, he is none of his." Romans 8:9*

**God can speak to your spirit in many ways for your spirit is strong because God dwells there.**

1. Within your spirit is the ability to make a million dollars. 1 Corinthians 2:9 10

2. Within your spirit is the ability to know the future. St. John 16:13

3. Within your spirit is the ability to overcome every sin. Romans 6:14

4. Within your spirit is the ability to heal your body. Proverbs 18:14

5. Within your spirit is the ability to worship God. St. John 4:24

6. Within your spirit is the ability to pray in an unknown tongue. 1 Corinthians 14:14

7. Within your spirit is the ability to sing with the spirit. 1 Corinthians 14:15

8. Within your spirit is omniscience wisdom and your spirit knows all things already. *For "ye have an unction from the Holy One, and ye know all things." 1 John 2:20*

From this day forward begin to exercise your spirit to make it strong and more receptive to the things and leading of God. You do this by meditating in the word of God. *"When I remember thee upon my bed, and meditate on thee in the night watches." Psalm 63:6, Psalms 1:2, 77:2, 119:15, 119:23, 119:48, 119:78, 119:148, Joshua 1:8, 1 Timothy 4:15*

- You do this by prayer and praying in the Holy Ghost. *"But ye, beloved, building up yourselves on your most holy faith, praying in the Holy Ghost." Jude 1:20*

- You do this by reading and studying the word of God. *"Study to shew thyself approved unto God a workman that needeth not to be ashamed, rightly dividing the word oftruth." 2 Timothy 2:15, Hebrews 4:12, Ephesians 1:17-18*

Your spirit man also become strong as you attend the place of worship and hear the word of God, as you listen to the word preached or taught by various means of audio, CD etc... Ephesians 4:8-16 Also, you build up your spirit by having a daily confession of the word of God in your mouth using affirmations to build up your inward man. *"For which cause we faint not; but though our outward man perish, yet the inward man is renewed day by day."* 2 Corinthians 4:16, Romans 7:22, 2 Corinthians 4:16, James 3:2, Proverbs 6:2, Genesis 1:3-24, Proverbs 18:21

Never fail to realize the power of your sleepless spirit always ready to avail you of answers, solutions and directions for your life. Within your spirit abides the awesome Spirit of God and you know all things, begin to allow God to speak to your spirit and direct your steps for *"ye have an unction from the Holy One, and ye know all things. But the anointing which ye have received of him abideth in you, and ye need not that any man teach you: but the same anointing teacheth you of all things, and is truth, and is no lie, and even as it hath taught you, ye shall abide in him."* 1 John 2:20, 27

# 10

# That Green Stuff

*"The amount of money that exist in this world staggers the imagination, truly there is no reason for anyone to be poor, money makes the world go around or make it stand still figuratively speaking, at this moment your world is moving rapidly or slowly according to the amount of green stuff in your possession."*

One of the wisest men who ever lived made a revolutionary statement that can change the life of any individual that will allow this statement to get in their spirit with a deliberate elimination of all influence, inducements and persuasion against the veracity of the authenticity of the statement. This one statement if you allow it to get into your spirit can change the course of your financial life forever. So said the wisest man who ever lived next to Jesus Christ *"Money answereth all things."* Ecclesiastes 10:19

Whatever state you're in at the moment it can be improved or worsen if suddenly you came into a windfall of that green stuff or suddenly you had an emergency situation that caused you to pay out an abundance of that green stuff. According to the amount of that green stuff that is presently in your account, you're living luxuriously, contently or scarcely. The individual that's living scarcely could easily live contently if they had more of that green stuff. The individual that's living contently could easily live luxuriously if they only had more of that green stuff in their possession. The reason that one class of people is able to live greater than another class is simply because of the abundance or lack thereof of that green stuff in their possession. Money is a subject that causes people to cringe, it's a subject that people don't want to talk about, and if they do talk about it, they're ready to get the conversation over quickly and talk about something else.

Well if a conversation about money scares you or causes you reservation at the mention of that word then you're reading the wrong book, no, I take that back you're reading the right book. This book is written to help break that spirit of fear and apprehension that comes upon you at the mention of the word money, if you want to keep that spirit and you're satisfied with your financial situation put this book down and read something else. In this book, we're going to talk about money uninhibited and without reservation like you've never heard before. I guarantee you if you finish this book and receive the words all your misconceptions and erroneous beliefs about money will be broken by the anointing that destroy every yoke.

Many individuals have a yoke around their head that tightens at the mention of money and puts distaste in their mouth at this marvelous word. Each chapter of this book will loosen that yoke around your head so that you can clearly understand how good it is to have money in your possession, until finally that yoke is destroyed. By the time you finish this book you're going to acquire a new taste for money like you've never had before, not because of a love for money but because the eyes of your understanding will have been enlighten. You will see that this green stuff is ordained by God to answer all your natural needs; you will see that this green stuff is not your enemy and that it can be a real good thing to have in your corner. That green stuff that you now have in your possession is not evil nor is it the root of evil, that green stuff does not favor any particular class of people over another. That green stuff that you now have in your possession is impersonal, it doesn't care about you it has no feelings, it doesn't care whose rich or poor, broke or have abundance, cursed or blessed, prosperous or lacking, totally supplied or barely making ends meet. That green stuff that you carry around with you has no feelings about you either way, if you love it, it doesn't love you, if you hate it, it doesn't hate you back it cares nothing for you one way or the other. Yet, many people love that green stuff and will kill over that green stuff just to have it in their possession.

Many individuals work sixty, eighty even a hundred hours a week to have it and some of these same individuals become irate when the subject of money is being taught. Why are you working so much for that green stuff, I'll tell you why, either because you love it or you realize what it can do by having an abundance of it in your possession. Let's take the advice of the wise man and realize that money is good not bad, realize that money answer all things, realize that you can do more good with money than you can without it.

1. *Get it in your spirit and mind that money is what you need to answer some of the problems and situations in your life.*

2. *Get it in your spirit and mind that God is not against money for he himself asks you to bring money into his house so that the needs of his house can be taken care of. Malachi 3:10*

3. *Get it in your spirit and mind that God is not against you having money and he wouldn't care if you had millions, billions or trillions in your possession, he just doesn't want money to have you.*

Realize that the more of that green stuff you have in your possession the more of a defense, protection and cover you can have over your family life, your own life and the more protection you can secure over the lives of others. For the scriptures says "*Money is a defence*" it's designed to help protect you, cover you, guard you and secure you from many of life's situations that you would not have to go through if you had the proper amount of money. God can use money to put a hedge about you that can enclose you off from attacks of the enemy and the attacks of others. This hedge can protect your family, your substance and give you a quality of life that you can order at your specification. A good example of an individual that had plenty of that green stuff and ordered his life to his arrangement and God was not mad at him and even voiced his idea about the man saying, *"Hast thou considered my servant Job, that there is none like him in the earth, a perfect and an upright man, one that feareth God, and escheweth evil?"* Job 1:8

Job's money was a defense about him and Satan could not get in and he voiced his opinion saying; *"Hast thou not made an hedge about him, and about his house, and about all that he hath on every side? Thou hast blessed the work of his hands, and his substance is increased in the land."* Job 1:10 Satan was saying to God, *you've blessed Job with plenty of that green stuff and it has put a protection and covering around him that I can't get through. He's able to pay all his bills without any problems whatsoever, his house is secure and luxurious, he has everything that's needed in it and he lacks nothing. He understands how money works and how to use it for good. Everywhere he turns he's blessed with an abundance on every side, you have blessed his businesses and all the work of his hands, his substance is greater than ever before and amplified in the land, you protect his children and all that he has I can't get in at all to touch him.*

When God made his statement about Job it wasn't because he was rich or poor, but because of the condition of his heart toward God and his dedication and commitment. But here's my point, Job's riches did not cause God to look down on him, his riches did not influence God at all, God looked at the man's heart. God likewise is not looking at your money but at your heart, but he knows that the more of that green stuff you have the better off your life is going to be. God knows that the more of that green stuff you have the more protection and covering over your life and the more secure your family and life will be simply because you have an abundance of that green stuff.

Your life financially can be as secure naturally as Job's but you must have plenty of that green stuff in your possession and we shall show you in this book how to get it and how to attract it. So says the wise man *"A feast is made for laughter, and wine maketh merry: but money (that green stuff) answereth all things."Ecclesiastes 10:19*

# 11
# Money Answers All Things

*"A feast is made for laughter, and wine maketh merry: but money answereth all things." Ecclesiastes 10:19*

In life everything has a purpose and place, at a feast individuals have a time of festivity and laughter as they enjoy themselves and each other. Often time individuals use wine to make themselves merry and their countenance cheerful. The wise man says *"To everything there is a season, and a time to every purpose under the heaven: A time to be born, and a time to die; a time to plant, and a time to pluck up that which is planted. A time to kill, and a time to heal, a time to break down, and a time to build up; A time to weep, and a time to laugh; a time to mourn, and a time to dance; A time to cast away stones, and a time to gather stones together; a time to embrace, and a time to refrain from embracing; A time to get, and a time to lose; a time to keep, and a time to cast away; A time to rend, and a time to sew; a time to keep silence, and a time to speak; A time to love, and a time to hate; a time of war, and a time of peace." Ecclesiastes 3:1-8*

Even though to everything there is a time and purpose, isn't it amazing that in just about everything we have to deal with the idea or thought of money plays a major role in these times and purposes? Money has been given a major part in every phase of our lives and without it purposes and plans are disappointed. God realized that money would have a vital relevance to things that pertain to this life so he put within his word this premise *"money answereth all things." Ecclesiastes 10:19* We can argue, dispute, express our opinions and squabble about how money isn't everything and how there are more important things than money. And all our squabbles and disputes will be correct but in the end we will still retreat back to the same premise *"money answereth all things."* The reason we will always retreat back to this premise is because God has affirmed and spoken a word for this natural life that will stand until the end of time and that word is just as powerful and sure as the word he spoke when he said *"Let there be light: and there was light." Genesis 1:3*

The word that God spoke is the answer to all your natural needs, desires, purposes and plans and that word is *"money answereth all things."* When God speaks a word, it's so powerful that the very foundation of the world is upheld by it and the power of God backs it. The scriptures says, *"that the worlds were framed (fashioned) by the word of God"* and *"God upholds all things by the word of his power." Hebrews 11:3, 1:3* When God stipulated in his word *"that money answereth all things,"* **(meaning all natural things)** he set forth a frame and fashion that cannot and will not be eradicated that the world must abide by. He used money to be seen as a medium of exchange and a resource to be accepted as a payment of bargaining, debt, purchase, pleasure and to meet needs. When your thoughts are contrary to God's about money and you only see money from a negative perspective then God will not allow money to be attracted to you but repelled. The reason most individuals cannot get beyond their needs being met is because they are consciously or unconsciously dispelling money on a daily basis by the negative thoughts that dominate their thinking about money.

You cannot attract money and repel money at the same time; money is operating in your life in one way or the other according to your attitude about it. It's nobody's fault if you're not where you desire to be financially but yours, you are the guilty party, and you are the financial failure or success of your own life. God is not against money he spoke the word about money and gave us a methodical system of how to acquire the things we need in life and enjoy life to the fullest. That methodical system is that God has established money as the process by which needs are met and the more money you have in your possession the more needs will be met and more defense will surround your life and make it more enjoyable. The word of God accentuates this fact saying, *"money is a defence."* *Ecclesiastes 7:12*

Without a full supply of money, you will not have an enjoyable life and there will be no defense that surrounds you and protects you from the attacks of life situations. When you have a full supply of money and able to enjoy life and lacking nothing you have entered into the gift of God for mankind. You have entered the place of rest where God desires every person to enter so that mankind can spend their time focusing on him and not worrying and concerned with money matters. In the book of Ecclesiastes it says, *"Behold that which I have seen: it is good and comely (beautiful) for one to eat and to drink, and to enjoy the good of all his labour that he taketh under the sun all the days of his life, which God giveth him: for it is his portion. Every man also to whom God hath given riches and wealth, and hath given him power to eat thereof, and to take his portion, and to rejoice in his labour; this is the gift of God. For he shall not much remember the days of his life; because God answereth him in the joy of his heart."* Ecclesiastes 5:18-20

What do you need right now that you don't have? If you had the money to get it you would have it, the only reason you don't have it is because you don't have the available resources in your possession. We have to get above our petty thoughts about money and come to the conclusion that it's the will of God for man and without it you can do nothing. Having plenty of money does not necessarily make you a lover of money; you can be poor and still love money more than the rich man that has plenty of it. Money of itself is neither good nor bad but it's the thoughts that follow the money that makes it either good or bad. Yet, in order to get the work of God accomplished in the earth we need the wealth of the land, we just have to be balanced in our thinking concerning money. There are many things that God desire to do in the land and it will take money to get it done, and God's not relying on the world to fund his projects but his own people.

- *Be not deceived God will use the tool of money to pay off that church building or to build that new building.*
- *God will use the tool of money to buy that equipment that's so badly needed.*
- *God will use the resources of money to make it so that Pastors can go full time in ministry.*
- *God will use the tool of money to feed the hungry and clothe those that need clothing.*

God has designed this world so that the tool of money will answer all these natural things. Ecclesiastes 10:19b Money is power and the more of it you have the more power you have in this world's system to do good and the more influence you can have for the glory of God and the good of man. When money is used in the right way for the glory of God and the good of mankind many benefits and blessings occur.

1. *Wealth is a protection. Proverbs 10:15, 18:11*
2. *Wealth can make many friends. Proverbs 14:20*
3. *Wealth puts one in a position of authority and causes their voice to be heard in the land. Proverbs 29:2, 22:9*
4. *Wealth enables you to be able to do more good, be rich in good works and enable you to*

*distribute your wealth to worthy causes. 1 Timothy 6:17 19*

5. *Wealth will enable you to be able to help spread the gospel to the ends of the earth by supporting missionaries and help pay for radio and television time for your personal ministry and other ministries that has the call of God on their life.*

So let us hear the conclusion of the whole matter *"A feast is made for laughter, and wine maketh merry:* **but money answereth all things**." *Ecclesiastes 10:19*

# 12
# Money Needs You

*"Without you money has no avenue to work through and is therefore nothing more than paper waiting to attach itself to the right person with the right ideas to use it."*

At this very moment money is waiting on your beckoning call. It is waiting to be put in use by the right person that will allow it to do what it was designed to do which is answer all things. You have been taught up to this point in your life that you need money, but in all actuality money is not the only thing you need, what you also need is an idea and a plan that will attract to you the money that is waiting to attach itself to the right person that will bring forth a worthy idea that will make society a better place to live as a result of their idea. Most individuals spend their days thinking about how they can get more money and the more they think about this the more money repels itself from them instead of attracting itself to them. Money is not designed to be chased after or pursued but to do the chasing and the pursuing. You must not love money, but it's ok to let money love you, *"For the love of money is the root of all evil: which while some coveted (craved) after, they have erred from the faith, and pierced themselves through with many sorrows."* 1 Timothy 6:10

However, if you will allow money to love you it will

pursue you with such vigor that it will almost make you ashamed at the ease that it attaches itself to you when so many are finding it hard just to make ends meet. Just like a man pursues a woman that he wants to have in his life money will pursue you in the same manner. Some couples would not be together today if the man had not pursued the woman with such tenacity and determination. The traits that were used by the man in his pursuit money use the same ones to find its lover and mate. Everyone has not set himself or herself up to be money's mate.

Money is very particular with the mate that it chooses to spend its life with and will not attach itself to just any old body that has not wooed it and convinced it to fall in love with them. There are certain things that money is looking for in a mate and one of the main things is compatibility. Money wants to make sure that the two of you will be together for a long time. Money is not looking for a booty-call or a one-night stand, but a long-term, lifetime commitment. Money wants to make sure that the person is going to be with it for a long time. Sure some people woo money in by tricking money into a false relationship with them but they will soon find out that money when treated unfairly and against its standards will fight back. When this happens money becomes a thorn in their life and neither fulfills their intended purposes. What are some of the things that money looks for in a mate?

1. *A Love for God-Proverbs 8:18,21, Ecclesiastes 2:26*
2. *Ideas-Proverbs 8:12*
3. *Compatibility-Amos 3:3*
4. *Unity-Psalms 133:1-3*
5. *The Right Attitude-Philippians 2:5*
6. *The Same Belief and Purpose for Money. 1Timothy 6:17-19*
7. *Personality*
8. *Character*
9. *Oneness*
10. *Obedience-Deuteronomy 28:1*
11. *Respect*
12. *Friend-Proverbs 18:24*
13. *Someone to think about it from time to time.- Philippians 4:8*
14. *Honesty*
15. *Sincerity*
16. *Kindness*
17. *Someone that desires it.*
18. *Communication*
19. *Someone that will not use and abuse it.*
20. *Someone that has a plan for it.*
21. *Passionate*
22. *Compassion*
23. *Unselfish*
24. *Faith*
25. *Hope*
26. *Belief*
27. *A true connection with it.*
28. *Appreciation*

*29. Gratitude*
*30. Confidence*
*31. Commitment*
*32. Harmonious*
*33. Pray for it.*
*34. Share it.*
*35. Not love it.-1 Timothy 6:10*

Money needs you and if you will allow money to come into your life it will make you a great partner and will answer all your natural needs.

## 13
## Find A Job In 30 Days

*God is good all the time and all the time God is good. God is the creator of the heavens and the earth and all things belongs to him. The earth is the Lord's and the fullness thereof, the world and all they that dwell therein.*

*Because I love God he has worked all things together for my good. God has supplied all my needs according to his riches in glory by Christ Jesus and because He is Lord of my life every need is supplied now. I am rich, I am wealthy, goodness and mercy shall follow me all the days of my life. I shall rejoice and be glad because I favor God's righteous cause and I will say continually let the Lord be magnified who has pleasure in the prosperity of his servants, let the Lord be magnified who has pleasure in the prosperity of his servant, let the Lord be magnified who has pleasure in the prosperity of his servant. I have the mind of Christ therefore THROUGH CHRIST I MASTER MY MIND AND THOUGHTS, THROUGH CHIRST I MASTER MY EMOTIONS, THROUGH CHRIST I MASTER MY ACTIONS AND THROUGH CHRIST I MASTER LIFE. HALLELUJAH IN JESUS NAME*

### HOW TO START YOUR DAY

- *"This is the day that the Lord has made, I will*

*rejoice and be glad in it."*

- *"I love them that love me; and those that seek me early shall find me." Proverbs 8:17*

When you start out the day, when you wake up in the morning the first thing that should come out of your mouth is; ***"This is the day that the Lord has made, I will rejoice and be glad in it."*** This is the start of your day and it can make you or break you. The majority of people in life their first hour of the day is breaking them in every area of their life. That first hour is the dawning of a new day and what you do in that first hour will determine the rest of your day.

We find throughout the scriptures the men and women of God that were used by God started their day off in a manner that would equip them to live a victorious day. Our first and main example in everything is our Lord and Savior Jesus Christ and it is written of him, *"And in the morning, rising up a great while before day, he went out, and departed into a solitary place, and there prayed." Mark 1:35*

The first hour of your day is the time to put forth the fresh manna from heaven; your first hour is not necessarily based on any particular time as much as it is based on what you do with that first hour you awake. Individuals work different schedules so the first hour for some may be 5:00 am in the morning and for others it may be 9:00 am in the morning. And for those that work a third shift job of 11:00 pm – 7:00

am you first hour when you awake after going home and sleep may be 3:00 pm or 4:00 pm. However, the important thing is what you do with that first hour no matter what time you arise.

The best way to start this off is to introduce you to two parts of your being that plays a vital part in your life throughout your day. These two parts are your conscious mind and your spirit. Your conscious mind is that part of you that reasons and chooses for you throughout your day and has chosen for you throughout your life. The most important thing that your conscious mind chooses is the thoughts and images that will dominate your thinking throughout the day. When you arise in the morning you can think negatively or choose to consciously think positive. You can arise and say, *"Oh man another day, I don't want to get up today."* Or you can arise and say, *"Man this is a great day and I am a winner today and all things will work together for my good this day."* Your conscious mind is the decision maker and for the majority of people it decides to start their day off pessimistic rather than optimistic.

Your spirit however accepts what you conscious mind decides for the day and will not refute it or dispute it. It will simply respond in kind to the decision and suggestion of your conscious mind. It does not matter whether the suggestion is negative or positive, bad or good, pessimistic or optimistic or devilish or godly. The scripture says, *"Keep thy heart with all diligence; for out of it are the issues of life."*

*Proverbs 4:23* Throughout the day your conscious mind is always active and feeding your spirit thoughts and suggestions. Your spirit readily receives it without rejection. Even though your spirit is in all actuality the stronger of the two your conscious mind is the reasoning factor and takes control over your spirit and rules it during the day by its decisions, thoughts and suggestions.

The two most powerful times of your day are when you first awake and when you drift off to sleep. In the morning your conscious mind right after waking is in abeyance or a half sleep / half wake state. At this point your spirit is most susceptible to thoughts and words that first come to it when you arise in the morning. Your conscious mind being in such a limbo or drowsy state does not fight your spirit as it does throughout the day because it has not completely awaken to its purpose and its operation and work of the conscious mind. Your spirit at this point is functioning at optimum because it's hasn't had the opportunity to be influenced yet by your conscious mind with negativity. At this stage it is more open to the divine and spiritual, positive and good thoughts, suggestions, affirmations and decisions that will enable it to be all that it was meant to be for today.

This is the time to impress your spirit by making a conscious and reasoning decision to give it those thoughts and suggestions that will start your day off positively and equip you for a victorious day. The scripture says, *"Finally, brethren, whatsoever things are true, whatsoever things are honest, whatsoever things are just, whatsoever things are pure, whatsoever things are lovely, whatsoever things are of good report; if there be any virtue, and if there be any praise, think on these things."* *Philippians 4:8* At the start of your day you have to begin to train your conscious mind to think on such things. Whatever your conscious mind believes and dictates to your spirit at the beginning of the day your spirit will accept it and act upon it and manifest it in your external world. If you want your spirit to be the powerhouse that it is and manifest in your life the spiritual and positive things that you want to see happen throughout your day and throughout your life you have to equip it with the right information to change your circumstances and situations. The scripture says, *"For as he thinketh in his heart, so is he."* *Proverbs 23:7a*

If you want to see more positive external changes in your circumstances you must begin at the start of the day to change the cause that are producing the effects that you are experiencing. It is all based on the law of absolutes, which is cause and effect. To change the effect simply change the cause and the changing of the cause begins at the start of the day when you make the conscious decision to start the day out with positive affirmations and an attitude of expectation.

## Start Out in Expectation

*"I wait for the LORD, my soul doth wait, and in his word do I hope." Psalms 130:5*

Since you were created with and for a great purpose it's time for you to begin to expect great things for your life. Therefore when you arise in the morning arise with an expectation of greatness in your mind. Make that conscious effort to begin your day on a positive note. Start your day by expressing the positive expectation that you desire to see happen in your life today and for the rest of your life. Start off by making such decrees and affirmations as.

- This is the day that the Lord has made I shall rejoice and be glad in it.

- This day I expect to succeed in all my endeavors.

- This day I expect to accomplish my goals.

- This day I expect to draw near to God and he will draw near to me.

- This day I expect greatness and for all things to work together for my good.

- This day I expect to be the head, above only, the lender and be blessed going and coming.

- This day I expect to find a job and to receive a call for employment.

You can make a list of anything that you personally want to see happen in your life and begin to voice these things in the morning when you arise.

Expectation is the missing key on the road to success. You will not get what you think you rightly deserve but you will receive what you believe and what you expect. Jesus said, *"Therefore I say unto you, What things soever you desire, when ye pray, believe that ye receive them (there is expectation), and ye shall have them." Mark 11:24* If you expect nothing then you will receive nothing. If you expect something then you will receive that which you're expecting, whether good or bad, so make sure that you only expect to receive good things for your life. When you start your day off in this manner in the morning you are supercharging your day and *"thereby good shall come unto thee." Job 22:21b "Thou shalt also decree a thing, and it shall be established unto thee: and the light shall shine upon thy ways." Job 22:28*

Expectation is like a magnet that will attract and draw to you that which you're expecting. Throughout the scriptures we see that the people that came to Jesus expecting to be healed receive that which they desired. In the story of the woman with the issue of blood she came with great expectation that if she could touch his clothes she would be whole. Here is the story, *"And a certain woman, which had an issue of blood twelve years, And had suffered many things of many physicians, and had spent all that she had, and was nothing bettered, but rather grew worse, When she had heard of Jesus, came in the press behind, and touched his garment. For she said, If I may touch but his clothes, I shall be whole (expectation). And straightway the fountain of her blood was dried up; and she felt in her body that she was healed of that plague. And Jesus, immediately knowing in himself that virtue had gone out of him, turned him about in the press, and said, Who touched my clothes? And the disciples said unto him, Thou seest the multitude thronging thee (but they were not touching him with expectation), and sayest thou, Who touched me? And he looked round about to see her that had done this thing. But the woman fearing and trembling, knowing what was done in her, came and fell down before him, and told him all the truth. And he said unto her, Daughter, thy faith (your belief coupled with your expectation) hath made thee whole; go in peace, and be whole of thy plague." Mark 5:25-34*

Your desire must be coupled with belief and expectation and then you *"shall have whatsoever you desire." John 16:23-24* Without expecting that you shall have that which you ask you are doing nothing more than daydreaming and wishful thinking. However, the moment you know within your spirit that you have that which you desire, believe and expect then you know that it shall be manifest in the external realm of reality. At that point as far as you are concerned the thing is already real and any opposition that try to persuade you otherwise is a lie.

At one point in my life I was staying in a homeless shelter for quite a while. After leaving there I went to a transitional house, it was a smooth transition and I was welcomed in. However, two weeks after I was in I went through the process of attending the job class that was mandatory for all that came in to attend. After the class was over we were told to go find a job which I had already begin seeking even before I begin the class. When we were sent out to find a job we were sent out without the necessary things needed to go locate a job. Our only means of transportation was catching the buses to get to and from our destination. We were only given two bus passes and each ticket lasted each way only one and a half hour before the ticket expired, and to go look for some jobs took catching three buses one way.

Many more individuals could have gotten jobs if they would simply have given us an all day passes which by cost standards was only fifty cents more but lasted all day while the two passes lasted only 3 hours. I don't know who came up with this wise idea but it was the most ignorant idea ever put forth in such a setting as this. Well, after the two weeks several individuals was told that we have two more weeks or a total of 30 days from the date we arrived to find a job or else we would be given a ten day notice to depart from the premises even if we had no place to go.

At this point I'm not worried nor fearful about the outcome for me of finding a job because I know who is on my side and also I now the absolutes and principles of how to make it happen. However, the other individuals have no knowledge of these things so they're basically up the creek without a paddle. During this ordeal I was constantly instructed to just go out and find any job so that I could have a job and start working. I had to see the individual that taught the job classes twice a week and her instructions was *"Dexter, you're not looking in other places besides the kind of work you want to do. You have to go out and find anything for right now."* But I was not willing to settle for any kind of job I wanted the type of work that I knew I could do and that I had done prior in past jobs. I was even told that this job will not come through for me.

Well, the time was winding down I was now up to 28 days with only two days left to go before I would receive a ten day notice that I had to depart. I was neither fearful, afraid nor dubious concerning the matter; I told the other young lady that I had to report to that God would bless me with a job before the time. On the next day I got a called from one of the interviews I had went on prior to come in for a second interview. I went in for the second interview and was hired on the spot and never had to get a 10 day notice to depart and go elsewhere. Unfortunately, the other individuals did not find a job in the 30 days and they received their 10 day notice and had to leave the premises on or around the tenth day.

Well you know I was praising God for his divine intervention on my behalf and for teaching me the things that I knew about finding a job in 30 days or less. These same absolutes, principles and truths will work for any and everyone if you will grasp this information and take it to heart. Here are some pointers that you must understand and which I stood on and refused to partake of.

Even though the job market at this time was bad as far as others were concerned and the news was daily reporting thousands losing their jobs daily and even as much as over five hundred thousand people lost their job in a single month. *"I never gave heart to this nor ever spoke negatively about the job market."* Everyone else around me was constantly speaking about how bad things were.

- I never focused on the woes of the economy and how bad things were or about businesses closing and laying off workers. I never allow my heart and mind to be influenced. I didn't give in to all the hype. I knew there was a job out there for me.

- I continued to speak and think positively in the face of bad reports and being surrounded by negative talking and thinking.

- I used everything I had read and learn about how to make things happen and not just sit back and wait for things to happen.

- I put faith in God who promised to never fail me nor forsake me and I gave God his word and took him at his word.

Likewise, every person that's reading this book that is in need of a job there is a job out there for you and you don't just have to settle unless you choose to settle. If you choose to settle there is still a job out there for you and I will show you how to attract it to you within 30 days or less.

Use spiritual truth to make it happen for you. As you have read in previous chapters about spiritual truths now is the time to find a word in the word that pertains to you finding a job. If you can't think of anything here is one that is certain to work on your behalf. *"Trust in the LORD with all thine heart; and lean not unto thine own understanding. In all thy ways acknowledge him, and he shall direct your paths."* *Proverbs 3:5-6* You know what to do with it according to the chapter entitled "The Truth."

Use mental truth to make it happen for you. Send your mind to seek for that job that you want according to what you learned in the chapter entitled "The Truth." Claim your job now not tomorrow, not next week, next month or someday. The scripture says, *"Now faith."* *Hebrews 11:1* This job you want you have it now and begin to praise God for the job in advance of the job. Expect that call with the assurance and mental belief and focus that you have it now. Change your thinking to all positive for when you change your thought you change your life.

Use spiritual and mental truth to begin changing your words from negative words to words that will produce life for you in the area of jobs. No more speaking that *"jobs are hard to find, nobody will hire me, it's rough out here, there are to many people out looking for work, the economy is too bad, jobs are laying out workers not hiring workers, etc."* Loose all this and let it go. Change your words and you change your circumstance and situation for *"Death and life is in the power of the tongue." Proverbs 18:21*

Use natural truth to make it happen for you. Begin to praise God for your job right now and sow a seed of faith and reap a harvest of blessings. Begin to use the law of sowing and reaping by sowing thoughts in your mind of success, employment, position, growth and career and you will begin to reap a harvest of success, employment, position, growth and career. Those thoughts will transcend space and time and will make contact with the individual(s) that have your position for employment, as sure as the night follows the day. Add spiritual truth with your natural truth and allow God to open doors for you that no man can close and attract to you favor from an employer as they view your resume or call you for an interview. When you sow praises to God here are the results, *"Let the people praise thee, O God; let all the people praise thee. Then shall the earth yield her increase; and God, even our own God, shall bless us. God shall bless us; and all the ends of the earth shall fear him."* Psalms 67:5-7

Use the Absolute of cause and effect to make it happen for you. Begin to visualize yourself working on that job. Plant the right cause in the earth and the right effect with spring forth. The Bible says, *"Where there is no vision, the people perish:"* Proverbs 29:18a Focus your mind on yourself working, see this day and night, go through the whole process of a fulfilled day at work. Imagine it in detail and see yourself doing it right now. Use your imagination to work for your good for it is a powerful tool that can be used for right and good. If you can imagine it and can believe it you can certainly have it and come forth as a master of circumstances and no longer a slave of situations.

Also, put the idea of employed in your spirit man at the time when it is most susceptible to ideas, suggestions and affirmations, when you are drifting off to sleep. As you drift off to sleep begin to say over and over until you are sleep, employed, employed, employed, employed, employed. Say it with confidence and with feelings knowing that you are employed. *"For verily I say unto you, That whosoever shall say unto this mountain, be thou removed, and be thou cast into the sea; and shall not doubt in his heart, but shall believe that those things which he saith shall come to pass; he shall have whatsoever he saith." Mark 11:23*

In conclusion let these two Psalms be the first thing you read in the morning and the last thing you read before going to be at night, read them with faith and feelings and you will begin to not only see your job situation change but your entire life will be followed by goodness and mercy.

*"He that dwelleth in the secret place of the most High shall abide under the shadow of the Almighty. I will say of the Lord, He is my refuge and my fortress: my God; in him will I trust. Surely he shall deliver thee from the snare of the fowler, and from the noisome pestilence. He shall cover thee with his feathers, and under his wings shalt thou trust: his truth shall be thy shield and buckler. Thou shalt not be afraid for the terror by night; nor for the arrow that flieth by day; Nor for the pestilence that walketh in darkness; nor for the destruction that wasteth at noonday. A thousand shall fall at thy side, and ten thousand at thy right hand; but it shall not come nigh thee. Only with thine eyes shalt thou behold and see the reward of the wicked.*

*Because thou hast made the Lord, which is my refuge, even the most High, thy habitation; There shall no evil befall thee, neither shall any plague come nigh thy dwelling. For he shall give his angels charge over thee, to keep thee in all thy ways. They shall bear thee up in their hands, lest thou dash thy foot against a stone. Thou shalt tread upon the lion and adder: the young lion and the dragon shalt thou trample under feet. Because he hath set his love upon me, therefore will I deliver him: I will set him on high, because he hath known my name. He shall call upon me, and I will answer him: I will be with him in trouble; I will deliver him, and honour him. With long life will I satisfy him, and shew him my salvation." Psalms 91*

*"The LORD is my shepherd; I shall not want. He maketh me to lie down in green pastures: he leadeth me beside the still waters. He restoreth my soul: he leadeth me in the paths of righteousness for his name's sake. Yea, though I walk through the valley of the shadow of death, I will fear no evil: for thou art withy me; thy rod and thy staff they comfort me.*

*Thou preparest a table before me in the presence of mine enemies: thou anointest my head with oil; my cup runneth over. Surely goodness and mercy shall follow me all the days of my life: and I will dwell in the house of the LORD for ever." Psalms 23*

## 14
## The Salary

*"In all labour there is profit." Proverbs 14:23*

*"Love not sleep, lest thy come to poverty; open thine eyes, and thou shalt be satisfied with bread. Yet a little sleep, a little slumber, a little folding of the hands to sleep: So shall thy poverty come as one that travelleth; and thy want as an armed man. How long wilt thy sleep, O sluggard? When wilt thou arise out of thy sleep: For the desire of the slothful killeth him; for his hands refuse to labour. But he that gathereth by labour shall increase. For the soul of the diligent shall be made fat." Proverbs 24:33-34, 20:13, 21:25, 13:4, 11*

A man's salary is the wages that he receives for his services it is payment for work rendered. In olden times, men worked and received other things for wages instead of money.

Some received animals, food, clothing etc. but today the general wages for work rendered is money. Money is also the number one medium of exchange used today in relations to purchasing goods. Without available money, mankind is limited in what he can do and what he can purchase, with a full supply of money he is unlimited in his purchasing power and his ability to do. If you want to have money the only right and legal method of getting it is by work.

Work will cause you to have money and money will give you a salary or a wage for work done. No work, no salary, no salary no money no money no ability to do things and no purchasing power.

If you want to discover wealth you must first have a salary in order for it to be revealed with the method and truth we're referring to here. For wealth lies hidden in your salary, in the beginning of acquiring increase, prosperity and wealth it has no bearing on the size of your salary. Wealth is not accumulated over night and there's no such thing as overnight riches, no such thing as get rich quick. All things requires work and time, if you will put forth the necessary effort (work) with the proper knowledge and give it enough time with God's help you can bring any kind of venture to pass.

## Our Main Focus

Our main focus in this book is your salary, it's the salary that gives God and you something to work with and work through. I'll define salary as any kind of income that you have coming to you on a weekly, bi-weekly or monthly basis.

Whether it's a government check, regular job, social security, child support, income from your son, daughter, husband, or business, if you have access to a steady stream of income we will define this as your salary. Salaries differ one from the other but the fact that you have a salary puts everyone on equal ground. Whether the salary is $1000 a week or $100 a week both individuals will be able to discover wealth that's hidden there.

## Without A Salary

A question may be asked in reference to salary stating what shall I do if I have no salary but desire to discover wealth that God has for me. The first thing you must realize is that in this day and time God always has something that he works with and work through. When Jesus performed the prosperity miracle of turning water into wine he used what they already had to perform the miracle, he didn't make wine out of thin air (even though he could have) he used the water that was available to make the wine. When he fed the multitude with two fishes and five loaves he used those available sources to feed the multitude, once again he didn't produce fish and loaves out of thin air. This is God's normal method of operation that he uses to perform his acts. Therefore having no salary gives God nothing to work with unless he chooses to supersede his normal plan of action and perform a miracle in your behalf out of his goodness and mercy. If God refuse to break his pattern or method then you will have to reap the consequences of lack, poverty and barely making ends meet because you have not wisely positioned yourself to lay claim on wealth.

Nevertheless, you can position yourself and refuse to live in the above manner regardless of where you are at the moment so that you can get where you need to be to fulfill the financial destiny that God has ordained for your life as a child of God. If you're presently without a salary of any kind, what you need to do is pray and ask the Lord to open a door for you to get a job, start a business or to receive some type of public assistance if you're unable to work. This is also an opportunity to use divine help (angels) to get your wealth. God wants you to work don't fool yourself into believing that God will supply your needs and you will not have to work in order to have money, this is a lie from Satan to keep you in poverty and lack disabling you from acquiring the abundant life God has for you.

You must have some type of income coming in to live, in 2 Thessalonians 3:10 it says, *"If any would not work, neither should he eat."* Simply put God is saying if you refuse to work and you can work you should starve, you don't deserve any of life's pleasures or financial and material blessing because you refuse to work in order to get them.

In 1 Thessalonians 4:11 it says, *"And that ye study to be quiet, and to do your own business, and to work with your own hands, as we commanded you."* Yet if you really want a salary to lay claim on your increase, prosperity and wealth, go to God in sincerity and humility and ask him to open a door of opportunity for you to get income coming in so you can work and make money. God knows where the jobs are and the public assistance that you need to help you get ahead in the game of life. Stating to God it's your desire to have a salary so that you can bring your tithes and offerings in the house of God, make money for you and your family, be a blessing to others and enjoy life. God wants you to have increase and prosperity more than you can ever imagine and even more than you desire to have increase and prosperity. The scriptures states, *"Therefore I say unto you, What things soever ye desire, when ye pray, believe that ye receive them, and ye shall have them. Ask, and it shall be given you; seek, and ye shall find; knock, and it shall be opened. Or what man is there of you, whom if his son ask bread, will he give him a stone? Or if he ask a fish, will he give him a serpent? If ye then, being evil, know how to give good gifts unto your children, how much more shall your Father which is in heaven give good things to them that ask him? Mark 11:24-26, Matthew 7:7-11*

You must have a salary of some sort in order to discover the wealth that's there and put these principles that you will learn in this book into action. Begin today to seek the Lord and watch God work on your behalf. When God open for you that door of opportunity don't forget God and begin to enjoy the blessings more than the blesser. If you already have a salary of any kind you're in good shape financially, you already have what you need to change your situation and circumstances and begin a new financial future. For within your salary God has placed your increase, prosperity and wealth and it's now awaiting your beckoning call as the following chapters show you how to make it work for you instead of against you.

# 15
# The Intents of the Heart

*"Keep thy heart with all diligence, for out of it comes the issues of life."*

Out of 100% of individuals, 95% are controlled in life by negative thinking and this type of thinking creates negative results. The Scripture says, *"For as he thinketh in his heart, so is he." Proverbs 23:7* This negative thinking in the area of finances block individuals from entering into a life of financial increase, prosperity, wealth and riches. What individuals fail to realize is what is in your heart is what will be evident in your life, whether it is there consciously or unconsciously. It's really a matter of the heart. The Bible states, *"The heart is deceitful above all things (your mind, your words, everything), and desperately wicked: who can know it?" Jeremiah 17:9* You don't know the innermost depths of your own heart, but God said, *"I know the heart, I try the reins, even to give every man according to his ways, and according to the fruit of his doings." Jeremiah 17:10*

The reason why you are where you are in your financial life is because you have been deceived and bamboozled by your own heart into believing a lie. You think you are positive in your heart, but in the reins and innermost part, you are really, really negative. And as a result of the negativity, you are poor, broke and constantly repelling financial increase, prosperity, wealth and riches from coming into your life.

You may be offended at this statement and want to defend yourself. But if you will accept this truth and allow understanding to enlighten your mind, *"You shall know the truth, and the truth shall make you free." John 8:32* If you have been poor and broke for years and desire to see financial increase, prosperity, wealth and riches in your life but can't seem to get it to manifest, then obviously something is truly wrong. The truth is that your heart has been deceiving you for years and has attracted to you what is really in the innermost depths of your heart. And for most individuals, the thoughts that has the ascendancy in the heart are **"I just can't seem to get ahead for nothing, things are tough, money is tight, I don't know how we are going to make it, etc..** It's really a matter of the heart. And the time would fail me to tell of all the complexities of the heart in one book, but I will give you several more scriptures to accentuate the importance of having the right (positive) thoughts to dominate the heart.

- *"And thou shalt love the LORD thy God with all thine heart, and with all thy soul, and with all thy might." Deuteronomy 6:5*

- *"But the LORD said unto Samuel, Look not on his countenance, or on the height of his stature; because I have refused him: for the LORD seeth not as man* seeth; for man looketh on the outward appearance, but the LORD looketh on the heart." 1 Samuel 16:7

- "He that hath clean hands, and a pure heart." Psalms 24:4a

- "Trust in the LORD with all thine heart; and lean not unto thine own understanding." Proverbs 3:5

- "The heart knoweth his own bitterness." Proverbs 14:10a

- "And ye shall seek me, and find me, when ye shall search for me with all your heart." Jeremiah 29:13

- "For where your treasure is, there will your heart be also." Matthew 6:21

- "A good man out of the good treasure (positive things) of the heart bringeth forth good things: and an evil man out of the evil treasure (negative things) bringeth forth evil things." Matthew 12:35

- "For verily I say unto you, That whosoever shall say unto this mountain, Be thou removed, and be thou cast into the sea; and shall not doubt in his heart, but shall believe that those things which he saith shall come to pass; he shall have whatsoever he saith." Mark 11:23

- *"As a man thinketh in his heart, so is he." Proverbs 23:7*

In many of these Scriptures we see over and over the words *"with all thine heart."* Now, what this accentuates is that individuals are doing things but not with all their heart and not with a true heart. According to the Scriptures when this happen you think you are in sync with things when in reality you are out of sync and doing things half-hearted and with a false heart. This is why individuals are experiencing more paycheck living and barely making ends meet than financial increase and prosperity. Most of society falls in the 95% negative category of thinking. This type of thinking and half-heartedness trickles down into every aspect of our life and keeps us on the bottom totem-pole instead of being at the top. According to statistics, 1% of individuals are the super rich, 4% are the rich and 90-95% are barely making ends meet or apart of the have not. This 90-95% are the ones in the financial aspect of life whose heart in their innermost parts are filled and dominated with negative thought, thereby producing negative circumstances and situations.

12% Underclass

13% Working Poor

30% Working Class

30% Lower Middle Class

10-15% Upper Middle Class

4% The Rich

1% The SuperRich
$1,000,000,000 or More

$1,000,000 or More

$100,000 - $200,000

$35,000 -$75,000

$16,000 - $30,000

Extreme Poverty

Government Reliance

However, be not dismayed for there is a way out of the deception that has the ascendancy in your financial life. I have taken the opportunity to put together a test that will show you where you are and help you to understand your dilemma and will show you how to come out victoriously. If you don't know whether or not negativity is controlling your financial life, you can easily know by simply taking this test, **The Money Attitude Challenge Test or TMACT.** This test will help you to discover why you are where you are in your financial life. Your feelings toward a thing play a major part in the outcome of that thing. Sadly, we have not been taught this and therefore we haven't realized that the way we feel in our heart (spirit) or innermost being is the real truth that determines our outer circumstances. Our mouth may say one thing, but the real truth is in our heart and that is what manifests in our life. On several occasions the scriptures emphasize this saying, *"For as much as this people draw near me with their mouth, and their lips do honour me, but have removed their heart far from me."* Isaiah 29:13a In Matthew gospel it says, *"This people draweth nigh unto me with their mouth, and honoureth me with their lips; but their heart is far from me."* Matthew 15:8

Therefore, *"As he thinketh in his heart, so is he."* *Proverbs 23:7* **The Money Attitude Challenge Test** will help you to determine your own heart and attitude. I have outline below 10 words that deals with money and life. Take your time and read each word, noting honestly and precisely what your first immediate mental attitude or train of thought is when you read each word. Your mind will immediately go toward a negative or positive frame of thinking. Note that frame for that is your answer. Write it down next to the word. Here are the words.

| The | Money | Attitude | Challenge | Test |
|-----|-------|----------|-----------|------|
| T | M | A | C | T |
| Wealth | Cars | House | Prosperity | Money |
| Giving | Success | Millionaire | Good | Abundance |

The feeling and words that immediately came to you is the true feelings of your heart (spirit) or innermost being. Up to this point your true feelings have placed you where you are in your finances and life. Your true feelings also tell you why you're there. According to the negative feelings and words that immediately came to you tell the real story. The words where you saw more negativity on are where you're having problems at right now in your finances and life. Most individuals in the 90-95% will have more negatives than positives.

You have to get your feelings in line with the positive feelings and eradicate the negative feelings out of your heart and mind. You have allowed your feelings to control your life in a negative and constructive manner and have thereby reaped negative circumstances and situations in your life financially.

Here is a list of negative and positive feelings and words that may have come up during the test.

| NEGATIVE | POSITIVE |
|---|---|
| • Wealth — Happens to others not me. I'll never be wealthy. | • Wealth — God gives me power to get wealth. I am wealthy. |
| • Cars — I need a new one. I want a new car. | • Cars — I have a new car. I can afford any car I want. |
| • House — I'm happy just to have a place to live. | • Houses — Houses and wealth belongs to me. I am blessed to own my own. |
| • Prosperity — I'm barely making ends meet. Living paycheck to paycheck. | • Prosperity — I always have more than enough. I am blessed going and coming. |
| • Money — Money doesn't grow on trees. Money is tight right now. | • Money — Money loves to fill my pockets. Money comes to me easily. |

| | |
|---|---|
| • Giving—I don't have nothing to give. I need to focus on me. | • Giving—I give and it shall be given back to me abundantly. |
| • Success—I haven't had much success lately. Times are tough. | • Success—Whatever I do shall prosper. Success belongs to me. |
| • Millionaire—I just want to be able to pay my bills. | • Millionaire—I am a millionaire. Wealth and Riches are in my house. |

| | |
|---|---|
| • Good—I need something good to happen to me sometimes. | • Good—Goodness and mercy follows me all day and everyday. |
| • Abundance—I am lacking so much in my life. I am in need constantly. | • Abundance—I am blessed going and coming. I have abundance. |

In taking this test you have just encountered your true self. Your innermost feelings tell the whole and true story. Most individuals have never known that their true feelings are negative and not positive. **Any feeling or statement that is not in the now is**

**negative, not positive.** Most go on doing business in the same old way but are expecting different results than what's in their heart. Not knowing that their heart is deceiving them and making them believe a lie. Individuals don't realize that the negative feelings within their heart produces negative energy around them and causes them to repel money instead of attract money to them. However, my words to you are FEAR NOT. Throughout this book you will be taught how to bring about a change in your attitude, feelings and the energy that surrounds you. As you master this it will bring about a change in your entire financial life. A change which will take you from lack to financial increase, from poverty to prosperity and then from barely making ends meet to wealth and riches.

### The Feelings Chart

Our feelings play a major role in the accumulation of money as well as in anything in life. According to the feelings that dominate your life they will either attract things to you or repel things from you. We have failed to realize the importance that our feelings play in our everyday life situations. If I mention the word money to you, immediately you feel either negative or positive about the thought of money. These feelings dominate your heart and have produced the issues of life that you are currently experiencing. The scriptures say, *"Keep thy heart will all diligence, for out of it comes the issues of life."* Proverbs 4:23 You are producing and have produced your current financial status in life. Many times we want to blame everyone and everything else, but the truth of the matter is we are the guilty party. No longer can you look at your success in life being hindered by anyone or anything. No longer can you blame:

- **The devil, because he is already a defeated foe.**
- **Any particular race, because people from all races have excelled in life.**
- **Circumstances, because many have come from circumstances just like yours and have achieved both financial and secular success.**
- **Lack of opportunity, because individuals have broken all barriers to achieve their dreams.**
- **No money, because individuals found the money they needed to do what they wanted to do.**

Two things that have held you back up to this point in your life is your attitude and your wrong feelings about life and money. Let's observe the feeling chart at this time. According to the feelings that dominate your life they will either attract things to you or repel things from you. We have failed to realize the importance that our feelings play in our everyday life situations. As stated above, if I mention the word money to you, immediately you feel either negative or positive about the thought of money. These feelings dominate your heart and have produced the issues of life that you are currently experiencing. Each stage of this chart portrays a certain feeling that you exert about money in accordance to the amount that you currently possess.

- **If you have zero dollars in your savings account at this time you are feeling something about having nothing in your account.**

- **If you have $100 in your savings account at this time you are feeling something about having $100 in your account.**

- **If you have $300 in your savings account at this time you are feeling something about having $300 in your account.**

- **If you have $500 in your savings account at this time you are feeling something about having $500 in your account.**

- **If you have $1000 in your savings account at this time you are feeling something about having $1000 in your account.**

What I want you to understand is that in each financial stage you are feeling differently about the amount of money you possess. You do not feel the same about having zero dollars as you do about having $100, $300, $500 or $1000. My objective is to get you from zero to $1000 in your savings within the next 12 months. I have outlined a methodical systematic approach of how to do this no matter where you are financially at this time. If you have zero in your savings account I need to first off change your thinking and your understanding of how to get your money to work for you instead of against you. I need to change your feeling about money, because if you have zero in your account it's because you're feeling zero financially. My goal is to get you feeling $1000 even at the zero level of your account. You have to conceive or birth in your spirit, heart, mind and feeling the idea of possessing $1000 right here, right now.

**Here is the feeling flow in reference to how a person feels at certain dollar levels.**

0. **Zero dollars =** Man this is pitiful; I don't even have enough money to buy a cup of coffee. I'm not able to do anything.

1. **$100 dollars =** Well this is a beginning; I am at least started in my savings.

2. **$200 dollars** = I have doubled my initial savings and I'm getting there one step at a time.

3. **$300 dollars** = This is good things are looking up financially. I've got a solid whole on this idea of saving.

4. **$400 dollars** = I am creating great progress in my savings and I'm happy about my continual financial success.

5. **$500 dollars** = I am making great strides financially and things are working in my favor.

6. **$600 dollars** = I'm feeling real good now and my understanding of saving money is continually increasing, I am excited about my progress.

7. **$700 dollars** = I'm feeling complete about my financial portfolio and I will see it to the full manifestation of my $1000 goal. (**Confidence is strong at this point.**)

8. **$800 dollars** = God has blessed me to get my finances to this point and this is a new beginning for me. My finances have taken on a new order and I am excited.

9. **$900 dollars** = This is great I've been able to save $900, more money than I've been able to do in years. I'm feeling real good now and my financial future is bright and promising.

10. **$1000 dollars** = Life is wonderful. I now have a $1000 in my savings. I have accomplished my goal completely and in perfect order. I feel blessed and fortunate and my finances are increasing continually.

My task at this point is to get you to the $1000 feeling even at the zero level feeling, $100 level feeling or the $200 level feeling, wherever you may be starting at. I will do this by applying a spiritual, mental, systematic and methodical approach, leaving nothing to chance but every act strategically planned to get you to be a thousandaire.

**Spiritually** = You must begin to confess the word of God in relations to financial increase in your life on a daily basis. Here are two scriptures in relations to your savings been blessed that you can quote daily? *"Blessed shall be my basket and my store. The Lord shall command the blessing upon thee in thy storehouses, and in all thou settest thine hand unto." Deuteronomy 28:5,8a*

**Mentally** = You must begin to change your attitude and feeling so that it corresponds to the attitude and feeling of the person that has already saved a $1000 in their savings account. You have to affirm this attitude and acquire this feeling at the zero, $100 or $200 level. The way to do this is to begin affirming the thought and feeling stated above at the $1000 level. *"Life is wonderful. I now have a $1000 in my savings. I have accomplished my goal completely and in perfect order. I feel blessed and my finances are increasing continually.*

**Mentally =** Next, you must begin to take out a time of meditation in meditating and seeing yourself in possession of $1000 in your savings. See yourself going to your bank and asking the teller for a balance in your savings account, and when she hands you the slip it says **$1000.** Do this for at least 10 minutes a day or as often as you can. Go to a quite place and begin to meditate on this scenario. **(We will talk more about meditation later in the book).**

**Systematic & Methodical Approach =** You will learn about the scientific, systematic and methodical approach of how to skillful become a thousandaire according to the plan that I have laid out for you in the chapter entitled **"Finanatomy, The Economic Plan For Ordinary People."**

Many books have been written about becoming a millionaire or having a millionaire mindset. Many books have also been written about attracting to yourselves wealth and riches and everything you desire to have in life. However, the sad truth is that most people that read these books fail to accumulate the wealth or acquire the lifestyle that the books say they will. One of the reasons is because the authors fail to realize that the readers of these books are not the 4% Rich or the 1% Super Rich, but the 95% that are part of the have-nots and the ones that are barely making ends meet.

These individuals' attitudes and feelings cannot even relate to what it feels like to be a millionaire, and therefore the success of their readers is few. These authors are trying to put a millionaire mindset in the mind of a person that has zero or little finances in their possession, ultimately it doesn't work. Even though the author sells millions of books the success rate of those that see results are few. This is what we have fail to see and the authors are walking away with millions from book sales but the readers are walking away disappointed because another book has promised results but instead they have come up empty and without substance to change their life.

In this book I don't want you to think about becoming a millionaire at this point, later on in the book I will show you how to make that a reality through another methodical systematic approach outlined for you in this book. However, before you think about becoming a millionaire I want you to become a thousandaire. A person that is a millionaire has at least a million dollars in asset or cash. A person that is what I call a thousandaire has at least a thousand dollars in cash or assets. My goal is to show you how to get a thousand dollars in your possession first and then show you how to become a multi-thousandaire and eventually move you up on the chart to the 4% Rich; and the ultimate goal should be to reach the 1% super rich if that's what you desire. That is my personal ultimate goal to be in the number of the 1% Super Rich, I have the methodical systematic approach of how to do it and it is the will of God for my life as well as yours if you desire it, work for it, learn for it and apply. *"Every man also to whom God hath given riches and wealth, and hath given him power to eat thereof, and to take his portion, and to rejoice in his labour; this is the gift of God." Ecclesiastes 5:19*

## Let's Begin the Journey

One of the keys to bringing about this change is to remove the negative thinking and feelings and replace them with the positive word of God in your thinking and allow it to engraft your feelings and soul, *"Wherefore lay apart all filthiness and superfluity of naughtiness, and receive with meekness the engrafted word, which is able to save your soul. But be ye doers of the word, and not hearers only, deceiving your own selves. "James 1:21-22*

You must renew your mind. The scriptures say, *"Be not conformed to this world (to this worlds way of thinking and feeling, 95% of the world's thinking and feelings are negative) but be ye transformed (to change in composition or structure, to change in character or condition, to cause (a cell) to undergo genetic transformation, a complete metamorphose, to change a thing into a different thing, implies a major change in form, nature, or function, an abrupt or startling change induced by supernatural power.) by the renewing (to make like new, to restore to freshness, vigor or perfection, to begin again, to replace, a restoration of what has become faded, negative or disintegrated, a return to an original state after depletion or loss, to supply that which is necessary to restore lost, strength, animation or power) of your mind (the element or complex of elements in an individual that feels, perceives, thinks, wills, and especially reasons. The attitude that dominates one thinking), that ye may prove that which is good, and acceptable, and perfect, will of God." Romans 12:1-2* Simply put you must renew your thinking and feelings from negative to positive, form satanic and evil thoughts to godly and good thoughts. In the chapter entitled "**Your Mind Is Your Money**", you will learn many positive scriptural affirmations from the word of God to renew your mind and become *"engrafted with the word which is able to save your souls." James 1:20*

Next, you can supercharge your heart in such a manner to get out the negative and build yourself up by operating in the spirit in the manner of speaking in tongues according to the word of God. In Jude it says, *"But ye, beloved, building up yourselves on your most holy faith, praying in the Holy Ghost." Jude 1:20*

When you pray in the Spirit in your heavenly language you are allowing the Holy Spirit who searches the heart to get your heart in line with the will of God for your life. In Romans 8:27-28 it says, *"And he that **searcheth the hearts** knoweth what is the mind of the Spirit, because he maketh intercession for the saints according to the will of God."*

The negativity in your heart may have been there for many years and it may take a spiritual surgery by the operation of the Holy Spirit to get down into the reins of your heart to eradicate the negative feeling and thoughts that have the ascendancy in your heart and spirit. In 1 Corinthians 14:14 it states, *"For if I pray in an unknown tongue, **my spirit prayeth,** but my understanding is unfruitful."* In other words, when you pray in tongues it is a deeper prayer than when you pray in your English language. Praying in tongues is moving out of the natural realm of praying and allowing your spirit or innermost being to pray. Your spirit through the Holy Spirit knows all things. *"For the Spirit searcheth all things, yea, the deep things of God. For what man knoweth the things of a man, **(in other words man doesn't know his own self)** save **the spirit of man which is in him** (in other words the only part of man that really knows man, is the spirit of man which is in the man being led by the Spirit of God)? Even so the things of God knoweth no man, but the Spirit of God. 1 Corinthians 2:10-11* Begin to spend time praying in tongues in your heavenly language, for you don't know what's really in your heart but the Holy Spirit knows and He knows what and how to pray through you to remove the negative and put in your heart the positive will of God. *"Likewise the Spirit also helpeth our infirmities: for we know not what we should pray for as we ought: but the Spirit itself maketh intercession for us with groanings which cannot be uttered."* Romans 8:26

Last, you must change those negative feeling in your heart to true positive feeling. The way to do this is as stated earlier through meditation in the word of God. In Joshua 1:8 it says, *"This book of the law shall not depart out of thy mouth; but thou shalt meditate therein day and night, that thou mayest observe to do according to all that is written therein: for then thou shalt make thy way prosperous, and then thou shalt have good success (or deal wisely in the affairs of life).* In Psalms 1:1-3 it states, *"BLESSED is the man that walketh not in the counsel of the ungodly, nor standeth in the way of sinners, nor sitteth in the seat of the scornful. But his delight is in the law of the LORD; and in his law doth he meditate day and night. And he shall be like a tree planted by the rivers of water, that bringeth forth his fruit in his season; his leaf also shall not wither; and whatsoever he doeth shall prosper."* In the chapter entitled **"Your Sleepless Spirit"**, go back and delve into the meaning and definition of what it means to meditate and how it can bring about a change in every area of your life. Read it thoroughly; digest it to get an understanding of how and why meditation works. Then allow it to work **"for good success"** in your financial life.

## 16
## The Hand of the Diligent

*"He becometh poor that dealeth with a slack hand: but the hand of the diligent maketh rich." Proverbs 10:4*

In life the God we serve is one of righteousness, justice and equity he does not favor one person above another but he has given every man the opportunity and right to increase, prosper and acquire wealth. *"But glory, honour, and peace, to every man that worketh good; to the Jew first, and also to the Gentile: For there is no respect of persons with God." Romans 2:11 "But let him that glorieth glory in this, that he understandeth and knoweth me, that I am the LORD which exercise lovingkindness, judgment, and righteousness, in the earth: for in these things I delight, saith the LORD." Jeremiah 9:24* If you would notice in the beginning scripture Proverbs 10:4 both of these individuals have been dealt a hand, however the choices that each made with the hand they were dealt determined their financial destiny. The first individual chose to take the hand he was dealt and become slack with it as a result he shall became poor. The second individual chose to take the hand he was dealt and become diligent with it as a result he shall became rich.

Poverty and riches are both choices, no one is destined to remain in poverty. If you want to become rich you can, many individuals from all walks of life that were once poor are now living a life of wealth and opulence. Simply because they used the power of choice to decide that they were not destined for a life of poverty and barely making ends meet. No one could make this choice for them; it's an individual personal decision they had to make. If you spend your time being slack you will not have financial increase and prosperity in your life. But will live a life beneath the will of God for your life.

Slack people are lazy people that refuse to put forth the necessary effort to better their life so that they can reach the next level.

1. Slack people are sluggards and God says *"Go to the ant, thou sluggard; consider her ways, and be wise: Which having no guide, overseer, or ruler, Provideth her meat in the summer, and gathereth her food in the harvest. How long wilt thou sleep, O sluggard? When wilt thou arise out of thy sleep? Yet a little sleep, a little slumber, a little folding of the hands to sleep. So shall thy poverty come as one that travelleth, and thy want as an armed man."* Proverbs 6:6-11

2. Slack people are great wasters and God says, *"He that is slothful in his work is brother to him that is a great waster."* Proverbs 18:9

3. Slack people are slothful and God says, *"The desire of the slothful killeth him; for his hands*

*refuse to labour." Proverbs 21:25*

4. Slack people will always end up in poverty because of their laziness, *"I went by the field of the slothful (lazy), and by the vineyard of the man void of understanding; And, lo, it was all grown over with thorns, and nettles had covered the face thereof, and the stone wall thereof was broken down. Then I saw, and considered it well: I looked upon it, and received instruction. Yet a little sleep, a little slumber, a little folding of the hands to sleep: So shall thy poverty come as one that travelleth; and thy want as an armed man." Proverbs 24:30-34*

Slack people will get nowhere in life and will end up with nothing or next to nothing. If your life represents one of slackness break free from this spirit and begin to change your thinking and your actions to become one of diligence. Only the diligent will have financial increase, prosperity and wealth and diligence isn't assigned to any class or race of people in particular, whosoever will may partake of a diligent life and began to advance and prosper in their undertakings. Diligent people are hard-working people, but hard work alone will not cause you to have financial increase or become rich, many people work sixty, eighty and even a hundred hours a week but still don't increase financially and never become rich. To be diligent means to not only work hard but also to work smart and have financial competence to know how to make your money work for you. You must have wisdom, knowledge and understanding in order to build a stable and secure financial future.

- *"Through wisdom is an house builded; and by understanding it is established: And by knowledge shall the chambers be filled with all precious and pleasant riches." Proverbs 24:3-4*

- Diligent and wise people shall be leaders and rule, *"The hand of the diligent shall bear rule: but the slothful shall be under tribute." Proverbs 12:24*

- Diligent and wise people realize that their mind is their money, *"The thoughts of the diligent tend only to plenteousness." Proverbs 21:5a*

- Diligent and wise people are diligent in their business, *"Seest thou a man diligent in his business? He shall stand before kings; he shall not stand before mean men." Proverbs 22:29*

- Diligent and wise people know what's going on in their lives and have it under control, *"Be thou diligent to know the state of thy flocks, and look well to thy herds." Proverbs 27:23*

- Diligent and wise people shall increase financially and become rich in mind and in

money, *"The soul of the diligent shall be made fat."*
*Proverbs 13:4b*

From this day forward, make up your mind that you will be a diligent and wise person and will have a life of financial increase, prosperity, wealth and riches. For what one person can do and accomplish in life another can do if they're willing to pay the price in time, effort and money.

# 17
# Finanatomy

In this book we will teach you about finanatomy, which is defined as the science of the shape and structure of financial increase, financial prosperity and wealth. This chapter will start you mentally on the road to what finanatomy is and how it can work for you. The word finanatomy is derived from two words joined together to make up one word, finance and anatomy. God gave me the concept of finanatomy in a dream, in this dream, I was riding on a bus and on this bus was another young man whom I know and respect as a man of God. In this dream, he made one simple statement to me that changed the course of my life and thinking about finances. He said, *"The human body and finances work the same. If you can understand the working of the human body finances work the same way."*

- Finanatomy is the beginning of financial increase it's the difference between prospering God's way and prospering the way of the world.

- Finanatomy takes you into the realm of the spirit and allows you to do warfare on behalf of your finances.

- Finanatomy shows you how to change your perspective on your finances by being transformed by the renewing of your mind.

- Finanatomy will teach you how to produce life in the area of your finances where death once reigned.

- Finanatomy will show you how to take what you presently have and through the law of cause and effect produce more than you've ever had.

- Finanatomy will show you how to get from where you are to where you desire to be.

- Finanatomy will teach you how to put vision and order in your finances.

- Finanatomy will unveil to you the Hidden Riches in Secret Places as revealed by the Holy Spirit to teach you God's method of financial increase, prosperity and wealth.

- The Secret Places where Riches are Hidden are *"nigh thee, even in thy mouth, and in thy heart."* Romans 10:8

- God works through the Hidden Riches to produce for you financial increase, prosperity, wealth and also financial miracles.

- Through finanatomy you don't have to wait until tomorrow to prosper, you can have prosperity today when you learn how to get *"the earth to yield her increase; God, even our own God, shall bless us. God shall bless us; and all the ends of the earth shall fear him." Psalms 67:6-7*

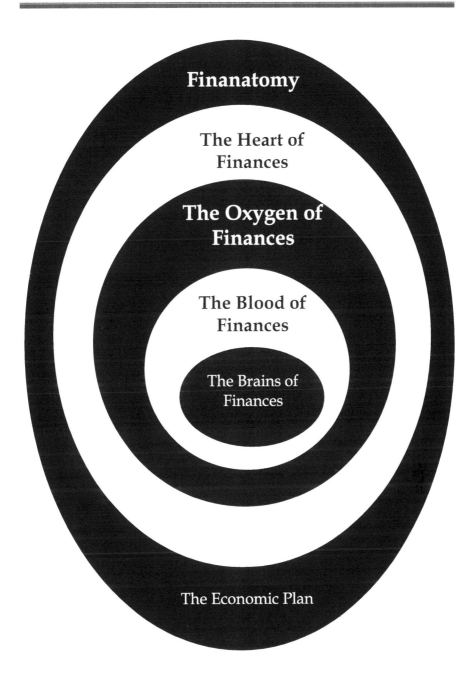

Finanatomy

The Heart of
Finances

The Oxygen of
Finances

The Blood of
Finances

The Brains of
Finances

The Economic Plan

# 18
# Shape and Structure

*"In the beginning God created the heavens and the earth. And the earth was without form and void; and darkness was upon the face of the deep." Genesis 1:1-2*

In Genesis 1, we have the story of creation it begins with these five words, *"In the beginning God created." Genesis 1:1a* In all things that are created there must also be a creator. The story of Genesis tells us who the creator is that created all things. Before God begin to create the heavens and the earth, *"the earth was without form and void, and darkness was upon the face of the deep." Genesis 1:2* In the beginning the earth was without shape and structure, it was in a chaotic and confused state (we know that something happened between Genesis 1:1 and 1:2 but we will not elaborate on that at this time). Whenever things are without form and void, without shape and structure it can only lead to confusion and failure. What you must realize is that from Genesis 1:2 unto the present most things have being operating with shape and structure. Remove the shape and structure from our world and it will return once again to a state of confusion and chaos and without form and void. Everything is this world has shape and structure (including finances). If you can find and follow the shape and structure of a thing that shape and structure will lead you to success in that thing.

Let's observe time, at one point there was only chaos and confusion but when time was given shape and structure the confusion and chaos left, and immediately we know when a day has arrived according to the shape and structure formed. If a day would have been shaped and structured to be 36 hours instead of 24 hours then that would have been the accepted shape and structure that all the world would abide by.

- **Today our time is shaped and structured first by seconds; these seconds are shaped and structured to make up a minute (60 seconds.)**

- **Minutes are shaped and structured to make up an hour (60 minutes).**

- **Hours are shaped and structured to make up a day (24 hours in a day).**

- **Days are shaped and structured to make up a week (7 days in a week).**

- **Weeks are shaped and structured to make up a month (4 weeks and 2 or 3 days).**

- **Months are shaped and structure to make up a year (12 months in a year) etc...**

Shape and structure brings **vision** and **order**, the opposite of vision is blindness and the opposite of order is confusion. Where there is confusion there is *"every evil work."* James 3:16b In finances the evil works are exemplified by **poverty, lack, financial loss, barely making ends meet, living paycheck to paycheck and financial imprisonment.** Every person in debt and experiencing these evil works are individuals with no vision and order in their financial life. Their finance has no shape and structure and as a result, they experience a financial life without form and void.

1.  **In order to get your finances in line you must begin to give them shape and structure.**

2.  **Giving your finances shape and structure will set them on a path destined to get you out of debt.**

3.  **Destined to break the cycle of paycheck living.**

4.  **Destined to break the cycle of poverty, lack and financial imprisonment.**

5.  **You are not destined to live in debt, poverty and lack for the rest of your life. God has a life of plenty, financial increase, abundance,**

overflow, prosperity and wealth waiting for you.

6. **You can remain where you are or you can choose from this day forward to take the initiative to change your financial course forever.**

In Jeremiah 29:11 God says, *"For I know the thoughts that I think toward you, saith the Lord, thoughts of peace* (**prosperity, wellness, health, safety, and happiness**)*, and not thoughts of evil* (**grief, calamity, sorrow, trouble, and affliction**)*, to give you and expected end* (**a future, a hope and success.**)

You can guarantee yourself financial success by following the shape and structure designed to prosper you financially. Follow the shape and structure and financial success is automatically yours. Avoid the shape and structure (or try to make up a new shape and structure) and your financial future will always end in chaos and confusion.

- **The majority of individuals have either avoided the shape and structure.**

- **Tried to make up a new shape and structure.**

- **Or have not come into the knowledge of what the shape and structure is.**

In this book, we will teach you about **finanatomy,** which is defined as the science of the shape and structure of **financial increase, financial prosperity and financial success.** This will start you on the road to financial increase today **GUARNATEED!** The word finanatomy is derived from two words joined together, finance and anatomy making up finanatomy. As mentioned earlier finanatomy was given to me in a dream, in this dream I was riding on a bus and on the bus was another young man that I know and respect as a man of God. In this dream, he made one simple statement to me that changed the course of my life and thinking about finances. The statement was, **"The human body and finances work the same. If you can understand the working of the human body finances work the same way."**

Now I had never heard such a thing, my thinking when I awoke was how do finances relate to the human body, this is absurd there are no relations between the two. Finances deal with money and the human body deals with anatomy or the science of the shape and structure of organism and their parts. Then the Lord allowed me to see how the example of the human body has been used to explain and emphasize other things as well. Anatomy also has been used by God to explain the scriptures in other instances. God used the metaphor of the body to illustrate His working and dealings in the church. In 1 Corinthians 12:12-31 it says, *"For as the body (anatomy the metaphor) is one, and hath many members, and all the members of that one body, being many, are one body: so also is Christ. For by one Spirit are we all baptized into one body, whether we be Jews or Gentiles, whether we be bond or free; and have been all made to drink into one Spirit. For the body is not one member, but many. If the foot shall say, Because I am not the hand, I am not of the body; is it therefore not of the body? And if the ear shall say, Because I am not the eye, I am not of the body; is it therefore not of the body? If the whole body were an eye, where were the hearing? If the whole were hearing, where were the smelling? But now hath God set the members every one of them in the body; as it hath pleased him. And if they were all one member, where were the body? But now are they many members, yet but one body."*

In the above example God breaks down the human body to show the church its order of operation. As long as the church follow the shape and structure for church operation and organization according to the word of God or churchanatomy, then the church will have vision, order and success. Yet, the moment the church gets away from the ordained shape and structure of churchanatomy or church operations it will immediately begin to experience chaos and confusion. If it continues in this manner, it will become totally without form and void operating simply by the will of man without any operation of the Spirit.

Following the shape and outlined structure of a thing guarantees you success in that thing over and over again.

- Are you discontent with your present financial situation?
- Are you tired of what life is dealing you financially?
- Are you ready to come out of financial imprisonment into financial freedom?

## THEN FINANATOMY IS FOR YOU!

1. Finanatomy will show you how to have **financial increase**.
2. Finanatomy will show you how **prosperity and financial success** can be yours.
3. Finanatomy will help you to understand that you no longer have to live in your **present financial situation**.
4. Finanatomy will show you how to have **plenty** where there was once lack.
5. Finanatomy will show you how to have **abundance** where there was once scarcity, how to have it **running over** where there once was just enough to make ends meet.
6. Finally, finanatomy will teach you how to have financial success where there once was financial failure.

Your financial destiny is not a matter of chance but a matter of choice. As you apply the shape and structure of finanatomy for a financial change, you are guaranteed to reap all the benefits for financial increase, prosperity and financial success.

The treasures of darkness and hidden riches of secret places belong to you child of God, *"that thou mayest know that I, the LORD, which called thee by thy name, am the God of Israel. I am the LORD, and there is none else, there is no God beside me: I girded thee, though thou hast not known me: That thou mayest know from the rising of the sun, and from the west, that there is none beside me. I am the LORD, and there is none else. I have made the earth, and created man upon it: I even my hands, have stretched out the heavens, and all their host have I commanded. The secret of the LORD is with them that fear him; and he will shew them his covenant."* Isaiah 45, Psalm 25:14

God has a banquet of prosperity ready and waiting for each of us; it's the perfect will of God that you now learn how to *"take your portion."* As Jesus spoke in the parable of the great supper to the guest *"Come; for all things are now ready."* Luke 14:17 Now let's go to the next chapters that breaks down finanatomy into the four most important aspects of the human body and finances so that we can discover the first hidden riches of secret place.

# 19
# Finanatomy — The Economic Plan
# for Ordinary People

*"For who hath despised the day of small things?, Though thy beginning was small, yet thy latter end should be greatly increased." Zechariah 4:10a, Job 8:7*

In one of my books entitled **"Hidden Riches of Secret Places"**, I wrote about the finanatomy concept. In that book I divided finanatomy into four different parts essential for financial increase, prosperity and wealth. I broke down finanatomy into four of the most important aspects of the human body and entwined those aspects into the realm of finances. In that book we emphasized those four aspects in this manner:

- The Heart of finances
- The Oxygen of finances
- The Blood of finances
- The Brain of finances

In this book however, we will focus on **the brain of finances.** The brain of finances reveals the natural aspect and principals that you must apply to bring about financial increase, prosperity and eventually wealth to you from a hands on strategic, systematic and methodical standpoint. Many books tell you what to do but they don't show you how to do it.

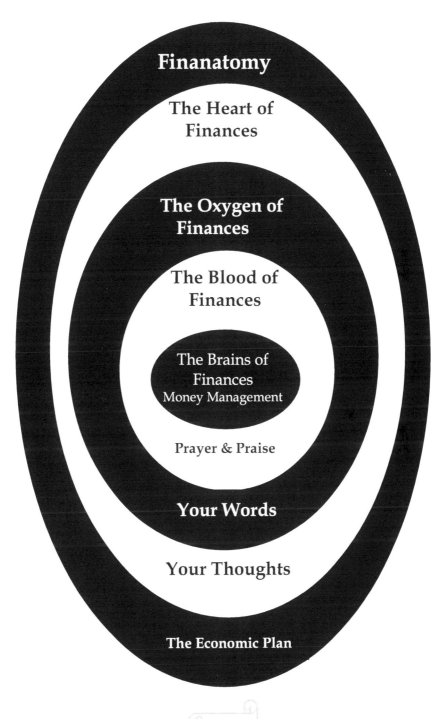

Finanatomy

The Heart of Finances

The Oxygen of Finances

The Blood of Finances

The Brains of Finances
Money Management

Prayer & Praise

Your Words

Your Thoughts

The Economic Plan

In this book we will engage in both, we will tell you through the written words and we will also show you through charts and diagrams how to begin so that you can end with all your financial goals achieved. The brain of finances is the fourth hidden secret of financial increase, prosperity and wealth. This hidden secret has been missing in both the Christian community and to the 85-95% of people that's in a financial dilemma. This is the part that has gone untaught in depth and as a result has caused a recession economically throughout the Christian community and the general population.

## The Human Brain

The brain in the natural body is the master control nucleus of the body. It consistently receives information from the senses about the inside and outside of the body. It takes this information and quickly analyzes it, and then sends out messages that control the body actions and functions. The brain is also the information center that stores past experiences which makes learning and remembering possible. The brain is also the arena where the emotions, thoughts and mood lie. Out of all of God's creations, humans have the most highly developed brains of all. The human brain consist of billions of interconnected cells which enables people to be creative, use language, plan and solve difficult problems. A network of blood vessels supplies the brain with the vast quantities of oxygen and food that it requires. The brain can only go without oxygen for three to five minutes before serious damage occur.

## The Brains of Finances

The brain of finances, the information center that analyzes and controls financial actions and functions which causes financial increase, prosperity and wealth are **the management of your finances or economics**. In managing your finances, there are a variety of things that you must consider, things that the church and the 85-95% have omitted in the financial realm. In this section, we will delve into topics that the average Christian and the 85-95% don't even consider. Topics that may seem elementary and things people should already know. Nevertheless, our objective is to simplify this area so that the average person can know how to manage their monies and make it work for them instead of against them. Knowing how to manage your finances is the key to financial increase, prosperity and wealth. **It's not how much money you make that counts but how you manage your money that counts the most**. A sad reality is that most people saved and unsaved alike fail to use their minds in the way most constructive. Most people simply do not think, people do not take out the time to use their mind to come up with constructive and profitable ways to get out of their financial situations.

A merciless truth but a truth nonetheless is that **Christians are some of the most financial illiterate people in the world**. They have no idea about how money works, how to make it increase, how to manage it, how to invest it or how to get it. Also the 85-95% whether Christian or not fall in the category also. Most Christians simply think that if you bring the tithes and offerings into the house of God money will come pouring in and the more you give the more you get. **For years, Christians have been bamboozled, hoodwinked and deceived into thinking in this manner and they're still no further financially than they were five and ten years ago**.

- Christians have not been taught how to manage their money so that God can use it to work for them instead of against them.

- Christians have basically been taught to bring the tithes into the house of God, yet haven't been taught what to do with the 85%-90% left over in their hands.

- Christians have not been taught how to use their minds to manage their monies, all they know about money is it's the medium they use to pay their bills with.

- Churches have basically done nothing much at all to help Christians to advance their finances in an intelligent and wise manner.

## Your Rightful Inheritance

To be financially stable is your rightful inheritance as a child of God. **It's the will of God for you to be prosperous financially, no ifs, and or buts about it**. Financial stability is your right, always has been and always will be as far as God is concerned. The word of God abounds with scriptures accentuating financial increase, prosperity, wealth, abundance and overflow. If this was not God's will then He wouldn't have interjected such an overflow of scriptures emphasizing this manner of living. In the book of Proverbs, we have scripture after scripture about increase, overflow, wealth and riches.

- *"Honour the LORD with thy substance, and with the firstfruits of all thing increase: So shall thy barns be filled with plenty, and thy presses shall burst out with new wine." Proverbs 3:9-10*

- *"Length of days is in her right hand; and in her left hand riches and honour." Proverbs 3:16*

- *"The rich man's wealth is his strong city: the destruction of the poor is their poverty." Proverbs 10:15*

- *"The blessing of the LORD, it maketh rich, and he addeth no sorrow with it." Proverbs 10:22*

- *"There is that scattereth, and yet increaseth; and there is that withholdeth more than is meet, but it tendeth to poverty. The liberal soul shall be made fat: and he that watereth shall be watereth also himself." Proverbs 11:24-25*

- *"A good man leaveth an inheritance to his children's children: and the wealth of the sinner is laid up for the just." Proverbs 13:22*

In these scriptures, God is trying to tell us something. He wants you to prosper in life and enjoy life to the fullest; however it's hard and difficult to enjoy life without money. God is not against you having money, increase, things, abundance and wealth, but he is against money, increase, things, abundance and wealth having you. God wants to be first and foremost in your life, he doesn't want to be second place in your life, finances or affairs. Having wealth does not make you a bad person you can be poor and greedy or rich and greedy. You can be poor and allow money to be your God or rich and have money as your God, either way you've made money your God. You can be poor and foolish with your money or rich and foolish with your money (yet you will not be rich long). The problem is not with money but with people's attitude about money and how they view money. Money can either be your servant or your master.

## Managing Your Money

In talking about the brain of finances, managing your money is of great importance. What I want you to understand is that it's not how much money you have or make that counts but how you manage it. God is tired of his people being ignorant and illiterate concerning finances. He's ready to bless his people financially. But why should he bless people that have no financial knowledge and give them wealth and abundance? **Solomon said, *"The prosperity of fools shall destroy them." Proverbs 1:32a***

- Christians are saying they're ready for wealth yet can't even balance their checkbook, if they even have one.

- Christians are saying they're ready for wealth yet don't even have $500 - $1000 dollars in a savings account and is undisciplined in the principle of saving.

- Christians think they're ready for wealth but haven't learned the first principles of how money works.

**Our churches have done a very poor job in the realm of finances, our churches have not taught the people about how finance works nor how to get ahead financially in life.** Christian leaders are well educated about how to get people to live holy, righteous and how to get to heaven, yet most are ignorant and illiterate when it comes to showing their people how money works. **They're ignorant concerning how to get money to grow, how to manage it, how to make it work for the people instead of against them, how to invest it, and how to get it.** If they're not ignorant and illiterate concerning financial matters then they're keeping this knowledge from the rest of their people in order to keep them financially imprisoned and financially bound. If this is the case then they're no better than the government who keep certain ones in financial slavery so that they will have a class of people to rule over and look down on.

**One of the most important teachings in the coming days will be financial management and financial prosperity. The church is going to rise up and demand that their leaders teach them how to prosper in the here and now!**

### Questions to Consider

The brain of finances is the one aspect of Hidden Riches of Secret Places that makes all the difference. It's an advent message that Satan in his subtle has divested from the body of Christ. He has diverted the church from their thinking, teaching and preaching about financial matters by relegating it to a position of earthly-minded thinking.

- **But here's my questions, where are you presently in heaven or on earth?**

- **When you go to pay your bills, do you pay it with a praise or money?**

- **When you go grocery shopping, do you tell the cashier you will pray for the business or do you give them money?**

Even if the cashier is a Christian, they will say that you have lost your mind, for its money that counts at the checkout line and God wants us to have some sense. Money is the number one medium of exchange on earth. Money is the answer to all natural things, that's why Ecclesiastes 10:19 states, *"A feast is made for laughter, and wine maketh merry: **but money answereth all things.**"* This aspect of the brains of finances is a topic that must be taught on a consecutive basis. It's not a one time, teaching or preaching to instruct or excite the people, but it must be a continual progressive message that's taught with consistency until each person that desires to can become financially literate and financially competent in the area of finances.

- Who said that economic and especially finanatomy can't be a subject taught weekly to the saints that desire to learn more about finances just like a Bible Study night?

- Who said that it's wrong to have a classroom setting to teach the saints just as a school or college has a course on economic for those who would like to enroll because they're tired of being financially illiterate and financially incompetent?

- Who said it and what are they doing to help the people's financial situation right now?

**To keep the financial and prosperity message out of the church is a trick of the devil designed to keep the saints ignorant, in poverty and lack**.

### Money Management

Money management is the brain of finances, what good is a healthy body with a sick brain? The brain (money management, economics) is the nucleus of financial increase, if every other aspect of finanatomy is working except the brain your finances will still be deformed. The brain (money management, economics) when working in a state of financial literacy and financial competence is the information center that takes finances analyzes them and then appropriately manages financial actions and functions thereby causing financial increase. The brain (money management, economics) is the arena where those thoughts of increase, prosperity and abundance are put into action. **If you don't learn how to manage your money now you will either be broke or barely making ends meet all the days of your life**. Because money is impersonal, it doesn't care who's rich or poor, broke or have abundance, cursed or blessed, prosperous or lacking, totally supplied or barely making ends meet. Money doesn't care it has no feelings about you either way and therefore you must take charge of your money and do it now.

## First How Do You Begin to Take Charge of Your Money?

You begin taking charge of your money by first realizing where you are financially, whether you have thousands or just one dollar. The first step is to know where you are financially. At this point take out a sheet of paper and write down where you are financially, if you have ten thousand dollars in your savings account write at the top of the paper and date it–**Total Money I Possess = $10,000**. If you only have one dollar to your name write at the top of the paper and date it- **Total Money I Possess = $1.00**. Now you know where you are financially, this is your starting point.

**Second**, you want to set a financial goal of where you want to be in one year, three years and finally in five years. When setting this goal make sure to be realistic don't try to set it as a faith goal (you've been there done this) set it as a realistic goal to be achieved if there is no divine intervention on your behalf. My objective here is to get you to use your mind and stop always looking for a miracle to get you out and over. If God wants to do a miracle, he can and he will, otherwise learn to focus on financial principles that God has set in the earth that will work for all. In later chapters we will talk about prayer and money.

Ecclesiastes 5:9 says, *"Moreover the profit of the earth is for all: the king himself is served by the field."* Let's use an example to lead you on the way, if you don't have $100 in a savings account now, to set a financial goal for $10,000 in a year is foolish, it's not faith it's foolish. Now you can be foolish and obtain nothing or you can intelligently use your mind and set a reasonable goal like $1,000. In order to save $10,000 within a year you will have to save up $833.34 per month for the next 12 months. Realistically how are you going to do this when you haven't been able to save up $500 in the last 3 years?

This may seem hard and tough but dear reader the devil is out to destroy you and your finances and he's not playing any games. If you want a change in your finances, you're going to have to get serious and tough. You're going to have to take what's yours from this world by force (spiritually, mentally and naturally). Matthew 11:12 Now let's say that you set your first financial goal for $1,000 a year from now. This is both a reasonable and intelligent goal for a person that's starting with a $100 or less in their savings or in their possession. In order to save $1,000 in a year time you will only need to save a total of $83.34 per month. Now doesn't this seem more realistic and attainable than trying to save $833.33 per month? You can start with this realistic goal as your first year objective or continue in the same way you've been going and accomplish nothing. The word of God says, *"For who hath despised the day of small things." Zechariah 4:10* If you believe that God is going to bless you with thousands of dollars and you haven't learned how to discipline yourself to save $100, you are deceived by the devil and will live in poverty and lack for many days. For *"he that is faithful in that which is least is faithful also in much: and he that is unjust in the least is unjust also in much." Luke 16:10*

### Rulers Over Much

As Christians, we desire that God make us rulers over much when we haven't learned how to be faithful in the least. We're like the man that received the one talent that did nothing with it, yet we want more talents nevertheless. In the parable of the talents the man that received one *"came and said, Lord, I knew thee that thou art an hard man, reaping where thou hast not sown, and gathering where thou hast not strawed.*

*And I was afraid, and went and hid thy talent in the earth: (in other words he did nothing with it) lo, there thou hast that is thine. His Lord answered and said unto him, thou knewest that I was an austere man, taking up that I laid not down, and reaping that I did not sow: Wherefore then gavest not thou **my money in the bank**, that at my coming I might have required mine own with usury? And he said unto them that stood by, Take from him the pound, and give it to him that hath ten pounds. (**And they said unto him, Lord, he hath ten pounds**.) For I say unto you, **That unto every one which hath shall be given; and from him that hath not, even that he hath shall be taken away from him**."* Luke 19:12-26

Three points I like to make here, **First**, the Lord called that servant wicked, in Matthew gospel he called him both wicked and slothful meaning lazy. **Second**, he told him the least he could have done was put the money in the bank so that he could have at least gotten some interest on it. **Third**, the Lord told those that stood by to take the pound from the wicked slothful servant and give it to him that has ten pounds. Their response was, Lord, he already has ten pounds, the Lords response in today terminology was **"the rich get richer and the poor get poorer**." *"For I say unto you, That unto every one which hath shall be given; and from him that hath not, even that he hath shall be taken away from him."* Luke 19:26

**Dear Reader, the point I am making here and want you to understand is that God will not give you thousands if you haven't learned how to contr-**

**ol hundreds**. Also, unless you quickly learn how to control hundreds even the hundreds you have will be taken away from you. Mismanagement, the law of cause and effect and the law of sowing and reaping will take it. God wants you to learn how to control the minimum first, if you can learn to manage and budget your paycheck from week to week this is a start? Once you can control hundreds you qualify yourself to control thousands, and then ten thousands, hundred thousands, millions etc. You qualify yourself as you show yourself unto God a person approved and ready for the next financial level. Now let's go back to an important point that the Lord made to the servant that's one starting point for financial management, increase and accumulation. The Lord told the wicked servant, *"Wherefore then gavest thou not my **money in the bank**, that at my coming I might have required mine own with usury." Luke 19:23*

The Lord told the servant the least, the lowest that you could have done was put my money in the bank. This is the least form of financial increase but it's at least a beginning of financial accumulation. Do you at this time have a savings or checking account? If not, start one immediately so that you can begin to have financial increase coming your way? Do you realize that when you're getting interest by having your money in an account you're making money, your money is accumulating more money and you're not even working for it. You can begin a savings or checking account at most banks with a $100, some banks less and some more.

If you don't have a hundred to start with, less observe another method that can help you get there. Begin from this day forward to save the change you have at the end of the day. Get a jar of some sort and put your change in it on a daily basis, discipline yourself to do this at all cost. If you can be faithful with this small beginning of saving your change God will bless you to do greater things, but if you can't even do this small thing how are you going to do greater things? (We will talk more about saving change and its many benefits).

## More Will Be Given You

On the finanatomy chart it outlined the heart of finances which are your thoughts and attitude about things and situations. Make up your mind with a positive attitude that you will daily put that change aside to start building your financial future. *(You will learn more about this in the chapter* **Your Mind is your Money***)*. Next, the chart outlined the oxygen of finances which is the words that you speak daily, daily let the oxygen of finances do its job as you speak words of increase, prosperity and success over your money. *(You will learn more about this in the chapter entitled* **Your Mouth is your Money***)*. Finally, the chart outline the blood of finances which is prayer and praise, let the blood of finances flow freely as you spend time in prayer asking God to help you be discipline in your endeavor to reach your financial goal. *(Your will learn more about this in the chapter entitled Prayer and Money).*

Remember that *"unto every one that hath shall be given; and from him that hath not, even that he hath shall be taken away from him. Luke 19:26* One reason that you have not had in the pass is because to *"every one that hath shall be given."* You have had nothing therefore nothing can be added to you but only taken away, nothing from nothing always equal nothing. Once you begin to have, then more will be given to add to that which you have. This is a law and a principle, God moves upon the earth to yield its increase to those that have. The hardest thing is to start your financial portfolio increasing, however the start doesn't have to be large it can be small but if you start small with continuity before long it will be larger than you've ever had before. If you are in the category with less than a $100 in savings, do as we stipulated above with the change. Many people in the world today can't put their hands on $500 right now. This is why I started with such a small amount, I am not writing this book to the Rich, the Super Rich, and the Capitalist that have millions and billions of dollars in the bank but to those who are barely making ends meet living paycheck to paycheck, in poverty and lack.

I am writing to those who long to leave this curse of a financial life behind and ready to move forward to obtain what's rightly theirs. A sad reality is that many Christians don't even have $500 in a savings account right now, definitely not $1000 yet we're saying that we will win the world for Christ.

A merciless truth but a truth nonetheless is that it's going to take money to win the world and God is not depending on the world to fund his work. God is looking to his own people to bring the tithes and offerings into his house to help reap this last day harvest of lost souls. (**See our book "Discover Wealth God's Hidden In Your Salary**) If you've already pass the hundred dollar savings, make your financial goal higher yet realistic. You can also begin to save money by the same method of change accumulation. There have been individuals that have saved hundreds and thousands of dollars in change alone. Every day you empty your change into your jar you're increasing financially. Each time you have saved $50-$100 in your jar take it and add it in your savings account if this is the method you've chosen to save by, whatever method you choose have a weekly and monthly goal that you have set aside to reach to add to your savings. You may scoff at the idea of change accumulation for such a person as yourself, but let me ask you something, are you among the ones that currently has less than $1000 in your checking or savings account?

If you are then obviously, you have not been a good money manager and if you keep on doing the same thing, you're going to continue to get the same results. If you want something other than what you've been getting then you must begin to take a different course of action. Just to show you how the idea of change accumulation can add up quickly and cause you to get on the road to financial increase and create financial miracles for you in the process, I want to relay this story.

When I begin to write this book and my other books, I had the idea of paying for it by using the change that I had accumulated over time, the book that you're reading either in e-book form or by paper back the publishing of it was paid for by the change I accumulated. Now any person knows that to get a book published is not cheap, it doesn't cost dollars to get it done but hundreds of dollars and in some cases even thousands. Yet, all the money that was needed to accomplish my goal of getting this book published was done by the change that I daily saved in jars to get it done. I had jars marked with the writing on it **"for book publication."** Other jars I had marked **"savings"**, **"long term savings"**, and **"emergency fund."** Daily in some and weekly in others I put something in these jars if it was only twenty five or fifty cents and over time the change increased and accumulated into much, so much that I could publish this book and do other things as well. You will be amazed what you can do when you have understanding and a road map of how to do what you need to do. Many individuals are spending money daily that they could using toward the attainment of their financial goals. Let's observe a brief concept of spending.

## Money Spent vs. Money Saved

Individuals spend an insurmountable amount of money on a daily, weekly and monthly basis without even realizing it. These same individuals then turn and say that they have no money to save to build their nest egg and their financial fortune. We will base our calculations on individuals spending $10 a day, $75 a week and $300 a month. Let's observe how people are spending money which they could be saving. You may not be spending money on all these things, but I will leave it up to you to figure out what you're spending money on daily. Most people will average around $10 a day without even realizing they're spending this kind of money daily.

| $300 Monthly Spent | | | |
|---|---|---|---|
| Money Spent | Spent Daily | Spent Weekly | Spent Monthly |
| $5-Coffee | 1.   $10 | 1.   $75 | 1.   $300 |
| $5-Breakfast | 2.   $10 | | |
| $5-Lunch | 3.   $10 | | |
| $2-for Break | 4.   $10 | | |
| $5-Cigarettes | 5.   $10 | | |
| $3-Lottery | 6.   $15 | | |
| $2-Daily Beer | 7.   $10 | | |
| Total--$27 | $75 | Weekly total--$75 | Monthly $300 |

## Money Spent In Years

- 1st  year = $3600
- 2nd  year = $7200
- 3rd  year = $10,800
- 4th  year = $14,400
- 5th  year = $18,000
- 6th  year = $21,600
- 7th  year = $25,200
- 8th year = $28,800
- 9th year = $32, 400
- 10th year = $36,000
- 15th year = $54,000
- 30th year = $108,000
- 40th year = $144,000

## Money Saved

Now let's look at the money that individuals are saving on a daily basis verses what they are spending on a daily basis. If you would have saved and invested that $10 a day, $75 a week or $300 a month and earned yourself a 10% annual return, you would be earning a magnificent nest egg for years to come. Let's take a moment to observe some financial figures.

## Money Saved In Years / Plus 10% Annual Return

- 1st year = $3600 @ 10% return = $3770

- **2nd year = $7200 @ 10% return = $7934**
- **5th year = $18,000 @ 10% return = $23,231**
- **10th year = $36,000 @ 10% return = $61,453**
- **15th year = $54,000 @ 10% return = $124,341**
- **30th year = $108,000 @ 10% return = $678,146**
- **40th year = $144,000 @ 10% return = $1,897, 224**

You have money to save; you just never understood how much money you were spending on a daily, weekly and monthly basis. The Bible says, *"Wisdom is the principal thing, therefore get wisdom, and with all thy getting get understanding."* At this point I have put together a chart that will show you how to go about saving money on a daily, weekly and monthly basis, I think you will like it. I have put together a very basic and simple financial plan of action. I have based this plan on an individual making a minimum of $200 a week. If you make more then you can do more or just stick with the plan, I wanted to make this plan accessible to the average person. If you follow these charts you will begin to see financial increase and as you continue to follow the other charts throughout this book you will be blessed with prosperity and eventually wealth.

### Your 3-Month Plan of Action

On this finanatomy 90-day plan of action you will notice that I have broken it down precisely for you so that you can accumulate at least $100 in the first 90 days. Of course you can do more but this is a minimum and a scientific start that is structured to help you put money aside yet not interfere with your money process. I want to first off get you to that $1000 that I guaranteed you that I could show you how to save.

| Finanatomy 90-Day Plan of Action | | | |
|---|---|---|---|
| **Change Goal** | | **Dollar Goal** | |
| Financial Statement | $45 | 90 Day Goal--$100 | $60 |
| Steps to 90 Day Goal **"Change"** | | Steps to 90 Day Goal **"Dollars"** | |
| 1st Save All Change for **"30 Days"** | $15 | 1st Put Aside $5.00 a week | $20 |
| 2nd Save All Change for **"60 Days"** | $15 | 2nd Put Aside $5.00 a week | $20 |
| 3rd Save All Change for **"90 Days"** | $15 Total = $45 | 3rd Put Aside $5.00 a week | $20 Total = $60 |

## Your 6-Month Plan of Action

Our goal is to get at least $1000 in a savings account for you within the next 12 month period. Let us go further and observe the finanatomy six month financial plan of action.

| Finanatomy 6 — Month Plan of Action | | | |
|---|---|---|---|
| **Change Goal** | | **Dollar Goal** | |
| Financial Statement | $60 | 90 Day Goal--$180 | $120 |
| Steps to 90 Day Goal **"Change"** | | Steps to 90 Day Goal **"Dollars"** | |
| 4th Save All Change for **"30 Days"** | $20 | 1st Put Aside $10.00 a week | $40 |
| 5th Save All Change for **"60 Days"** | $20 | 2nd Put Aside $10.00 a week | $40 |
| 6th Save All Change for **"90 Days"** | $20 Total = $60 | 3rd Put Aside $10.00 a week | $40 Total = $120 |

## YOUR STEP BY STEP PLAN OF ACTION

### Your 9-Month Plan of Action

In the next 3 months you will be in your 9-months of financial increase by simply following the finanatomy concept of change and dollars accumulation. Let's go further and see where you will be when you conclude your 9-month economic plan.

| Finanatomy 9—Month Plan of Action | | | |
|---|---|---|---|
| **Change Goal** | | **Dollar Goal** | |
| Financial Statement | $110 | 90 Day Goal--$350 | $240 |
| Steps to 90 Day Goal "Change" | | Steps to 90 Day Goal "Dollars" | |
| 7th Save All Change for "30 Days" | $37 | 1st Put Aside $20.00 a week | $80 |
| 8th Save All Change for "60 Days" | $37 | 2nd Put Aside $20.00 a week | $80 |

| 9th Save All Change for **"90 Days"** | $37 Total =$110 | 3rd Put Aside $20.00 a week | $80 Total = $240 |
|---|---|---|---|

## YOUR STEP BY STEP PLAN OF ACTION

### Your 1-Year Plan of Action

As you will come to the stretch of your 1-year journey you will notice several things, one in particular is that you now have money in your account and it's earning interest. At this point you will have at least $630 that you possess in a savings account of your very own. Hallelujah, this is definitely a time to get your praise on. Maybe you were not in as bad a shape as I was but I can't remember having this amount in quite a while in a savings account. However, we're not done yet, we will now bring it on home to the final 90-day stretch and you will end up with over $1000. Let's observe how we will do this.

| Finanatomy 1-Year Plan of Action | | | |
|---|---|---|---|
| **Change Goal** | | **Dollar Goal** | |
| Financial Statement | $120 | 90 Day Goal--$480 | $360 |
| Steps to 90 Day | | Steps to 90 Day Goal | |

| Goal "Change" | | "Dollars" | |
|---|---|---|---|
| 10th Save All Change for "30 Days" | $40 | 1st Put Aside $30.00 a week | $120 |
| 11th Save All Change for "60 Days" | $40 | 2nd Put Aside $30.00 a week | $120 |
| 6th Save All Change for "90 Days" | $40 <br> Total = $120 | 3rd Put Aside $30.00 a week | $120 <br> Total = $360 |

YOUR STEP BY STEP PLAN OF ACTION

## THE FINANATOMY STAIRWAY
## PLAN OF ACTION

I have now shown you how much money you're spending and the various ways you're spending it. Also I have given you an understanding through my concept of finanatomy on how to save money in a theological, scientific, systematic and methodical manner for financial increase. The charts are designed to show you how money is saved and spent. The majority of individuals don't have a clue of what is going on in their financial life.

## EXPAND YOUR MIND FOR INCREASE

While you're in your saving mindset, begin to expand your mind to look for new ways of financial increase and prosperity. Begin to think about how to increase your finances even further by doing what most individuals ever hardly do, use your brains to help solve your problems. Most individuals act like God doesn't want them to use their brains to think about how to logically get ahead in the game of life. Many believe that God will tell them everything to do and every step to make, if so then why would he give you a brain? Remember that we stated how the brain is used and for what. Let's reiterate here, the brain in the natural body is the nucleus of the body functions. It consistently receives information from the senses both about the inside and outside of the body. It takes this information and quickly analyzes it, and then sends out messages that control the body actions and functions. The brain is also the information center that stores past experiences and makes learning and remembering possible. The human brain consist of billions of interconnected cells **which enables people to be creative, use language, plan and solve difficult problems**.

Here dear reader is what I want you to understand, even as a Christian your brain was given you by God to play a part in your life. This may seem elementary **but the majority of people do not use their brain to be creative, plan or solve their difficult problems**. A mind is a terrible thing to waste yet daily millions no billions of individuals are wasting their minds by not using them to do new and creative things. **Most individuals do not use their minds to think, to plan, to strategize or to visualize the future they desire to have. Their brains are simply in their head like old clothes in a closet just hanging there not used at all but there to take up space**. When you begin to think then you are taking your future into your hands and using your God given mind to be creative, to plan, to be strategic, to visualize and to solve difficult problems. I repeat most people do not use their minds to think, their minds are simply kept in storage nothing more.

- When was the last time you used your mind to plan your financial future, to plan how to get the salary you desire in life?

- When was the last time you used your mind to plan your savings, how to get the amount you desire to have in your savings account.

- When was the last time you used your mind to plan your financial retirement, how to have the money that you would like at your retirement age.

All these things take thinking and planning, they don't just automatically happen or happen just because you're a Christian or part of the human race.

You must take the initiative to make these things happen or they will never happen. If you don't you will come to the end of your life broke, busted and disgusted.

## PLAN YOUR FINANCIAL FUTURE

You must come to the realization that your financial future is in your hands and no one else. If you don't make it happen then it will not happen, you can't sit around and wait on **"luck"** or a **"break"**, you must go forth and make your own break and luck is nothing more than what happens when a prepared person is ready for an opportunity when it arrives.

- **Start immediately to plan your financial future, take a note pad and at least one hour a day write down 5 ways to reach your desired salary goal.**

- **Next, write down at least 5 ways to reach your savings goals.**

- **Finally, write down at least 5 ways to reach your retirement goals.**

Do this on a daily basis Monday through Friday and watch the ideas that God bless you to come up with because you have taken the initiative to use your mind. Some of your ideas will be good and some will not, nevertheless write them down and begin to put the good ones into action as soon as possible. As you continue to do this, you will find that God will begin to bless your mind with more and more new ideas about how to increase your finances. One idea can change your financial status completely and thereby change your life forever. I have given you your first idea and plan of action to get you started; I took my mind and used it to create a plan of action for financial increase. It has worked for me and brought me out and it will do the same for you. Others have used this plan and have overcome their financial situations also.

The beauty of it all is that if you simply keep following this Financial Plan of action it will simply keep increasing you financially. You don't have to change a thing, just keep doing the same thing and you will keep getting the same results. Here's how it will look.

1. **Your second year you will be up to $2,000.**
2. **Your third year you will be up to $3,000.**
3. **Your fourth year you will be up to $4,000.**
4. **Your fifth year you will be up to $5,000.**
5. **And it can and will go on and on as long as you keep doing the same thing.**

For an individual that doesn't want to go any further this can be your plan for the rest of your life and you will simply increase year by year. You will not decrease because you are applying the principle of cause and effect and sowing and reaping. Your finances will continue to climb and you will become more and more prosperous. When you begin to use the Finanatomy Concept for financial increase you'll be on your way to becoming financially competent.

## FINANCIALLY COMPETENT

In order to prosper financially you must become financially competent, therefore begin to read more or listen to audio, video or CD's about finances, prosperity, wealth etc. So that you can become financially literate and competent about making money, investing money, learning how to make money work for you and how to get money. In the book of Deuteronomy 8:18 it says, *"But thou shalt remember the LORD thy God for it is he that giveth thee power to get (to create, to produce, to harvest, to acquire) wealth, that he may establish his covenant which he sware unto the fathers, as it is this day."*

- **God wants to establish his covenant with you and you are the one who decides if you want it established.**

- **God has done his work he's now waiting on you to go and increase your finances and get the wealth that he has provided for you.**

- You are a co-laborer with God, God and you work together to fulfill the financial destiny for your life.

- Now God wants to work with you to teach you how to make money work for you.

## THE PROSPERITY PLAN

In order to get money working for you one thing you must have is a budget. Do not let the word budget frighten you; a budget is simply a map that will help you get from where you are to where you want to be.

1. A budget doesn't have to be complex; it can be simple and precise, uncomplicated yet ingenious.

2. A budget can be your best friend to help you come out of financial imprisonment into financial freedom.

3. A budget will help you realize your expenses and also save up for what you want.

4. Finally, a budget is a plan that lays out what you have to do with your money and also helps you to plan for the future.

If you don't like the term budget but prefer a more sophisticated and likable term, you can prefer to it as your **Prosperity Plan**. If you were to ask the people that you know that's prosperous and not living paycheck to paycheck how they're doing it they will more than likely tell you they live by a budget (prosperity plan). They were once where the majority of people are today but thank God, they begin to think and use their brain to put together a prosperity plan. When you write out your prosperity plan you're doing something that the majority of people never do, you're using your brain to think and help solve your financial problems. The majority of people never get this far in rectifying their finances and that's why so many individuals remain in poverty and financial lack all the days of their life.

**If they would have simply, taken the time to think and come up with a prosperity plan as you will do and put that plan into action their life would have been tremendously different financially**.

Now that you know that you must have a prosperity plan if you want to prosper in life here is a simple system for planning your prosperous future. This is a system that will lay out for you your income, expenses and spendable income. On a clean sheet of paper or on your computer, or in this book record your annual income from all sources that you have money coming in. Here's an example:

- Yearly Salary Made = $_____/ Year
- Gross Income Per Month/ Monthly Income = $_____
- Tithes = (10%)_____Offering =_____
- Taxes = (%) _____
- Pay Self = (10%) _____

Now we will work with your Net Spendable Income left after taking out the above amounts, showing whether the amount you're spending is different from the amount you should be spending. We will put a plus sign (+) to show you could spend more or a minus sign (-) to show you should be spending less.

**Fill in the correct amount on the sheet according to the difference you should or shouldn't spend. Let's look at an example to show what we mean.**

- Ex. Housing Cost/Utilities= 35% of your (Net Income left) let's say your net spendable income is $1,250, your housing cost should be 35% of $1,250 which comes to $437.50. If you're spending $537.50 for housing, you have a minus (-) $100 difference. Meaning you are spending $100 more for housing than you should.

After going down each category total up to see what's the difference between your spendable income and your monthly cost? If you're in the negative you need to adjust your spending and cut some cost or do something to increase your income.

NET SPENDABLE MONTHLY INCOME = $_____
Category Spendable Income Monthly Cost Difference

1. Housing/Utilities 35%_____
2. Food Cost 15%_____
3. Auto Cost 13%_____
4. Auto Insurance 5%_____
5. Life Insurance 4%_____
6. Debts 2%_____
7. Entertainment 3%_____
8. Saving 7%_____
9. Medical/Dental 2% _____
10. Clothing 5%_____
11. Miscellaneous 3%_____
12. Investments 4%_____
13. School/Child Care 2%_____
14. Total 100%_____

Having a prosperity plan is the best way possible to manage your money so that you can live as well as you possibly can on the money you make. You must make up your mind to faithfully and consistently follow your prosperity plan; if you do you will always know how much you can spend monthly in each category.

Along with your prosperity plan you need to get in the habit of keeping track of everything that you spend daily, get receipts of your purchases (you'll be amazed at the money you're wasting, as stated earlier). You can keep track of your purchases by recording them daily on a daily purchase sheet that you can make from a simple sheet of paper. If you have a computer you can log it in on a file on your computer, I personally prefer this method and just keep the receipts stapled together by the week. You should review your prosperity plan at least once a week to see how you're doing. When you know exactly where you are on a weekly basis, this will make it easier to stick to your plan. This may be one of the hardest things you have to do sticking with and reviewing your prosperity plan, but if you will stick to this plan, you're guaranteed to come out of your financial dilemma.

**This is something you must do if you want to experience financial freedom**. Such a plan separates the winners from the losers (financially), it separates those that remain in financial imprisonment from those that become financially free. Remember, with finances it's not how much money you make that counts but how you manage your money that counts the most. Have a livable plan that will allow you to enjoy life along the way without jeopardizing your present income. The key to it all is simple management of your finances.

Now that you understand the necessity and importance of having a prosperity plan, the importance of saving money and how to begin a simple saving plan of change accumulation this is a great start. A great start for the average person to begin seeing financial increase immediately. Financial sickness does not have to be your lot in life when financial health can be so easily attained. You no longer have to live paycheck to paycheck, in poverty, lack and barely making ends meet, there are enough finances in this world for everyone to live abundantly. Start where you are and with what you have, follow the principles and laws for increase, prosperity, overflow, abundance, and wealth and you will be among those that increase financially, prosper and eventually become wealthy.

Don't be in such a desperate hast to be rich, financial increase, prosperity and wealth will come as you follow the concepts laid out in this book. As surely as the night follows the day it will happen, financial freedom will be yours. It will not happen overnight but it will happen in due time and with the right plans laid out and daily tasks followed. Becoming financially prosperous isn't the result of a single task but the result of doing prosperous things on a daily basis. Becoming financially prosperous is nothing more than a lot of successful, self disciplined string of days strung together into weeks, months and years. Your goal will be reached by a continuation of successful tasks done on a daily basis. Daily budgeting, daily putting aside that change, daily tracking your spending, daily saving, daily planning, daily using your note pad and daily staying focused. When these daily things become a habit then you have grasp the one thing that has made the difference between those that win financially and those that lose. Every financially successful person has used these methods in one form or another and it has taken them from one financial level to another because they have allowed their daily tasks to become a habit.

## YOUR FINANCIAL PROSPERITY
## CAN BE PREDICTED

Luck as many suppose has nothing to do with financial increase, your financial prosperity can be predicted and guaranteed. Anyone that wants a financial breakthrough can have it by following the finanatomy concept. Before you realize it, you will be out of your financial sick situation and on your way to financial prosperity and success. Every financial goal you reach will bring you enthusiasm, confidence and the faith that with God's help you can reach financial heights that others only dream of.

- Financial heights for the kingdom and glory of God.

- Financial heights for your family and yourself.
- Financial heights for the uplifting of all mankind and the betterment of society.

There are no heights to your financial success if you're willing to go the extra mile and do what others will not do. Begin to use your brain as never before, God gave it to you to use. Learn all you can about how money works, making money, investing money and making your money grow. Don't be a financially illiterate and ignorant person, but be a wise and intelligent person. Once you start your savings account, delve further to learn all you can from your bank about building an investment strategy. Such a strategy requires careful planning and a commitment to put the plan you create into action. Don't be afraid go for it! Take advantage of what your bank has to offer, talk with an investment manager; the sooner you can put your plan into action the sooner you will be able to reap the benefits. Time can be your friend or your enemy you can let it work for you or against you. The sooner you begin learning about investing the better your chances for achieving the financial goals you set for yourself

## THE MANY WAYS OF FINANCIAL INCREASE

- **There are many ways for financial increase,**

**you can become self employed and own your own business.**

- **You can start right in the privacy of your own home on a part time basis.**

- **There are literally thousands of business ideas to choose from, use your brain to come up with ideas to start making money today.**

Going into business for yourself is the best way to become wealthy it will not be easy but anything worth having is worth working hard for. You'll never have to worry about your job again wondering if you may be laid off next month or next year. You can succeed regardless of education, previous experience (although experience is good to acquire) or background. Develop a business plan then proceed to follow it. You don't necessarily need a great deal of money to start but you do need to gain the necessary knowledge and put it to work for you to succeed. You should choose the type of business that fits your special skills, talents and gifts. You can take control of what you do today and create the financial destiny of your choice.

## ANOTHER DAY OF OPPORTUNITY

Tomorrow is a new day no matter where you are financially today you can be further tomorrow.

Despise not small beginning, making progress financially is a daily goal and you are the one with God's help that can start the financial flow in your behalf. Don't wait for chance or that old lie luck, luck is what happens when a prepared person is ready for the opportunity that has presented itself. Every day God gives you, he is giving you another opportunity to start afresh, another opportunity to get your finances on the right track.

- Another opportunity to **bring shape and structure** into your world of finances.

- Another opportunity to get **the heart of finances** pumping the word of God into your life to get the thoughts that dominate your mind about your finances in their proper perspective.

- Another opportunity to get **the oxygen of finances** (the words of your mouth) working for you, the thing that provides the source of life to the heart (the thoughts) and cause it to grow and develop properly for financial increase, prosperity and wealth.

- Another opportunity to get **the blood of finances** (prayer and praise) the river of life that flows through your finances flowing of which your finances cannot live without that causes financial increase, prosperity and wealth. As you allow the blood of finances to flow *"Then shall the earth yield her increase: and God, even our own God shall bless us. God shall bless us; and all the ends of the earth shall fear him."* *Psalm 67:5-7*

- Another opportunity to get **the brain of finances** (the management of your finances, economics) the information center that analyzes and controls financial actions and financial functions, which causes financial increase, prosperity and success working on your behalf. **Each day that you have is another day that the Lord has made and given you. You should rejoice, think according to the word, speak words of life, have times of prayer and praise, plan and put your plan into action, be productive on a daily basis knowing that daily habits produces a lifetime of rewards.** *"For as you sow, so shall ye reap."* Galatians 6:7

### The Parable of the Pounds

Here is a parable that carries much weight in the idea of financial prosperity and wealth. If you are satisfied with a yearly accumulation of $1000 then that's what you will acquire year after year as long as you follow the first phase of the finanatomy concept.

However, for those that desire to go further into the realm of prosperity and wealth there is yet more to learn and more to do. I am not satisfied with stopping at financial increase for financial increase only helps me; my desire is to be blessed to be a blessing. If you want to go further this parable of the pound gives us a good example of prosperity and wealth that can be acquired for those that are willing to pay the price in time, money and effort. *"A certain nobleman went into a far country to receive for himself a kingdom, and to return. And he called his ten servants, and delivered them ten pounds (a pound is equivalent to $17), and said unto them, Occupy till I come."* Luke 19:12-13

Here we have a most interesting parable that portrays the difference between the diligent and the slothful, or those that are willing to go further and receive all that is open for them to acquire. Before God will give you that which is great He will start you out with that which is least. This is also another reason that we started out our pursuit of financial increase with change and dollar accumulation. If you are faithful there you will be faithful here, but if you will not be faithful there, surely you will not be faithful with greater things. In this parable there are many interesting facts that show us the way to prosperity and wealth. Things, which we can use today, that will help us to understand how the servants prospered or fail to prosper.

As the parable continues, *"And it came to pass, that when he was returned, having received the kingdom, then he commanded these servants to be called unto him, to whom he had given the* **money,** *that he might know how much every man had* **gained through trading."** *Luke 19:15* At this time the nobleman commanded that his servants be called to him because he wanted to know what they had done with the **money** he delivered to them. Two key phrases here in reference to what they were supposed to do with the **money** is the phrase **"Occupy till I come** and **gained through trading." Luke 19:13b** What the nobleman was telling them **(and they knew this)** was too busy themselves with **trading and other business endeavors.** The word trading is a Greek word pronounced dee-ap-rag-mat-yoo-om-ahee and it means **to earn in business.** The dictionary defines trade as *to give in exchange for another commodity, to barter or to engage in the exchange, purchase, or sale of goods or service to another.*

In other words those servants were to either go into business for themselves or lend their money out to the exchangers that could in return make their money grow for them. *"Then came the first, saying, Lord, thy pound hath gained ten pounds. And he said unto him, Well, thou good servant: because thou hast been faithful in a very little, have thou authority over ten cities." Luke 19:16-17*

- Now this servant had taken his money and

either went into business or lent the money to the exchangers in the form of investment for a return on his money. From his $17 he had made $170, a profit of $153, a nine hundred percent profit.

*"And the second came, saying, Lord, thy pound hath gained five pounds. And he said likewise to him, Be thou also over five cities." Luke 19:18-19*

- Now this servant hat taken his money and either went into business or lent the money to the exchangers in the form of investment for a return on his money. From his $17 he had made $85, a profit of $68, a four hundred percent profit.

*"And another came, saying, Lord, behold, here is thy pound, which I have kept laid up in a napkin: For I feared thee, because thou art an austere man: thou takest up that thou layest not down, and reapest that thou didst not sow. And he said unto him, Out of thine own mouth will I judge thee, thou wicked servant. Thou knewest that I was an austere man, taking up that I laid not down, and reaping that I did not sow: Wherefore then gavest not thou my money into the bank, that at my coming I might have required mine own with usury." Luke 19:20-23*

- Now this servant took his money and neither went into business nor lent it to the exchangers in the form of investment for a return on his money. He did not even put it into the bank; he simply hid it away in a napkin. This servant did what most individuals are doing today, being controlled by the spirit of fear of what might happen if they lose their money in seeking to gain more. As a result they are unworthy of being entrusted with more. This servant did what the majority of people are doing today, refusing to allow their money to work for them instead of against them. This servant was reprimanded for his actions and his foolish use of the nobleman's money. He thought that the nobleman would commend him for his consideration and for being protective of his money. However, the nobleman was furious and spoke harshly to him saying, *"Out of thine own mouth will I judge thee, thou wicked servant. Thou knewest that I was an austere man, taking up that I laid not down, and reaping that I did not sow."* Luke 19:22 The nobleman did not give him the money for safekeeping but to trade so that his money could make more money. At this point in your life you are either portraying the manner of the first two servants or the last servant with your Lord's money. Which servant are you portraying? Let's observe the least this wicked servant could have done with the nobleman's money.

*"Wherefore then gavest not my money into the bank, that at my coming I might have acquired mine own with usury (interest)." Luke 19:23* The least this servant could have done was put his Lord's money in an interest bearing savings account. Now let me tell you the reasons that you find it hard to attract money to you and get ahead in the game of finances.

1. Because you are operating just like this wicked servant.

2. Because a spirit of fear is controlling your life, this spirit tells you that you will lose your money if you try to use it to gain more money. What you fail to understand is that no one that has become wealthy has attained that status without some losses, but the winners refuse to quit or be controlled by fear in spite of their losses. Also, winners realize that you trade with money that you can afford to lose not with money that you need.

3. Because you refuse to learn what to do to make your money work for you.

4. Because you have taken the path of least resistance.

5. Because you are perishing financially because of your lack of knowledge concerning money matters.

6. Because you have no mentors that can enlighten and counsel you about your financial status and that can bestow the wisdom upon you that you need. *"In the multitude of counselors there is safety." Proverbs 11:14b*

7. Because you think you are wise but you're really foolish and you're perishing financially.

Therefore in order for you to increase financially the first and least thing you must do is get your money out of your hands and into the bank, so that you can have your money automatically deducted into money saving and money making accounts (we will inform you about how to do this in the chapters ahead). If you do not get that money out of your hands you're going to end up just like that wicked servant, with nothing all the days of your life. The first thing, which the nobleman demanded concerning the wicked servant, was a command to get the money out of his hand. Here's what he said, *"Take from him the pound, and give it to him that hath ten pounds, (do you see how the wise servant just had more money attracted to him?)" Luke 19:24* If you still refuse to get that money out of your hands you will come to the end of your days, totally broke, busted and disgusted financially. You have to put your finances on autopilot and automate everything dealing with your finances so that the law of sowing and reaping and cause and effect can begin to work in your life, producing for you financial increase, prosperity and wealth. *"(And they said unto him, Lord, he hath ten pounds.) For I say unto you, That unto every one which hath shall be given; and from him that hath not, even that he hath shall be taken away from him."* Luke 19:25-26

## A Money Making Business

*"We have failed to realize the power and potential of a money making business. A money making business can prosper you financially in ways that nothing else can. You are one money making idea away from prosperity and wealth."* The Bible has much to say about business, but as Christians we have failed to pursue this most profitable avenue for prosperity and wealth. Just about everyone has the ability to go into business and make that business a profitable money making venture.

- *"Seest thou a man diligent in his business? He shall stand before kings; he shall not stand before mean men."* Proverbs 22:29
- *"Not slothful in business."* Romans 12:11
- *"The soul of the sluggard desireth, and hath nothing: but the soul of the diligent shall be made fat."* Proverbs 13:4
- *"Wealth gotten by vanity shall be diminished: but he that gathereth by labour shall increase."* Proverbs 13:11

- *"A faithful man shall abound with blessings: but he that maketh haste to be rich shall not be innocent."* Proverbs 28:20

Starting a business is not a difficult task; it just takes finding out what you need to do to legally operate a business in your state. This information can be found by researching at your local library or you can take a Small Business Course to become informed. You can always contact the Small Business Association on-line or locally to get all the information that you need to know how to get started in business. There are also plenty of books that you can read that will thoroughly instruct you about the ins and outs of starting a business. The main thing you will need to do is take action, don't be intimidated by fear or the things you have to learn to go into business for yourself, it's not as hard as you think. There are a variety of ways you can do business, such as:

1. A Home-based business.
2. A regular store or office type business.
3. An on-line business.
4. A network marketing or multi-marketing type business.
5. A delivery business of some type, etc..

The easiest way to start your business (*and we will get more into this in the next chapter*) is to begin by doing something that you already know. Everyone has a skill of some sort, a talent or gift that can be used as a business venture. In business, you must have some type of product or service that you can offer clients in return for money. All of the large companies today started out with one or two products, today they are million and billion dollar corporations. Every business with the proper knowledge and application has the potential to take you into prosperity and wealth. Individuals have become prosperous and wealth in practically every business. Some business can be started with as little as a hundred dollars or less, some may take a couple of thousands but with the proper knowledge, determination, a definite plan and a burning desire you can succeed. The business that you may have in mind somebody somewhere is prospering doing it or something similar. What one person can do another can do, you must not just dream about doing a business you must actually go forth and do it here and now. *"Faith without works is dead, being alone."* *James 2:17* That gift or talent that you have needs to be put to use, it can become a moneymaking cash register that can ring on a daily basis. Here are some pertinent questions that can evoke a stream of ideas for you.

- What do you do as a hobby that can become a money making idea?

- What skills do you have that you can turn into a business?
- What do others rave about that you do?
- What type of work do you do that can be turned into a business?
- If you lost your job tomorrow and knew that it would take a whole year before you could find another one what would you do to make money?
- What is fun to you?
- If money were no object what would you be doing now?
- What ideas did you have as a kid?
- If you were homeless what would be your next step (think outside the box)?
- What business concept or product do you just rave about? Why don't you try and sell it or find a way of marketing it?

This is a list of nuggets that can help provoke your thinking and get you on the right track to getting your business stared. Do not allow your skills, gifts and talents to lie dormant or just be used to make others prosperous and wealthy.

### Make Your Own Self Prosperous and Wealthy.

It's time for you to step up to the plate, if you don't do it for yourself then no one will. You can't sit back and wait on luck or base your future on winning the lottery. There are four types of people in this world and each of us fit into one of these categories, see where you fit in and begin to take immediate action to orchestrate your destiny by your own efforts.

1. Those who watch things happen
2. Those who wait for things to happen.
3. Those who make things happen.
4. Those who say what happened.

Your business is your personal cash register that can ring everyday and make money for you. Those skills, gifts and talents you are using for others you can now begin to use them for yourself. You do not need to start out big and elaborate in business, but begin doing something that you're already skilled at and allow that to become your first money making venture. Skills and talents vary with each individual and others have become prosperous and wealthy doing a variety of things. Here is a brief list of things to observe that others have made their personal cash register.

- Some individuals are great cooks; this could be your cash register.

- Some individuals are great at decorating; this could be your cash register.

- Some individuals are great sales people; this could be your cash register.

- Some individuals are great with numbers and could be accountants; this could be your cash register.

- Some individuals are great beautician; this could be your cash register.

- Some individuals are great seamstress; this could be your cash register.

- Some individuals are great teachers and could teach in private settings, workshops or seminars; this could be your cash register.

- Some individuals are good with people and could be great counselors; this could be your cash register.

- Some individuals are good in handling money situations and could become financial planners; this could be your cash register.

- Some individuals could go into Real Estate; this could be your cash register.

- Some individuals may love animals; this could be your cash register.

- Some individuals may enjoy working with their hands and the possibilities are endless here; this could be your cash register.

If you have to go back to school to get more education for your business, then by all means do so, begin to chart your destiny and create the financial future that you desire.

## Biblical Individuals That Were Entrepreneur

*"And Abram was very rich in cattle, in silver, and in gold." Genesis 13:2*

*"Then Isaac sowed in that land, and received in the same year an hundredfold: and the LORD blessed him. And the man waxed great, and went forward, and grew until he became very great: For he had possession of flocks, and possession of herds, and great store of servants and the philistines envied him." Genesis 26:12-14*

*"And the man (Jacob) increased exceedingly, and had much cattle, and maidservants, and menservants, and camels, and asses." Genesis 30:42-43*

*"There was a man in the land of Uz, whose name was Job; and that man was perfect and upright, and one that feared God, and eschewed evil. His substance also was seven thousand sheep, and three thousand camels, and five thousand yoke of oxen, and five hundred she assess, and a*

very great household; so that this man was the greatest of all the men of the east." Job 1:1,3
"King Solomon was not only king but also a businessman with many ventures. 1 Kings 5:13-18"

"Peter and Andrew were fishermen – And Jesus, walked by the Sea of Galilee, saw two brethren, Simon called Peter, and Andrew his brother, casting a net into the sea: for they were fishers." Matthew 4:18

"James and John were fishermen – And when he had gone a little further thence, he saw James the son of Zebedee, and John his brother, who also were in the ship mending their nets. And straightway he called them: and they left their father Zebedee in the ship with the hired servants, and went after him." Mark 1:20

"Luke – the beloved physician, and Demas, greet you." Colossians 4:14

"Paul was a tent maker- After these things Paul departed from Athens, and came to Corinth: And found a certain Jew named Aquila, born in Pontus, lately come from Italy, with his wife Priscilla; (because that Claudius had commanded all Jews to depart from Rome and came unto them. And because he was of the same craft, he abode with them, and wrought: for by their occupation they were **tentmakers.**" Acts 18:1-3

**"Pastors –** I included Pastors here (the ones that are truly called of God) because they have the most awesome work on the planet. They are called for *the perfecting of the saints, for the work of the ministry, for the edifying of the body of Christ: Till we all come in the unity of the faith, and of the knowledge of the Son of God, unto a perfect man, unto the measure of the stature of the fullness of Christ: That we henceforth be no more children, tossed to and fro, and carried about with every wind of doctrine, by the sleight of men, and cunning craftiness, whereby they lie in wait to deceive." Ephesians 4:7-14*

If you look at the natural aspect of Pastors they are like CEO's of corporations and their ministry is run like an ordinary business in many aspects. There is the business side of ministry that is indeed run like a business. In order to have a successful and prosperous ministry financially they must apply many aspects of running a ministry just like the business man runs his business. Their product is the word of God and according to their delivery and anointing they will acquire more or less people in their congregation. Ministries that become sloppy in the business aspect of their ministry will also soon find themselves in much legal conflict and will cause much trouble for their ministry. Make it therefore your business to become like the wise servant in the parable and make your money work for you by trading it either by business or by investments. From this day forward, make up your mind that you will be a diligent and wise person and wealth and riches will be in your house. For what one person can do another can do if they're willing to pay the price in time, money and effort.

Take time and meditate and think about all the things you have learned in this chapter before you go on to the next. You've been given much information with charts and diagrams that show you the way to financial increase. The next chapters will take you even further into an understanding and application of the course to prosperity and wealth.

# 20
# Finanatomy — Part 2
# The Two Courses of Life

*"Every man to whom God hath given riches and wealth, and hath given him power to eat thereof, and to take his portion, and to rejoice in his labour; this is the gift of God." Ecclesiastes 5:19*

In life there are two courses that you can take, one will lead you on to a life of success, prosperity, abundance, wealth and riches, the other will lead you on to a life of failure, lack and insufficiency. God's will for you as revealed in our above scripture is a life of success, wealth and riches which is the gift of God. The word course is defined according to Webster as *the way in which something progress or develops. A procedure adopted to deal with a situation. A direction followed or intended.* In the book of Acts Paul talked about a course that he was following that would ultimately lead him on to victory and enable him to testify the gospel of the grace of God saying, *"But none of these things move me, neither count I my life dear unto myself, so that I might finish my course with joy, and the ministry, which I have received of the Lord Jesus, to testify the gospel of the grace of God." Acts 20:24*

And in the book of Timothy he reiterated this again but from a different perspective, this time he was stating that he has **finished his course** and his reward is waiting, saying, *"I have fought a good fight, I* *have finished my course,* I *have kept the faith: Henceforth there is laid up for me a crown of righteousness, which the Lord, the righteous judge, shall give me at that day: and not to me only, but unto all them also that love his appearing."* 2 Timothy 4:7-8 Paul here was referring to a course that was laid out for him that if he followed would end up with great dividends on his part, but he had to follow the course in order to receive the rewards. In orchestrating your destiny for success, prosperity and wealth we must have an infallible and absolute course designed to get you there with complete certainty and accuracy. Well, in this book I will lay out for you the **financial course** that has already gotten multitudes there. A course that will enable you to not only get on the right track but will equip you with the essential knowledge necessary for attracting success, prosperity, wealth and riches into your life.

I have organized this into two simple concepts to insure balance and understanding for the reader. I call them the **Money Course** and the **Poverty Course.** These two concepts will give you an understanding of the process of how the money course and poverty course works and develops. The money course and the poverty course show you **what people do**, and the stairway to prosperity and the stairways to poverty shows you **how people do it**. The things about these two concepts are that every person either follows one course or the other. The courses will show you what happens when it's done right and what can happen when it's done wrong. Each stage of the money course will show you the proper steps that one should take on the right course. It will instruct you in the right way so you will not waste precious time, money and energy. However, if you try to get around the stages you will get off course and likely end up in disaster or off the path destined for financial success. You will end up as Paul stated **"running as one that beateth the air."** Paul in his exhortation said, *"I therefore so run, not as uncertainly; so fight I, not as one that beateth the air. So run that you may obtain."* 1 Corinthians 9:24b, 26 Once you get pass stage 1 and 2 on the money course and enter into stage 3 you will learn that stage 3 is the key on the journey to increase, prosperity, wealth and riches. Our objective in presenting to you the **Money Course** is to get you on the right track as early as possible or as soon as possible so that you can begin to enjoy the fruits of your labor, for this is the gift of God.

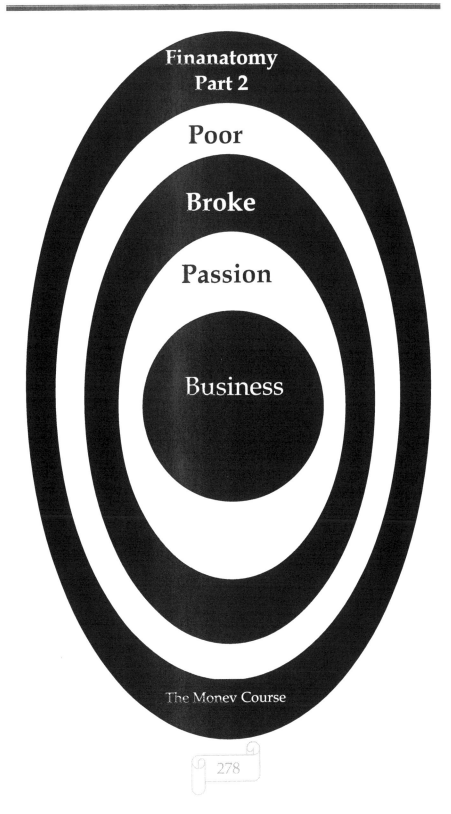

Finanatomy
Part 2

Poor

**Broke**

Passion

Business

The Money Course

## The Money Course Defined

1. **Poor** = We will use this as the starting point of the majority of people. We will define poor not from a monetary standpoint but from a mental perspective. Poor is a state of mind; riches and poverty both begin in the mind. We all have thoughts that come into our mind; however the thoughts that dominate our thinking control our life. Your thoughts are dominate in either the abundance realm or the poverty realm. The individual on the money course have dominating thoughts of:

- **Plenty**
- **Abundance**
- **Success**
- **Wealth**
- **Riches**
- **Prosperity**
- **Good**

The starting point for a changed financial life begins in the mind. Therefore the individual on the money course takes the initiative to renew their mind. This person starts doing this immediately and their life begins to transform into that which is good, acceptable and the perfect will of God. Romans 12:1-2 You cannot be rich in thought and broke in your finances. For *"as a man thinketh in his heart, so is he."*

*Proverbs 23:7* On the journey to your way to financial increase, prosperity and wealth you may experience a life of lack and insufficiency, but this is only a temporary situation and not a permanent destination. *(We will talk about this more in the chapter, "Your Mind Is Your Money.)"*

2. **Broke** = This stage is exemplified in both courses. This stage is designed to only be a temporary situation or a pit stop along the way. To the person following the money course that's exactly what it is, unfortunately for the majority of people it becomes a lifelong situation. The individual that follows the money course refuses to settle for a broke life of financial insufficiency and lack. Individuals create their own destiny according to their thoughts and the true intents of their heart. God will answer you not according to what you think you should have but according to the thoughts of your mind and the true intents of your heart. **Therefore your dominating thoughts should be thoughts of:**

- **Plenty**
- **Abundance**
- **Success**
- **Wealth**
- **Riches**
- **Prosperity**

- **Good**

The person on the money course cannot remain broke for their thinking will attract to them the life style of their dominating thoughts. On their journey this person walks by faith and not by sight. 2 Corinthians 5:7 They are not hemmed in by their temporary situation, because their situation is not in what they see with their physical eye but what they believe in their heart and their heart is engulfed with the right thoughts. The person on the money course trains them self to think contrary to sight, they train them self to think according to their state of mind. They realize that both riches and poverty are a state of mind and they choose the state of mind that will produce wealth and riches.

3. **Passion** = A person's passion is their heart cry for purpose. It's that one thing in them that calls them to come forth to be birthed in the earth.

- **Your passion speaks to you day and night.**
- **Your passion beckons you to begin it now.**
- **Your passion is the desire of your heart.**
- **Your passion is the purpose of your life.**
- **Your passion is effortless to do.**

Most individuals wonder all their life, *"what am I called to do"*? You're called to do your passion and it will bring you prosperity, wealth and riches. You don't need to do everything just do the main thing that you would like to do more than anything. My passion is writing and teaching, I love to do these things more than anything. My writing passion brings forth my other passion of teaching and they both work hand in hand. However, if I could only do one passion it would be writing. There are many different passions that we as individuals have been given to do. All our passions make the world go round and function in accordance with the creator's plan. Some of the passions we have are:

- **Catering**
- **Writing**
- **Researcher**
- **Computer skills**
- **Administration**
- **Selling**
- **Helps**
- **Music**
- **Interior Decorating**
- **Seamstress**
- **Cosmetologist**
- **Contractor**
- **Fashion Designer**
- **Pediatrician**
- **And the list goes on....**

You will learn more about how your passion and purpose is your money further in the book. But for now, find your passion, develop it, become skillful in it and be the best you can possibly be. The first three letters of the word prosperity is **pro.** Become a pro in your passion and prosperity will follow you as the night follows the day.

4. **Business =** A business comes in many shapes and forms. The problem that most people have encountered with a business is that they have started a business more for monetary gain than for the joy of just doing business. Many individuals jump from one business to the next, all with the hope of getting in at the right time to make the most money. Well let me inform you about the correct way to get into a business. The right way to do business is to do a business centered on your passion. If you do business from this perspective and acquire the necessary skills for business success you will make money and enjoy it with the utmost pleasure. However, if business is not your passion you can still reach the top using your passion whatever it is. Let me give you an example. If you love to cook but you have no passion for the business aspect of it, you can partner up with someone that has a passion for business and can see the passion within you for cooking. You can take care of the cooking part

while they take care of the business side and you both have taken your passion to another level that will produce prosperity, wealth and riches for both of you. There are many types of business to choose from:

- **A home based business.**
- **An Internet business.**
- **A store front business.**
- **A business on the move.**
- **A partnership business.**

Whatever businesses you choose to pursue just make sure it's in direct line with your passion. Diligence is the key in business. The scripture says, *"Seest thou a man diligent in business, he shall stand before kings, he shall not stand before mean men."Proverbs 22:29*

5. **System =** This is the final phase on the money course and the step which can take you to unlimited wealth and riches. In business you are trading time for money. Therefore, you can only be at one business yourself at one time. You can only cook at one restaurant at a time, as a cosmetologist you can only do one hairstyle at a time, as a writer you can only sell one book at a time, as a interior decorator you can only decorate one place at a time, etc. Therefore you are limited to the point of your

physical location at any one time. When you are constrained by your physical location there is only so much money you can make, therefore you are limited in your financial accumulation. However, if you could simply duplicate your system or method of what you do at one location by doing that same thing at another location you have just doubled yourself and now you're making twice the money.

When you teach someone how to do what you do, you have just enabled your system or method to work in another location without you being present to do it. **At this point you are no longer trading time for money; you are now trading money for time.** No doubt you are familiar with the Franchise opportunities available today through many fast-food restaurants as well as many other businesses. Here's how it works, you purchase the Franchise package from the company and they teach you how to run the business just as they run it, you are simply duplicating their system. Well, you can go and do likewise with your passion, which you turn into a profitable business and then sell the system or method of doing it for a particular cost. The Franchisee pays you an upfront franchise cost, and then for the life of the business they pay you royalties for the purchase of your system. A win-win opportunity for the Franchiser and also for the

Franchisee. You as the Franchiser duplicate your system and you can do it over and over again.

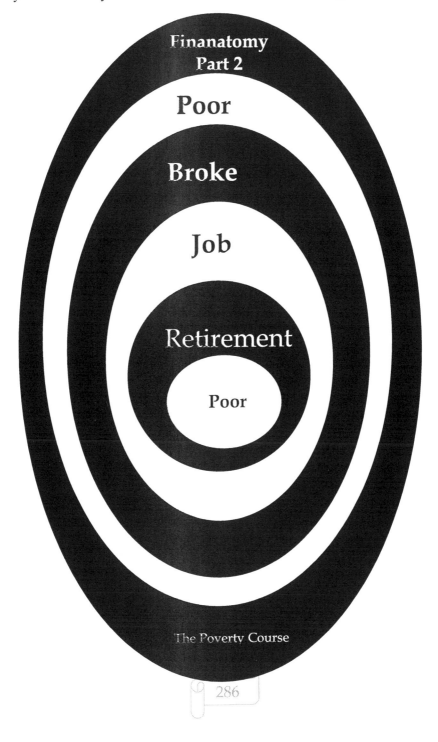

*"The destruction of the poor is their poverty."* Proverbs *10:15b* The one thing which is destroying the poor is their poverty. Yet the poverty of the poor is a result of their poor mentality. It is true those individuals who are experiencing a life of financial lack and insufficiency are in need of financial assistance. However, simply giving the financially poor more money will not solve their problem, because both poverty and riches begin in the mind. Financial poverty is a result of mental poverty. In observing the two courses one will lead you on to a life of increase, prosperity, wealth and riches. The other course will lead you on to a life of lack, insufficiency, paycheck living and barely making ends meet. We already explained according to the scriptures how Paul had a course and finished it. That finished course led him to life; if he would have gotten off that course he would have gotten off course and ended up in the way of death.

The Poverty Course is the course we want to deter you from, for the end thereof is the way of a dead financial life and financial failure. As we explain to you the 90-95% poverty way this is the way the majority of the world is following. The 90-95% poverty way will give you an understanding of how the poverty course works and develops. The poverty course shows you what most individuals do. Both of these concepts are arranged to let you know what the end result will be when these methods are followed. Our objective with the poverty course is to reveal to you the outcome of pursuing this course which will eventually cause you to spend all your life trading time for money

## THE SPIRIT OF POVERTY

Financial prosperity is a subject that I love to talk about because it's God's highest wish that his people prosper. In 3 John 2 it says, *"Beloved, I wish above all things that thou mayest prosper and be in health, even as thy soul prospereth."* However, many of God's people are living more in poverty than in prosperity, sure there are some saints prospering but the majority is barely making ends meet. There are several reasons for poverty I will list three in particular:

1. The first reason is sin, the second is man's own laziness and slothfulness the third is a spirit of poverty.
2. The first came as a result of the fall, the second is a result of man's unwillingness to take the initiative to act and do in order to prosper.
3. The third is a spirit whose focus is to bind mankind in the area of finances; this spirit's main focus is to keep you in lack, limitation and barely making ends meet no matter how much you work.

If it seems as though no matter what you do you

still aren't able to get a breakthrough financially maybe you're in bondage by a spirit of poverty. In the gospel of Luke Jesus loosed a woman that was bound by a spirit of infirmity, even though she was a daughter of Abraham and had rights according to the covenant she was yet in bondage by this spirit. Jesus stated, *"And ought not this woman, being a daughter of Abraham, whom Satan hath bound, lo, these eighteen years, be loosed from this bond on the Sabbath day?"* Luke 13:10-16 Maybe you've been bound for many years by this spirit of poverty while yet being the seed of Abraham and heirs according to the promise. You should be loosed now from this bond. *Galatians 3:29*

Until that spirit of poverty is broken over your life, it could hinder the manifestation of your confession from coming forth. This is the problem of many, that spirit must be broken so that you can be loosed from this bond so that the fullness of your blessings can come forth. Let's pray this prayer right now so that the spirit of poverty can be broken over your life. Pray it with boldness and authority.

*"Father I thank you that those which the Son set free are free indeed. In the name of Jesus Christ, I command this spirit of poverty to be broken over my life now. I bind it on earth Father as you bound it in heaven. I command you spirit of poverty to go forth from me and never return in the name of Jesus Christ. I now loose the abundance and Divine supply of God to be manifest for me now in rich appropriate form. God is now opening the way for my*

*immediate blessings and I receive it now, financial increase, prosperity and wealth shall be manifested in my life for I am an heir of God and joint-heir with Jesus Christ. I am the seed of Abraham and have a right to increase, prosperity and wealth. In Jesus Name, I receive it now, Amen.*

## Your Financial Prosperity Right

Financial prosperity belongs to you; everyday you're surrounded with an abundance of things, everything that you could possibly wish for has been placed within your easy reach. God certainly intended that everyone that wishes for an abundance and is willing to work for abundance should have abundance, for in life there is enough and to spare. God desires that you prosper, Jesus died to deliver you from the curse of poverty. Poverty was not God's original intention for man, God established a covenant saying, *"But thou shalt remember the LORD thy God: for it is he that giveth thee power to get wealth, that he may establish his covenant which he sware unto thy fathers as it is this day." Deuteronomy 8:18*

Financial freedom can be yours, many individuals started right where you are some in worse situations yet they rose above their circumstances to fulfill their financial dream. Your financial destiny is within your hands affirming or confessing your financial prosperity starts you out right.

## FINANCIAL PROSPERITY AFFIRMATIONS

- *"It is God that gives me power to get wealth, that he may establish his covenant which he sware unto the fathers, as it is this day. I am getting wealthier everyday." Deuteronomy 8:18*

- *"Prosperity is working right now and continually finding ways to come into my life."*

- *"The LORD is my shepherd I shall not want, all my bills are paid in full now." Psalms 23:1*

- *"But my God shall supply all my need, according to his riches in glory by Christ Jesus." Philippians 4:19*

- *Money loves to fill my pockets therefore my pockets are filled with money now.*

- *Money comes to me easily and abundantly I am blessed going and coming. Deuteronomy 28:7*

- *"Wealth and riches are in my house." Psalms 112:3*

- *"I am the head and not the tail I am above only and never beneath I am the lender and not the borrower, I am blessed of God.*

God is the creator of the universe he is both rich and wealthy and he is now showing me how to claim my own God given wealth. He is now moving on my behalf and opening the way for my immediate blessings.

## FINANCIAL PROSPERITY CONFESSION TARGET

When you are in pursuit of something it makes sense to have an objective or goal at which to aim for, in this case you have your prosperity target. Your goal is for you and not to be measured by anyone else's goal. Your prosperity target is what you will shoot for and what you shall attain to, now what we will do is give you a formula for confessing your target in an orderly manner that will cover your financial goal and cause you to boldly confess it outwardly. As you get started confessing your prosperity target, realize that your confessions are a powerful means for conditioning and renewing your mind so that you can perform in every area of your life with an optimist attitude. Romans 12:1-2 Next to building up your spirit, nothing is more important than a healthy state of mind. As your mind is renewed, it in turn affects your spirit and you become strong in both mind and spirit. A healthy and strong mind and spirit conditions you for life situations and then nothing shall be impossible unto you. Mark 11:22-24

## GUIDELINES FOR AFFIRMING CONFESSIONS

Always confess that something is happening here and now do not confess that something will happen in the future or that something is going to happen. Such confessions are actually negative confessions, which says **"Someday I will be wealthy or I am going to be wealthy." Place the results in today let it be now, "Now faith is." Hebrews 11:1** One thing I want to bear hard in mind in this section is that even though some confessions happen immediately the majority of them do not happen overnight. Here's something that you need to understand about confession, the moment you begin to confess a thing that thing begins to draw toward you from the time that you begin confessing until the time the confession is manifested before your very eyes.

The more you confess a thing the closer the thing gets to you that you're confessing, when you start out you may not have full faith that the thing you're confessing shall happen, but cast that thought aside and know that your confession is drawing the thing to you at every confession. Understand that it want happen just because you say it once or twice but the moment you really get that thing in your spirit and believe it your confession at that point is a reality. At that moment it has become just as real to you as if you already have in your possession the thing you've confessed. When your confession has gotten into your spirit, it's alive and active and your belief is a thousand times stronger than any belief you can have in your mind alone. When your confession has found a home in your spirit then it has become a part of you, then you shall have that which you've confessed and nothing shall be impossible unto you.

## Confession Plus Action Equals Financial Success

As you do your confession on a daily basis there are several ways that God will bring your confession to pass. In one instance you may begin to notice that you have hunches or inspirations that come to you to do certain things that will cause that which you've confess to come to pass. Another method that God may use is by means of other individuals, he may have an individual to tell you something that you need to know that's the answer to what you've been confessing. Or he may use a person to give you that which you've been confessing. In many cases of confession individuals have simply come to the one doing the confessing and given them money, clothes etc.

The individual doing the giving may not necessarily know they're the instrument that God is using to bring your confession to pass only God and your family member will know about your confession for you're doing it in secret, but God will reward you openly. Matthew 6:4 God can use a number of methods to bring your confession to pass he is God and he has all the answers and methods that's needed to make it happen. If God uses the method of hunches or inspiration by speaking to your spirit about something to do or say, don't be slothful put it into action immediately. Proverbs 12:24, 27, 15:19, 18:9, 19:15, 24, 21:25, 22:13

The thing to remember is whatever way God chooses you must take action for therein lives your breakthrough. If you do not take action then all your confessing would have been nothing more than a chasing of the wind, you are confessing something that you desire to see happen in your life now let it happen. Your confession shall come true it's your job to recognize God's method and move when God move and always give him praise for the answer, for therein lies your destiny your answer and God's manifestation of your confession. The key word is action, make that move, act now and receive your confession, do your confession at least twice daily, morning and night before you go to sleep. James 2:26

## FINANCIAL PROSPERITY CONFESSION

(Here write your financial prosperity target) Confess: I am a very prosperous person, I _____(say your name) Now have in my possession _____(say your financial prosperity target) which have come to me from time to time and all at once. Money have come to me from many sources, the divine supply of God has brought substance of increase, prosperity and wealth to me now. I have this money in my possession now, I now see it before my eyes (actually see yourself in possession of the money) I now touch it with my hands, it is now transferred to me because I have given of my tithes and offerings and confessed it in return for it. God has opened up the windows of heaven for me now, fresh ideas, new understanding, knowledge and wisdom I now receive. The Holy Spirit has directed abundance to me from God's riches in glory by Christ Jesus. The wealth of the sinner is given to me now, financial increase and prosperity is in my possession. I am blessed of God, I am blessed going and coming, I am the head and not the tail, I am above only and never beneath, I am the lender and not the borrower. Hallelujah, I am financially blessed and prosperous. I have received my prosperity target of _____ money loves to be in my possession.

## The Poverty Course Defined

1. **Poor =** As stated earlier we will use this as the starting point of the majority of people. We will define poor not from a monetary standpoint but from a mental perspective. Poor is a state of mind; riches and poverty both begin in the mind. As individuals we all have thoughts, these thoughts dominate our thinking in the poverty realm or the abundance realm. The individual on the poverty course has dominating thoughts of:

- **Lack**
- **Insufficiency**
- **Failure**
- **Poverty**
- **Barely making ends meet.**
- **Paycheck living.**
- **Bad**

The starting part for a changed financial life begins in the mind. Yet, the individual on the poverty course refuses to renew their mind, and their lifestyle has conformed according to their dominating thoughts. Proverbs 16:9a, 23:7 When you are poor in your thought life you will also be poor in your financial life. *"For as a man thinketh in his heart, so is he." Proverbs 23:7* Lack and insufficiency is not supposed to be a permanent situation in your life but only a temporary destination. However, when the person on the poverty course refuses to renew their mind it then becomes a permanent way of life.

2. **Broke =** This stage likewise is exemplified on both courses. This stage is designed to be only a temporary situation or a pit stop on the journey to wealth and riches. An individual whose life has been a life that's only followed the poverty course is a sad life indeed. Most of the time individuals on this course see no way out and begin to settle for this permanent situation, hoping one day to

maybe hit the lottery as their way out. Such a one has failed to realize that God is answering the thoughts of their mind and the true intents of their heart. Those dominating thoughts of their un-renewed mind of:

- **Lack**
- **Insufficiency**
- **Failure**
- **Poverty**
- **Barely making ends meet.**
- **Paycheck living.**
- **Bad**

Such a person will remain broke all the days of their life for their thinking will attract to them the lifestyle of their dominating thoughts. On their journey this person walks by sight and not by faith. They are hemmed in by their temporary situation, which eventually become permanent. This person on the poverty course will not train himself or herself to think like the individual on the money course, and therefore their poor state of mind creates poverty in their situation and circumstances.

3. **Job** = The person on the poverty course have dominating thoughts of surviving and not dominating thoughts of thriving. Their objective in life is just to get a good job, not

realizing that j.o.b. is by definition a brief word for being Just Over Broke. A job is indeed a blessing but if you want to thrive in life and live abundantly you will need more than just a job. A job is a good start but as you can see on the chart it is a bad end. A job can be a steppingstone to make money to use to get you to financial increase, prosperity, wealth and riches, and this we will show you later in this book. According to statistics at the age of 65, a majority of Americans are living in poverty. Out of 100% of Americans 90-95% are living beneath the American dream by a long stretch.

- **54% are wholly dependent on Social Assistance.**
- **36% are Dead.**
- **5% are still Working.**
- **4% are the Rich.**
- **1% are the Super Rich**

So 90-95% of the individuals are dead, dependent on the help of social assistance or still working at the age of 65. These are the individuals that spent their whole life working on a j.o.b.. If the 36% were not dead, they would also be either still working or receiving social assistance. We know that Jesus said in the scriptures, *"The poor you have with you always."*

But you do not have to be in the number, the 90-95% condition is not your guaranteed destiny. It becomes your destiny when you choose to follow the poverty course instead of the money course. A job can be a steppingstone to enable you to position yourself for your passion. If you decide to stay on the poverty course it will automatically take you to the next stage of life, retirement, and if you're not in the 36% which are dead you will be in the 54% wholly dependent on social assistance or the 5% still working. If you stay on the poverty course and keep doing **the same thing as others before you,** you are going to get the same results **as others before you**. You can't expect different results following the same pattern.

A j.o.b. will bring you to the end of your life and openly **welcome you into the club of the have not.** You could have just as easily been in the 4%, which are rich, or the 1% that are the Super Rich, and welcomed into the club of the haves. You are not destined to be just over broke. You were created for greater things, you are full of potential and God has put His stamp of approval upon you and called you a god, now act like one.

4. **Retirement** = When one reaches that age of retirement this is the phase of life that's designed for them to be able to enjoy the fruits of their labor. A time of reflection and a time to be able to enjoy life and do just about whatever they want to do. However,

individuals on the poverty course do not have that privilege. These individuals are forced to depend upon social assistance in order to even partially make it in life. Even though social assistance gives them no freedom and very little to live on this is the lifestyle and course they've chosen. Therefore, an individual on the poverty course comes to the end of their days, broke, busted and financially disgusted.

5. **Poor** = Even after reaching the age of retirement some of the individuals on the poverty course must return to a job. These individuals at the end of their life now know that they've done something wrong. They've taken the wrong course in life, the 90-95% poverty way. They have traded time for money, now they're about to run out of time and they still have no money. They have ended right back where they started, poor and broke. Poor, because at the beginning they refused to renew their state of mind. Broke, because they went the way of the 90-95% before them and now that which was supposed to be temporary has become permanent. If you are one of those that find yourself at age 65 or beyond, you may ask what can I do now? You can do two things. One, you can continue on the course you've

chosen for many years or you can now get on the money course and begin your journey on the road to increase, prosperity, wealth and riches.

- **Colonel Sanders was well over 60 when he began Kentucky Fried Chicken.**
- **Moses was over 80 when God begin to use him.**

As stated earlier, if you keep doing the same thing you're going to get the same results. But if you want something that you've never had then you must do something that you've never done. No matter what your age, you can begin again and it starts with attitude, renewing that poor mind from:

- **Thoughts of lack to thoughts of abundance.**
- **Thoughts of insufficiency to thoughts of plenty.**
- **Thoughts of failure to thoughts of success.**
- **Thoughts of poverty to thoughts of wealth.**
- **Thoughts of barely making ends meet to thoughts of riches.**
- **Thoughts of paycheck living to thoughts of prosperity.**
- **Thoughts of bad things happening to you to thoughts of good things happening to you. Jeremiah 29:**

For *"As he (mankind) thinketh in his heart, so is he."* *Proverbs 23:7* What you must realize and understand from this day forward is that you're already wired for success, increase, prosperity, wealth and riches. You are a money magnet and your passion will attract to you all the money you need. Your mission (**if you decide to accept it**) is to find your passion and develop it to be the best that it can be and follow a well-planned route for success, and prosperity and wealth is yours as sure as the night follows the day. All of this is in your make-up as a child of God. You are wired into the source of all success, all energy and all life and that source is God. God is the creator of the universe; He is the Alpha and Omega of all things. The scripture says, *"In the beginning God created the heavens and the earth."* *Genesis 1:1* That creator resides in you and has given you the ability to go forth and create your own destiny and financial future. You are a co-laborer and co-creator with God for the financial success of your choosing. God will not do it for you, but there is no limits what God can do with you.

It is within you to be a millionaire, a multi-millionaire, a billionaire and a multibillionaire. You are wired for this; you can truly have it all. When God sent Moses to Egypt to deliver the children of Israel from the hand of Pharaoh, Moses said *"Whom shall I say sent me? God said to tell them, **I Am that I Am."** That same I Am is in you. The source of all power and energy is in you now. When you realize who and what you are and begin to say, believe and think I Am, then financial miracles will begin to take place for you. Tell yourself from this day forward:

- **I am a millionaire.**
- **I am rich and wealthy.**
- **I am a money magnet.**
- **I am living the abundant life.**
- **I am a god.**

God is for you and He's ready to move on your behalf and move heaven and earth around if need be to bring you into a life of abundance. But you must first take responsibility and allow faith to have the preeminence in your heart. The things that you're seeking are also seeking you. God wants you to have all you need to live a fulfilled life in this world. In order to live that fulfilled life you need things and money answer all things. Make it your business to get rich for only as you're rich will you be able to afford all the things you need to fulfill your passion in its ultimate phase and accomplish all your dreams. It's the will of God that *"wealth and riches be in your house."* You need money and the more money you have the more things you can do. God told Abraham *"And I will make of thee a great nation, and I will bless thee, and make thy name great; and thou shalt be a blessing. And the LORD hath blessed my master (Abraham) greatly; and he is become great: and he hath given him flocks, and herds, and silver, and gold, and*

*menservants, and maidservants, and camels, and asses."*
*Genesis 12:2, 24:35* You need to be rich so that you can
be blessed financially and also that you can be a
blessing financially. Many are waiting on you in a
positive way to get rich, so that you can assist and
help them:

1. **Students that need to go to college are waiting on you.**
2. **People with good ideas but no money are waiting on you.**
3. **Ministries with a call and message to change people lives but no money are waiting on you.**
4. **Authors with books in them but no money to publish them are waiting on you.**
5. **Musician with songs and great gifts but no money is waiting on you.**

You do not want to get rich for just you and your
immediate family but you also want to be a blessing
to whomever God leads you to bless financially. You
can make a difference in this world but you need
wealth and riches to make a true impact. A poor man
may have a desire to make a difference but his/her
poverty stops them from fulfilling their desires.
There is nothing good about being poor and broke,
the scriptures say:

- *"The destruction of the poor is their poverty."*
  *Proverbs 10:15b*

- *"The poor is hated even of his own neighbor: but the rich hath many friends." Proverbs 14:20*
- *"All the brethren of the poor do hate him: how much more do his friends far from him? he pursueth them with words, yet they are wanting to him." Proverbs 19:7*
- *"Wealth hath many friends; but the poor is separated from his neighbor." Proverbs 19:4*
- *"The poor man's wisdom is despised, and his words are not heard." Ecclesiastes 9:16*

How is that for being poor? **Get rich, get rich, and get rich**. You will be able to do more for yourself and for others.

- **You are unique.**
- **You are powerful.**
- **You are energy.**
- **You are full of potential.**
- **You are here to get rich.**
- **You are a god.**

Now go forth and show the world who you really are and let them see the ability of the true God in you. For the scripture says, *"Let them shout for joy, and be glad, that favour my righteous cause: yea, let them say continually, Let the LORD be magnified (in you), which hath pleasure in the prosperity of his servant." Psalms 35:27*

## 21
## Finanatomy — Part 3
## Tithe to Yourself

We're all familiar with the biblical command to bring the tithes into the house of God according to Malachi 3:10 which states, *"Bring ye all the tithes into the storehouse, that there may be meat in mine house, and prove me now herewith, saith the LORD of hosts, if I will not open you the windows of heaven, and pour you out a blessing, that there shall not be room enough to receive it." Malachi 3:10*

Tithing is a biblical principal that's based upon the fact and truth that if you will first honor God with a tenth of your income God will in return honor you. When you honor God with a tenth of your income, it shows him that you honor him above the things of this life and as a result He will honor you with the things of life in abundance. The will of God for your life is that when you follow His principle and command to tithe, he will give the increase and cause the ninety percent left over to increase and flourish. Along with the tithes, God wants you to bring an offering saying, *"Will a man rob God? Yet ye have robbed me. But ye say, Wherein have we robbed thee? In tithes and offerings." Malachi 3:8*

One of the fallacies that has hampered the Christian church is that we have been well instructed about bringing the tithes in God's house but we have been ignorant about what to do with the 90% left over. It's going to take more than just bringing your tithes, offering and seeds to prosper and get wealth in your house. In this book we will instruct you about what to do and how to do it. We will not leave you to figure out your finances on your own and simply tell you to hold on to God's unchanging hand. Or tell you that God will work it out for you just believe and keep bringing your tithes into God's house. Let me be the first to tell you, it's going to take more than that. If you believe that's all it will take you've been bamboozled, hoodwinked and deceived. It's time to learn some things and get the information and know how about how to prosper in life with the principles, truths and laws that God has instituted in the earth that will work for all.

- **Why is it that some individuals are wealthy while some are poor?**
- **Why is it that some people can attract money while others barely make ends meet?**
- **Why is it that some people seems to be like a money magnet while others can't seem to get money to come to them if their life depended on it?**

One reason is because those that have wealth and riches do what those are poor and lacking doesn't do. They use their minds and their money to make more money. While the poor come up with all kinds of reason why something will not work the wealthy find ways to make things work.

1. The poor will give you many reasons or excuses why they're poor.
2. The wealthy will let you know they've been there but they came out and so can you.
3. The poor will blame everyone but themselves.
4. The wealthy blames no one and tells you to take your destiny in your own hands.
5. The poor will say no one will give them a break.
6. The wealthy will say go out and make your own break.
7. The poor will say they don't have the money to get out of their circumstances to make their life better.
8. The wealthy will say money is all around you go and find it.
9. The poor will say it takes too much work.
10. The wealthy will say anything worth having is worth working for.

I am reminded of a scenario I was engaged in with a young lady who was telling me how bad her situation was and the lack of opportunity where she was living. As I begin to listen to her she told me every bad and negative reason why she and others around her could not come out of their situations.

She went on and on telling me just how bad things were and how there was nothing that she could do about it. After I heard enough I jumped in to try and enlighten her about how she could change her situation, but she was adamant and continued telling me how she don't need to follow principles to get her out, she could just have faith and obey the word. Well no doubt she had been doing this for years and it wasn't working for her and it's still not working, she was going about asking her relatives and friends for this loan and that loan to pay her bills. She begin also to sell her material things to get **money** to pay her bills and all this time she is telling me that she knows how to get what she needs and God always make a way for her. She actually believes that is God's best for her life. So after about 30 minutes of trying to enlighten her so that she could have some understanding I just decided to let her be and had to come to the conclusion that there are some people that you're not going to be able to help no matter what. She thinks she is wise but she is foolish and if she doesn't learn how to accumulate wealth she is going to pass this same mentality, belief and lifestyle down to her children.

I pray that you are a person that will listen, hearken and obey instructions. What I am teaching you here can and will bring you out, it has brought me out and I follow these principles and concepts faithfully. I ask you also to follow the finanatomy concept for one year and watch where your life be financially in that time. We can be wise and faithful or we can be foolish and slothful and barely make ends meet when we could have *"spent our days in prosperity, and our years in pleasure." Job 36:11* In orders to give you further understanding of the finanatomy concept I think it could best be illustrated in the parable of the talents as Jesus told it. So it goes, *"For the kingdom of heaven is as a man travelling into a far country, who called his own servants, and delivered unto them his goods. And unto one he gave five talents, to another two, and to another one; to every man according to his several ability; and straightway took his journey. Then he which had received the five talents went and* **traded with the same,** *and made them other five talents. And likewise he that had received two, he also gained two. But he that had received one went and digged in the earth, and hid his lord's money."*

Now this parable is relevant to the parable that we looked at before in the parable of the pounds. In that parable the pound was equivalent to $17, in this parable a talent is equivalent to $29,085 or somewhere near that. Now this man gave his servants talents according to their ability to see what they would do with the talent(s), however, in this parable he did not tell them what to do as the nobleman did in the other parable. This man simply delivered unto them his goods and went his way, however, he still wanted them to make that money work for him and they knew this even though it wasn't stipulated according to the scriptures. As it goes on the scriptures says, *"After a long time the lord of those servants cometh, and reckoned with them."* In other words this man after his return came back and called his servants unto him to compare their accounts to see what each had done.

*"And so he that had received five talents came and brought other five talents, saying, Lord, thou hast deliveredst unto me five talents: behold, I have gained beside them five talents more. His Lord said unto him, Well done, thou good and faithful servant thou has been faithful over a few things, I will make thee ruler over many things: enter thou into the joy of thy lord. He also that had received two talents came and said, Lord, thou deliveredst unto me two talents: behold, I have gained two other talents beside them. His lord said unto him, Well done, good and faithful servant; thou hast been faithful over a few things, I will make thee ruler over many things: enter thou into the joy of thy lord. Then he which had received the one talent came and said, Lord, I knew thee that thou art an hard man, reaping where thou hast not sown, and gathering where thou hast not strawed: And I was afraid, and went and hid thy talent in the earth: lo, there thou hast that is thine. His lord answered and said unto him, Thou wicked and slothful servant, thou knewest that I reap where I sowed not, and gathered where I have not strawed: thou oughtest therefore to have put my money to the exchangers, and then at my coming I should have received mine own with usury."*

In the parable of the pounds we observed how the two wise servants took their noblemen money and traded it, we noted that the servants either went into business for themselves or lent their money out to the exchangers as an investment that could in return make their money grow for them. We noted that because the wise servants made their money work for them they increased and prospered and received favor from the nobleman. The other servant refused to trade his money and it was taken from him and given to a more worthy servant. In either case the wise servants multiplied their money while the foolish servants refused to trade their money so that it could make more money. In the past the church has operated their money like the foolish servants and as a result has lived a life of paycheck living and barely making ends meet. Let us observe some reason why this has happened:

- Because our leaders have failed to teach us proper financial knowledge.

- Because we have failed to take the initiative to learn proper financial knowledge.

- Because our leaders have failed in realizing that we're not in heaven yet and therefore we need financial education continually while we're here on earth to stay ahead of the game, seeing that money is so important and that it answers all things.

- Because we have failed to realize that the world may not end tomorrow and could last another 50 years or more, but we have omitted to become financially literate in order to prosper.

- Because our leaders teach us many things but have failed to teach us how to become financially competent about how to make our money work for us.

- Because we have failed to be like the wise servants and become financially competent even if no one tells us how or teach us how.

- Because our leaders have failed to realize that we not only need consistent Bible classes weekly but also consistent financial classes weekly.

- Because we have failed to realize that even if our leaders don't teach us weekly financial classes we can still attend seminars, workshops and classes that teach individuals how to manage their money and make it work for them instead of against them.

- Because some of our leaders just don't care as long as they get theirs.

- Because some of us don't care and we rather just barely make ends meet and get by than do a little extra work to get us out of our financially sick situation. We make and receive all kinds of excuses, we're like the men in the scriptures that say, *"There is a lion without, I shall be slain in the streets. The sluggard will not plow by reason of cold, therefore shall he beg in harvest, and have nothing. I went by the field of the slothful, and by the vineyard of the man void of understanding; And, lo. It was all grown over with thorns, and nettles had covered the face thereof, and the stone wall thereof was broken down. Then I saw, and considered it well: I looked upon it, and received instruction. Yet a little sleep, a little slumber, a little folding of the hands to sleep: So shall thy poverty come as one that travelleth; and thy want as an armed man." Proverbs 22:13, 20:4, 24:30-34*

So you may ask, Minister Dexter, how do we come out of this dilemma, how can we breakthrough and become like the wise servants and prosper financially for the Lord, others and ourselves? I'm glad you asked and here are the answers. In order to become like the wise servants I would say this a thousand times if I could, **it's going to take more than just bringing your tithes, offerings and planting financial seeds in order to prosper.** It's going to take operating your life like the wise servants, **if you will notice the servants did not increase and prosper just**

**because they brought their tithes, offerings and seeds. They increased and prospered because they traded their money.** This is the one thing that we're not doing. We're not trading our monies and as a result we're perishing financially, for nothing makes money grow like **trading it in business or investments.**

Let's see if I can break this down so that clarity and understanding can be exemplified. Within your salary is all the money you need to increase, prosper and through a process become wealthy.

- You start out with 100% of your income.

- Ten (10%) of your income goes toward your tithes.

- Three (3%) of your income goes toward offerings. (This is only suggested).

- Two – twenty (2-20%) for starters goes towards tithing to yourself (we will discuss this later).

- Two (2%) of your income goes toward helping the poor. (This is only suggested).

- This comes to 17-35% (this 35% is on the high end and is not for beginners, so we will say about 17 – 25%) of your income is dispersed.

- Five (5%) of your income should go toward saving in an automatic withdrawal where money is taken out of your checking account on a weekly, bi-weekly or monthly basis and invested in a mutual fund, money market account, stocks, bonds, IRA, etc. whichever you prefer to invest in.(More of this will be discussed later).

- You still have 65-75% of your income left for house, insurance, food, auto, etc.

This gives you a general idea of how to manage your money for economic gain. Now we will observe another one of the main keys that have been omitted by so many and they're suffering for it, if you will take this key here and apply it to your life you will become prosperous and wealthy without limits and you will never be in want again.

### Tithe to Yourself

Here is a principle for economic stability that I taught about in the book *"Discover Wealth Hidden In Your Salary"*, however because this principle is the basic foundation of wealth building I will offer it here also. Yet, within this chapter I will elaborate more on this particular subject. The concept is called *"Tithe to Yourself"*, to understand this concept further I came across a most interesting and shocking analogy.

When we think about the scriptures that emphasize to bring our tithes to the house of God in Malachi 3:10 so that there may be meat in God's house, let's look at it also from another perspective. I believe that we have overlooked a concept of vital importance. When we bring our tithes to the house of God in obedience to God's word we realize that the tithes already belong to Him. We're not doing God a special favor by doing this; we're simply returning to Him what is already His. However, if you will amuse me with myself for just a moment I want you to take a look at this analogy that God allowed me to see, and then I will show you the conclusion of the whole matter. I want you to take a look at the chart below that will show you how much money you have brought to the house of God in tithes, offerings and seed money over an extended period of time. I will use 5 simple figures for you to determine where you fit in reference to what you've brought to God's house in years gone by and what you will bring in the future.

**Figure 1.1 – Tithes Brought To God's House Over**

| Tithes Monthly | Number of Years | | | | |
| --- | --- | --- | --- | --- | --- |
| | 1 | 5 | 10 | 20 | 30 |
| $100 | $1,200 | $6,000 | $12,000 | $24,000 | $36,000 |
| $200 | $2,400 | $12,000 | $24,000 | $48,000 | $72,000 |
| $300 | $3,600 | $18,000 | $36,000 | $72,000 | $108,000 |
| $400 | $4,800 | $24,000 | $48,000 | $96,000 | $144,000 |

| $500 | $6,000 | $30,000 | $60,000 | $120,000 | $180,000 |

## Figure 1.2 Offering/Seed Brought To God's House

## Number of Years

| Monthly | 1 | 5 | 10 | 20 | 30 |
|---------|-----|-------|-------|--------|--------|
| $10 | $120 | $600 | $1,200 | $2,400 | $3,600 |
| $20 | $240 | $1,200 | $2,400 | $4,800 | $7,200 |
| $30 | $360 | $1,800 | $3,600 | $7,200 | $10,800 |
| $40 | $480 | $2,400 | $4,800 | $9,600 | $14,400 |
| $50 | $600 | $3,000 | $6,000 | $12,000 | $18,000 |

Now I want you to look through figure 1.1 and figure 1.2 and see where your monthly and yearly tithes, offering and seed fit according to the time length that you have been bringing the tithes, offering and seed. Is this amazing or what? Did you have any idea that you've brought this much money to the house of God in your length of time? Let's say that you've been doing this for 10 years and monthly your tithes have been **$300** in a 10-year period, you've brought **$36,000** in tithes. If your offering/seed has been **$30 a month** in a 10-year period you have brought **$3,600** in offering/seed. This comes to a total amount of **$39,600 in a 10-year period.** However, if you were to look at this in a 30 year period, it would come to **$108,000 in tithes and $10,800 in offering/seed** for a total of **$118,800.** *Now* *here is the big question, how much money do you have in your own house or account at this present time in comparison to what you've brought to God's house?*

Now we have a dilemma, do you think that a fair, righteous and just God is pleased with you bringing either **$39,600** or **$118,000** to his house, yet in your own house or account you probably don't even have **$1,000?** According to statistical facts and sources of information from the U.S. Census Bureau and U.S. Department of Labor and other sources:

- **Over 70% of Americans live from paycheck to paycheck.**

- **Nearly 90-95% of Americans 65 years and older retire or die broke.**

- **Nearly 1 out of 8 people living in America live in poverty.**

- **Over 70% of Americans have less than a $250 net worth in cash.**

- **Over 50% of marriages end in divorce due to money problems.**

Now if you fit in either of these categories then you've lived a life of false balance and have brought much to God's house but have little in your house.

According to the scriptures, *"A false balance is abomination to the the LORD: but a just weight is his delight." Proverbs 11:1* If there ever was a false balance it's you bringing all this money to God's house and yet living relevant to the things mentioned above. Now a just weight would be relevant to you bringing all this money to God's house while you have the equivalent in your house (account).

So how could such a thing happen? How could God's people get caught up in such a false balance and today be suffering financially for doing the right thing and the God thing according to his word?

1. **How could this happen to obedient Christians following God's word?**

2. **Are we going to allow another generation of obedient tithers to endure this?**

3. **Are we going to allow another generation of offering and seed givers to face such a false balance?**

4. **Are we going to just stand by and give such a place to Satan?**

5. **Or are we going to rise up and do something about this situation?**

The reason that we have arrived at this dilemma is

because our leaders in churches have not emphasized the concept of how to **tithe to ourselves.** At this time I want you to go back and look at the charts, yet this time observe it from the perspective of what you would have had in your house (account) at this present day if you would have tithed to yourself those same amounts. Also, keep in mine those figures are without you receiving interest, if you would have had that same amount in a 401(k), money market account, mutual funds, bonds, etc. then your total amount would have surpassed and exceeded those amounts. Let's say you had that amount which you've given in tithes in an account that earned you a 10% annual return, and then your total would have looked something like this:

- **A $300 a month tither for 10-years total $36,000, with a 10% annual return would have been $61,453, a difference of $25,453.**

- **A $300 a month tither for 30 years totals $108,000 with a 10% annual return would have been $678,146, a difference of $570,146.**

Because no one has taught us this method for financial increase for our own life it appears that we've been bamboozled, hoodwinked and led astray because we have not been given the whole truth. God is tired of his people and all people being ignorant and illiterate concerning finances and money matters.

He's ready to bless people financially but why should he bless people that have no financial knowledge and give them wealth and abundance? Solomon said, *"The prosperity of fools shall destroy them." Proverbs 1:32a*

- **People are saying they're ready for wealth yet can't even balance their checkbook.**

- **People are saying they're ready for wealth yet don't even have $500 in an account and is undisciplined in the principles of savings.**

- **People think they're ready for wealth but haven't been taught nor learned the first principles of how money works.**

I must say that our churches have done a very poor job in the realm of finances; our churches have not taught the people about how to get ahead financially in life. One of the most important teachings in the coming days will be financial management and financial prosperity. The church is going to rise up and demand that their leaders teach them how to prosper in the here and now. Luke 18:28-30, Mark 10:28-31 However, until that time comes the remainder of this book will teach you more things of what to do and how to do them here and now! You may ask, Minister Jones, do you have any ideas of what can be done to get God's people and people in general on the right track? I am so glad that you asked. Here are some suggestions and ideas.

1. *Get this book into the hands of every person so that they can see the truth of the matter and the false balance we're caught up in.*

2. *Teach the Tithe to Yourself principle on a consistent basis.*

3. *Churches and other places can have a Prosperity Class that will teach money matters on a weekly basis just like a Bible study night for those who want to participate.*

4. *Let it be a classroom setting to teach the people of God financial increase, prosperity and wealth principles just as a school or college has a course on economics.*

5. *Let it be a class that charges so those that take it will appreciate it and invest to become financially literate and competent. However have a grant or church fund set aside for those that are serious but just don't have the money.*

To keep the financial and prosperity message out of the church and other settings is a trick of the devil designed to keep God's people and all people ignorant, in poverty and lack. If you don't learn how to manage and invest your money you will either be broke or barely making ends meet all the days of your life. Individuals rarely think of taking a portion of their money and paying themselves just as faithful as they would bring their tithes to the house of God or pay their bills. Tithing to yourself is based on the principle of taking a tenth of your salary and putting it aside for you. This is money that you will use to build your fortune and bring about financial increase, prosperity and wealth in your life.

- *Most individuals take their salary and pay everyone but themselves, but when you learn the value of tithing to yourselves you have just discovered the key that will unlock the door to a flow of continual financial success.*

- *When you come to the realization and decide with conviction that for all your hard work a part of what you earn is yours to keep, you would have found the road to abundance and prosperity that can lead you on to wealth.*

### A Tenth Belongs To You

A tenth of what you make belongs to you. You must realize this here and now and make up your mind that you will begin to acknowledge and appropriate this into your life.

*1. If you fail to do this all you're doing is work-*

*ing for others and putting money in their pockets making them wealthy while your pockets go lacking.*

2. *Until you allow this principle to work in your life you'll never truly change your situation and circumstances. If it changes at all it will only be a small mediocre change and nothing that will bring you to your desired financial goal.*

3. *Until you begin to apply this principle of tithing to yourself you will continue to pay everyone but yourself. Your labor will be only for others with nothing for yourself, they will continue to increase while you continue to decrease.*

## Slave or Master

When you continue to pay everyone but yourself you might as well be a slave working for a master and giving him your salary as soon as you make it. You must decide here and now whether you will continue to be a slave or become a master. Tithing to yourself accentuates the idea that you're ready to take charge of your finances.

## Here's How It Breaks Down According To Cycles

A cycle is a consistent and continuous pattern in

one's life, events and circumstances. Cycles consist of weeks, months or years and there is a **cycle of lack, a cycle of need, a cycle of want** and **a cycle of wealth.**

- **Cycle of Lack** = In this cycle you continually live a life of being without, barely making ends meet, paycheck living and poverty, day after day, week after week and year after year. **By either refusing to tithe to themselves from their income or not knowing the principle of tithing to themselves from their income, this happens.**

- **Cycle of Need** = In this cycle you continually live in a state where you have a consistent permanent and continuous pattern of all needs met. It's a repeated flow of met needs week after week, month after month and year after year. *This is the cycle of financial increase.* **By tithing to yourself 4.5-10% of your income and following the principles in this book.**

- **Cycle of Want** = In this cycle you have entered into a place of abundance and plenty. Here you are financially stable to the point where you have an overflow of finances and you're able to purchase things when you want without any financial concerns. If you need to buy something that cost you ten or twenty thousand dollars you're able to do it without any financial hurt. This is the cycle of prosperity. **By tithing to yourself 15% of your income and following the principles in this book.**

- **Cycle of Wealth =** In this cycle money is no object to you for you have more than enough for life necessities and cares. Financially you're one to be reckoned with. God has blessed you to amass a fortune and your wealth opens doors for you and people are clamoring for your attention. You're rich and wealthy to say the least! **By tithing to yourself 20% of your income and following the principles in this book.**

### Seed Money

The tenth that you'll keep for yourself is the seed that you will use to produce a great harvest after its kind. Genesis 1:11-12 What small fortune would you have had if you would've taken a tenth of your salary and saved it for a year? If your salary were a minimum of $250 a week, a tenth of that would be $25 a week. In a month's time that would equal out to $100 a month and $1200 a year. If your salary equals more than your tenth would be more and so would your yearly total. That $25 is potential, its possibility crying out to become what you want to see manifested in your financial life. However, the past is gone but begin from this day forward implementing the concept of tithing to yourself. That tenth is the starting point that makes all things feasible, performable, achievable, accessible and obtainable.

- *That accumulation of money that you will have as a result of tithing to yourself has within it the ability (with the proper knowledge that we will teach you in this book) to become the $100's, $1000's, $10,000's, $100,000's, $1,000,000's, $1,000,000,000's or whatever you financially desire.*

Within this concept of tithing to you lives the increase, prosperity and wealth that you've always longed for and which we teach you in this book how to save it effortlessly without much discipline on your part.

## Automate Everything

The word automate is defined as *"to operate automatically using mechanical or electronic devices, to convert to automatic operation, an involuntary act, an act made so that certain parts act in a desired manner at the proper time.* For those of you who have told me that you have a problem disciplining yourself with saving, your solution is *"allow your money to operate automatically by using the electronic devices designed to act in that desired manner at the proper time.* That electronic device can take the time to save your money for you in a saving account, IRA account, 401 (k), mutual fund, stock, bonds etc. This is the **idea of having your money automatically deducted from your checking account or into your 401 (k) plan.** It's the idea of setting it up at your bank and allowing your money to be automatically deducted from one account and sent to another account on a weekly, bi-weekly or monthly basis according to your pay period.

1. **One method of doing this is that you can have the tithe to yourself money automatically sent into your 401 (k) plan, or you can have 10% sent to the account of your choice for savings or investments.**

2. **Another method of doing this is if your employer doesn't offer a 401 (k) plan, when you cash your check at that precise time put your tithe to yourself money into your checking account immediately and let it be automatically deducted from there.**

This is a plan worth its weight in gold and it takes the responsibility out of your hands and put it into the hands of **automatic deduction**. You are no longer required to be disciplined because you would have automated everything.

## Your Economic Well Being Account

*"Go to the ant, thou sluggard; consider her ways, and be wise: Which having no guide, overseer, or ruler, Provideth her meat in the summer, and gathered her food in the harvest." Proverbs 6:6-8*

This account is based on the idea of having a certain amount of money set aside in case life throws you a curve and things happen. The amount of money that you need in your economic well being account will depend on the amount you will need to have to feel comfortable covering your expenses for a limited time. However, I think individuals need to have **at least 3 months worth of cash** to start out with that cover their expenses and allow them to continue living without interruption in their lifestyle. Let's say that your monthly expenses are **$2,000,** this is what you spend every month to cover all expenses and to live comfortably. You will therefore need to have **$6,000** available cash for **3 months on hand.** Once you have reached the **3 month mark** don't stop there, let your next goal be to have at least **6 months** worth of cash that covers your expenses and allow you to continue your lifestyle without interruption.

- Six months worth of cash at $2,000 a month

equals $12,000. Finally, let a great goal for this account consist of 1-year's worth of cash that covers all your expenses.

- One year's worth of cash at $2,000 equals $24,000.

## Another Method of Savings

Another method of saving is to put money in a place where you will earn interest on your money. You will not earn any interest stuffing your money under your mattress or socked away in a piggy bank or your safe at home. A good method for doing this is to put your money in a money market account that invest this money for you and give you a good return. The beauty of opening a money market account is that with many institutions there is no minimum required to invest. You can find money market representatives by simply looking in your phone book yellow pages, on the Internet or through seminars. Many times you can find them under the titles **Investment Securities or Stock & Bond Brokers.** Be sure to talk with them at length and question them concerning their money market accounts and what is required to open it and what fees you will encounter. Do your own personal investigation of these companies and check out their track record with the **Better Business Bureau** and other Institutions to see the pro and cons of each.

Tithing to yourself is one personal wealth builder and an awesome key to having a secure financial future and building a wealth base that will make you stable for the time to come.

## 22
## Finanatomy — Part 4
## The Economic Team

*"And Moses' father-in-law said unto him, The thing that thou doest is not good. Thou wilt surely wear away, both thou, and this people that is with thee: for this thing is too heavy for thee; thou art not able to perform it thyself alone. Moreover thou shalt provide out of all the people able men, such as fear God, men of truth, hating covetousness; and place such over them, to be rulers of thousands, rulers of hundreds, rulers of fifties, and rulers of tens: And let them judge the people at all seasons and it shall be, that every great matter they shall bring unto thee, but every small matter they shall judge: so shall it be easier for thyself, and they shall bear the burden with thee."* Exodus 18:17-18, 21-22

We faced an economic crisis of astronomical proportions during the years 2008-2011, the worst it has ever been since the great depression. Who has the answers and what is to be done.

- **Most Pulpits don't have the financial answers; they only have the spiritual answers.**

- **The Bestselling Authors doesn't have the answers, the only ones that are increasing financially are the authors themselves.**

- **The Internet Gurus doesn't have the answers, the majority of their Internet money making schemes are shrouded in deception.**

- **The Seminar and Workshop Teachers doesn't have the answers, you buy their materials at these events and they walk away rich and you walk away with supposed solutions that turn out to be information geared towards those that already have some money in the bank.**

However, be not dismayed, there is someone that has the answers and he is the Author and Finisher of everything and his name is Jesus. Every person that increases financially, prosper and eventually accumulate wealth has one thing in common; each of these individuals has a **team** working on their side to help them in their endeavors. The Super Rich and the Rich has a team on their side working to make them a success both financially and in their pursuits. The problem with the other 90-95% is that they have no team to help them in their endeavors. Without a team your success will be slow in coming because you will have to do everything yourselves. A team works with you to enable you for a successful journey. Well I want to be the first to inform you, that you do indeed have a team already set and awaiting your beckoning call to go to work on your behalf, a spiritual team. Also, I will inform you about the natural team that you will need to put together.

**Your Spiritual Economic Team will consist of the following:**

| Your Spiritual Economic Team |
|:---:|

| God | Jesus | Holy Spirit | Angels | This Book |
|:---:|:---:|:---:|:---:|:---:|

1. **God the Father**. The creator of the universe and the greatest economic strategist in the world. If you doubt this look at Genesis 41 and you will see how God delivered Egypt through the man Joseph whom God gave a scientific, systematic and methodical approach to financial increase, prosperity and wealth.

2. **Jesus the Son.** By far the greatest businessman and organizer the world has ever witness. If you doubt this look at Matthew 10 at the team He put together and the works they did. Then go over to Acts 17:6 where it says, *"These that have turned the world upside down are come hither also."*

3. **The Holy Spirit.** The Paraclete or Comforter, the one that is called along side to help you. Jesus said, *"And I will pray the Father, and he shall give you another Comforter, that he may abide with you for ever; Even the Spirit of truth; whom the world cannot receive because it seeth him not,*

*neither knoweth him: but ye know him; for he dwelleth with you and shall be in you. I will not leave you comfortless: I will come to you. But the Comforter which is the Holy Ghost, whom the father will send in my name he shall teach you all things, and bring all things to your remembrance, whatsoever I have said unto you. He will guide you into all truth: and he will show you things to come."* John 14:16-18, 26, 16:13

4. **The Angels.** Who the Father has sent to ENCAMP ABOUT YOU and DELIVER YOU. Who the Father has given CHARGE OVER YOU, to keep you in all your ways. Who the Father has sent to go before you, to keep you in the way, and to bring you into the place (of financial increase, prosperity and wealth) which God has prepared for you. The Father has sent the angels to minister on your behalf. *Psalms 34:7, 91:11, Exodus 23:20, Hebrews 1:14*

*"Are they not all ministering spirits, sent forth to minister for them who shall be heirs of salvation."* Hebrews 1:14

In the accumulation of wealth we must realize that God is our source, in 1 Chronicles 29:11-12 David said *"Thine O LORD is the greatness, and the power, and the glory, and the victory, and the majesty: for all that is in the heaven and in the earth is thine; thine is the kingdom, O LORD, and thou art exalted as head above all. Both riches and honour come of thee, and thou reignest over all; and in thine hand is power and might; and in thine hand it is to make great, and to give strength unto all."* God in his wisdom has assigned to mankind angels that assist him in his great work. Angels are sent forth to minister on our behalf for we're heirs of salvation and they therefore assist us in our work. Angels are the divine helpers to assist you in life situations and circumstances.

- *Angels can go before you and prepare your way to make it prosperous. Exodus 23:20-22*
- *Angels can help you prosper in areas of your life. Psalms 91:11-12*
- *Angels can work on your behalf and help bring things to pass. Judges 6:11-22*
- *Angels are sent forth to minister on your behalf. Hebrews 1:14*

The word minister means to serve they will serve you in whatever capacity you need them to help you in, they will not do what you can do but they will help you in what you cannot do. We have failed to realize the assistance of angels; as a result we have omitted the help of God's secret agents. We do not have the authority or right to charge angels as some teach or tell them what to do, this authority and right is assigned to God. Yet, we see angels in many capacities throughout the scriptures:

- *We see angels as they wait upon Christ. Luke 22:43*
- *We see angels as they help Abraham's servant find a wife for his son Isaac. Genesis 24:7, 40*
- *We see an angel speak to Jacob in a dream and give him a business idea of how to prosper. Genesis 31:9-13*
- *We see angels assigned to keep the saints from evil. Psalms 91:10-12*
- *We see how angels are assigned to God's people to bring them into the place God has prepared for them. Exodus 23:20*

Angels are the neglected agents of God that aren't doing a portion of the work they could be doing in the earth because man has failed to realize who they are, what they can do and how they can assist us in life. You can have divine help in getting your wealth as you ask God to let his angels go forth and minister on your behalf to prosper you in your ways. The angels of God can assist you in many situations and circumstances that may be held back from you by the hand of the enemy. Angels can help you in finding a job by going before you to prosper your way. Angels can help you in business by prospering your way and moving upon customers to visit your business or move upon old customers to return.

1. *Angels can speak to man in visions and dreams to direct their steps. Acts 10:3-7, Matthew 2:13*

2. *Angels can move upon your boss man to give you that raise that's due you but has been held up by the will of man. Who knows what has been held up from you that should be yours but satanic forces have blocked your good from coming and you have not asked God to let his angels minister on your behalf to help you. In the book of Daniel we see how the answer to his prayers were held up by satanic forces that blocked the way from him receiving his answers, but the angels of God assisted Daniel and brought the answer forth.* "Then said he unto me, Fear not, Daniel: for from the first day that thou didst set thine heart to understand, and to chasten thyself before thy God, thy words were heard, and I am come for thy words. But the prince of the kingdom of Persia withstood me one and twenty days: but, lo, Michael, one of the chief princes, came to help me; and I remained there with the kings of Persia. Now I am come to make thee understand what shall befall thy people in the latter days: for yet the vision is for many days. Then said he, Knowest thou wherefore I am come unto thee? And now I will return to fight with the prince of Persia: and when I am gone forth, lo, the prince of Grecia shall come." Daniel 10:12-14, 20-21

3. *Angels can give us divine help in many areas of our life where assistance is definitely needed; here is a prayer that I like to pray in asking*

*God for divine help in the assistance of angels. You can make it your own.*

## AFFIRMATION OR PRAYER

*"Heavenly Father, I give you praise and thanks for your goodness and mercy. I thank you for being the LORD that exerciseth lovingkindness, judgment and righteousness in the earth. Jeremiah 9:24 I acknowledge you today and I need your help in all things. You said in all our ways to acknowledge you and you will direct our paths. Proverbs 3:6 Father today I ask you to send forth your angels to minister on my behalf for I am an heir of salvation. I am not sufficient of myself as to think anything of myself, but my sufficiency is of thee. 2 Corinthians 3:5*

*Father, according to your word you have given your angels charge over me to keep me in all my ways, today I need you to let your angels minister on my behalf to _____(here name what you need God to let the angels go forth to do to minister on your behalf. Example: give me favor in finding a job, help me to sell my product, get new customers, etc.), I ask you to let your angels go forth now, I desire _____ (Here name what you desire from God. Example: to find a good paying job, to sell 30 bottles of my product, my business sells to increase, etc.) Mark 11:24*

*Thank you heavenly Father for your blessings now, I believe it and receive it now and I shall have what I desire. Thank you for your faithfulness, for your word will not go out and return void but it shall accomplish that which it was sent to do and it shall prosper therein, in Jesus name Amen. Isaiah 55:11*

Now begin to visualize and see yourself receiving that which you have requested of God by faith, see the angels going forth and ministering on your behalf for you're an heir of salvation. See the angels in your imagination going forth and doing exactly that which you've asked God to send them forth to do. See yourself already in possession of that which you've asked, see yourself doing that which you would do as if your request was answered in reality and you shall have that which you requested. I make a constant use of this practice in my business and it never fails to bring forth the answer, if I need more customers to call in to make sales I just do as stated above and the calls begin to come in as the angels go forth to minister on my behalf. If I need more customers to come by to purchase my product, I just go through the affirmation and prayer above and customers begin to come forth and purchase my product. It's one of the most amazing things as you see it manifested before your eyes and become a reality in your life, many times I have prayed this and within minutes customers have come forth to buy the product. It's time to get divine help in getting your wealth as you ask God to let his angels minister in your behalf for you're an heir of salvation.

5. **The Book, Money Answers All Things.** The one and only book that gives you the

FINANATOMY CONCEPT. The science of the shape and structure of financial increase, prosperity and wealth. A God given scientific, systematic and methodical approach to financial increase, prosperity and wealth. Time honored principles and financial increase strategies guaranteed to get you ahead in the financial game of life. In this book I lay everything out in a simple don't make me think approach that a child can follow and have financial increase. I give you easy to understand charts and graphs throughout the book that simplifies things for you to help get you to the next financial level in life.

All of those that are part of the 1% Super Rich and the 4% Rich has gotten there as a result of their natural team and some have the spiritual team that has enabled them to reach their goal and destination. The sad reality is that the 85-95% has not been taught that they need a team in order to reach their financial goals in life.

- **The Church has not taught them.**
- **The Schools has not taught them.**
- **Most Book Authors has not taught them.**

The sad reality is that **the Pastor has a team** that enables him/her to have a successful ministry, but says nothing to the congregation about an economic team for their financial increase, prosperity and wealth.

The sad reality is that **the Schools/Colleges have a team** that enables them to run a successful school/college, but does not teach the students about an economic team for their financial increase, prosperity and wealth.

The sad reality is that **the successful Book Authors** has a team that enables him/her to become a bestselling author, but does not teach its readers about having a team that will help them become successful in their endeavors. Without a team it's almost a sure thing that you will not be able to become part of the 1% Super Rich and the 4% Rich. As early as the Bible day's men and women of God had a team that enabled them to do great works and accomplish exploits in life. One of the first instances we see is in the book of Genesis 41-44. Here we have the story of Pharaoh of Egypt that had a dream concerning future events about things that were coming upon the earth. He would need someone to be the Chief Officer in command and other officers and workers that would make up the team to accomplish the goals of the kingdom.

As his dream was revealed by Joseph, Joseph informed him that he needed to put together a team in order to do this. *"Now therefore let Pharaoh look out a man discreet and wise, and set him over the land of Egypt. Let Pharaoh do this, and let him appoint officers over the land, and take up the fifth part of the land of Egypt in the seven plenteous years. And let them gather all the food of those good years that come, and lay up corn under the hand of Pharaoh, and let them keep food in the cities. And that food shall be for store to the land against the seven years of famine, which shall be in the land of Egypt; that the land perish not through the famine. And the thing was good in the eyes of Pharaoh, and in the eyes of all his servants."* Genesis 41:33-37

We see that Pharaoh had enough sense to realize that a plan was needed in order to preserve his kingdom and his people in the time of famine. He saw that he needed someone to oversee the financial increase, prosperity and the wealth of the land and he put Joseph as his second in command to attend to the economy of the kingdom. Our second example is in the book of Exodus 18. Here we have the story of Moses that God had used to deliver the children of Israel out of Egypt. Moses was in charge and the Chief Officer and Overseer of the people, but Moses was doing it all himself. His father in-law saw the vanity of Moses trying to lead all these people by himself with no team to assist him in this endeavor.

*"And it came to pass on the morrow, that Moses sat to judge the people: and the people stood by Moses from the morning unto the evening. And when Moses' father-in-law saw all that he did to the people, he said, What is this thing that thou doest to the people?* **Why sittest thou thyself alone**, *and all the people stand by thee from morning unto even? And Moses said unto his*

*father-in-law, Because the people come unto me to inquire of God: When they have a matter, they come unto me; and I judge between one and another, and I do make them know the statues of God, and his laws. And Moses father in- law said unto him,* **The thing that thou doest is not good.** *Thou wilt surely wear away, both thou, and this people that is with thee: for this thing is too heavy for thee; thou art not able to* **perform it thyself alone.** *Hearken now unto my voice, I will give thee counsel, and God shall be with thee: Be thou for the people to God-ward, that thou mayest bring the causes unto God: And thou shalt teach them ordinances and laws, and shalt show them the way wherein they must walk, and the work that they must do. Moreover thou shalt provide out all the people,* **able men,** *such as fear God, men of truth, hating covetousness; and place such over them, to be rulers of thousands, and rulers of hundreds, rulers of fifties, and rulers of ten: And let them judge the people at all seasons: and it shall be, that every great matter they shall bring unto thee, but every small matter they shall judge: so shall it be* **easier for thyself**, *and they shall* **bear the burden with thee**. *If thou shalt do this thing, and God command thee so, then thou shalt be able to endure, and all this people shall also go to their place in peace. So Moses hearkened to the voice of his father-in-law, and did all that he said. And Moses chose able men out of all Israel, and made them heads over the people, rulers of thousands, rulers of hundreds, rulers of fifties, and rulers of tens. And they judged the people at all seasons: the hard causes they brought unto Moses, but every small matter they judged* *themselves." Exodus 18:13-26*

Also our President realizes that he must have an economic team that can help him to get the economy back on track. He realizes that this is not a one man operation and having a team will enable him to more expediently get the economy of the nation back in order. As a part of the 90-95% group likewise you must have an economic team, you already have your spiritual team ready to go to work for you. Likewise you must have a natural team that will enable you to reach your financial goals and pursuits in life.

**Your Natural Economic Team will consist of the following group of people.**

| Your Natural Economic Team |
|---|
| 1. A Financial Institution or a Bank |
| 2. A Secretary |
| 3. A CPA |
| 4. An Attorney |
| 5. Mentors |
| 6. An Investment Manager |
| 7. A Financial Planner |
| 8. A Philanthropic Advisor |

This is the economic team you will need in order to prosper financially and get ahead in the game of life. Everyone that legally prospers financially has this team on their side working in their behalf. I don't have the time to go into the depths of all these different team members and their roles, but you can research each of these individual and institutions in order to learn more about what they do and how they do it. As a person who starts out reading this book you are probably in great financial strains and you wonder how will you be able to afford such a team. Well the truth of the matter is most of these team members are already at your disposal.

1. **The Bank** = This is the financial institution that you will put your savings in as you appropriate the finanatomy concept as instructed.

2. **A Secretary** = In the beginning you can be your own secretary or get your spouse to do the secretarial work of keeping exact records on your financial status.

3. **A CPA** = This is a team member that you will not need in the beginning. While are simply in the first phase of finanatomy this team member is not a vital concern. However, when you enter the second phase of finanatomy and on and begin to operate a business or get into investments then you will need to hire you a CPA. But my advice is don't allow them to write your checks for you, write you own checks when you have to pay bills or

employees. Don't give that kind of control and assess to your CPA there are many horror stories of CPA thefts, not all are the same but this is simply my advice, you use your own discretion.

4. **An Attorney** = This is another team member that you will not need in the beginning. While you are simply in the first phase of finanatomy this team member is not a vital concern. However, when you enter the second phase of finanatomy and on and begin to operate a business or get into investments then you will need to hire a attorney.

5. **Mentors** = You will need mentors throughout your life. Some of your mentors you may be able to meet in person and some you may only meet through reading their books. Make sure to have you mentors that can pour into you and help equip you to reach your financial destination. Their books contain their methods.

6. **An Investment Manager** = You can begin to talk with an investment manager right from your bank, simply make an appointment with your bank to talk with an investment manager.

7. **A Financial Planner** = You can have an Financial Planner just like the rich. You may

not need one in the first phase of finanatomy but you can still have a Financial Planner in phase one by simply going to the bookstores and purchasing books of the Financial Planner of your choice. Read what they have written and follow their advice as you will and you will have your own personal Financial Planner. I personally have several Financial Planners and their advice has been golden for me.

8. **Philanthropic Advisor =** This is the individual that will help you to develop your personal strategy to reach your charitable objectives. Through your charitable giving you will help make a difference in the ministry that you support; the charities that you give to and also as you build a foundation to help others. In the beginning you or your spouse can oversee this aspect of your Economic team, as you progress financially you can do as the rich and hire someone to take care of these concerns. There you have your own Economic team that can help enable you to reach your financial goals and acquire the lifestyle that you desire.

# 23
# You Must Do
# Something Different

*"Prepare thy work without, and make it fit for thyself in the field: and afterwards build thine house."* Proverbs 24:27

*If you want something that you've never had, then you must do something that you've never done. If you keep repeating the same process, you're going to keep getting the same results; you can't expect different results following the same pattern. If you want different results than what you've had in the past, then you must choose a different course of action for the future. It's all in the power of your choice. You're where you are today as a result of the choices that you've made yesterday(s). Some of your choices were bad some were good, whether bad or good you're where you are as a result of them. The clothes you wear, the car you drive, the church you attend, the job you work, the salary you have, your wife or husband, all are the result of your choices.*

## THE DIFFERENCE THAT MAKES
## THE DIFFERENCE

At any time, you can change any of the choices you've made and the change will produce for you a different set of results that you will have to deal with.

1.  You are not bound to the life you're currently

experiencing if you're unhappy in any area, you can change it by simply choosing a different course of action.

2. If you're not happy with your current financial status, you can change it if you're willing to make both mental and natural changes.

3. If the course of action you're currently following isn't bringing you closer to your fortune and financial goal then you need to do something different than what you're doing.

4. You can't keep doing business the same old way and expect different results.

Taking a different course of action doesn't have to be anything drastic but it must be something different than what you're doing now. As an example let us observe one idea that we'll elaborate on more in the other chapters. If you having been trying to save up $1000 but have not been successful you must begin to take a different course of action to save that $1000. One course of action may be to begin taking out 10% of your income and put it into a savings account and refuse to touch it for any reason, if you can't put aside 10% then begin with 5%. The idea is to begin taking a different course of action and begin it now. I remember once when I was on a mission to save up one thousand dollars in a savings it seemed that I could not save up a thousand dollars for nothing. I was trying to save it up by doing the same old things that I had been doing in the past yet expecting a different result, however there was no different result that came forth for me simply because I wasn't taking a different course of action.

One day I decided to do something different to help me reach my goal of saving a thousand dollars, this different course of action was by no means easy but thank God, I realized that if I wanted something different then I must do something different. So I begin to sacrificially take out fifty dollars a week or 10% of my income, fifty dollars that I did not have but if I wanted to reach my goal I had to do this in spite of my situation and circumstances. As a result of my different course of action, I was able to save the one thousand dollars and this was the beginning of my financial increase. As you will learn in this book, money of itself is neither good nor bad, it's the thoughts that follow the money that makes it either good or bad.

Also, with money it's not how much you have that's important but how you manage what you have that's the key to financial increase and prosperity. Nothing happened for me until I begin to take a different course of action only then did I begin to get the results that I had been seeking for quite some time. If you want more than you've had in the past then you must go further than where you've been.

If you want to reap a different financial harvest then you must begin to plant different financial seeds.

Your financial future is wrapped up in the choices that you will make from this day forward. Refuse to allow your next three years to be like your past three years, however good or bad they were it can be better. You are the one that can make it better God gave you the power of choice and you have the authority to change it and make it better, your future is in your hands.

## 24
# Wealth And Riches In Your House

*"Wealth and Riches shall be in his house: and his righteousness endureth forever." Psalms 112:3*

God's plan for man is one of prosperity, good health and soul prosperity. The individual that will serve God wholeheartedly and renew their mind can certainly claim this promise and lay hold on the wealth and riches that rightly belongs to them. It's amazing that people try and refute this scripture and deny it's meaning and begin to say it's spiritual wealth and riches that' he's referring to here, instead of taking the scripture as it is and allowing it to speak for itself.

Wealth and riches is your inherited right and God desires that it be in your house, here we're not talking about being a little better off than you are we're talking a great quantity of substance and resources. We're talking opulence, plenty, abundance, and a large amount of finances and possession. We're talking millions of dollars in your name in your bank account so much money that you even has several accounts; so much that you certainly don't know the total amount. Throughout the scripture, we see many of God's people that were extremely rich and wealthy and still served God with their whole heart.

- We see Abram in scripture portrayed in this manner *"And Abram was very rich in cattle, in silver, and in gold." Genesis 13:2*

- We see Jacob in scripture portrayed in this manner *"And the man increased exceedingly, and had much cattle, and maidservants, and menservants, and camels, and asses." Genesis 30:43*

- We see Isaac in scripture portrayed in this manner *"And Abraham gave all that he had unto Isaac. Then Isaac sowed in the land, and received in the same year an hundredfold: and the LORD blessed him. And the man waxed great, and went forward, and grew until he became very great: for he had possession of flocks, and possession of herds, and great store of servants." Genesis 25:5, 26:12-14*

And what shall I more say for the time would fail me to tell of Moses, Joshua, the children of Israel, King David, King Solomon, the Priests, Job, the Apostles and the early church who all had an abundance of wealth and riches in their house. The scripture abounds with great emphasis on wealth and riches being in the possession of the people of God for the glory of God, for your own blessings in life and to be a blessing to others. Why be poor and live barely making ends meet when God has so much to offer you in this world and even greater wealth and riches in the world to come. Don't fall for the old tradition and saying of man about you will get your wealth and riches in the bye and bye, let them get theirs in the bye and bye you can have yours now plus in the bye and bye. Jesus said, *"Fear not, little flock; for it is your Father's good pleasure to give you the kingdom."* Luke 12:32 God wants you to have wealth and riches in this life and also everlasting life and blessings in the world to come. Don't settle for a piece of bread when God has promised you the whole loaf, you can have it you can have it all in Jesus name. On one occasion the disciples were astonished at a remark which Jesus made concerning

*"How hardly shall they that have riches enter into the kingdom of God! And the disciples were astonished at his words. But Jesus answereth again, and saith unto them, Children, how hard is it for them that trust in riches to enter into the kingdom."* Mark 10:23-27 *Then answered Peter and said unto him, Behold, we have forsaken all, and followed thee; what shall we have therefore (a very legitimate question don't you think)? And Jesus answered and said, (notice Jesus answer, he did not say in the by and by, he did not even begin the answer talking about heavenly and eternal blessing) Verily I say unto you, There is no man that hath left house, or brethren, or sisters, or father, or mother, or wife, or children, or lands, for my sake, and the gospel's, But he shall receive an hundredfold now in this time (not in the by and by, no, but right here right now), houses, and brethren, and sisters, and mothers, and children, and lands, with persecutions; and in the world to come eternal life."* Mark 10:23-30,

*Matthew 19:27-29*

Here we have Jesus own words out of his mouth; he wants you to have wealth and riches right now because that's the kind of God we serve. We don't serve a God that's just out for him; asking a man to leave all and follow him and then tell the man you can't have and enjoy life's financial and material blessings. If any man tells you such a thing that's a man made gospel and not a Jesus gospel for the word of God declares *"For ye know the grace of our Lord Jesus Christ, that, though he was rich, yet for your sakes he became poor, that ye through his poverty might be rich."* 2 *Corinthians 8:9* As Christians we have to understand the kind of God we serve because if we follow the words of man he will have you living a hand to mouth existence while he live a life of abundance and wealth.

- Driving around in their fine cars and every family member a new car while you drive around in an old car.

- Living in their fine luxurious homes with all the amenities of life, living luxuriously while you live in an old house with old furniture because you can't afford a better place and better furniture.

- Money in their several bank accounts not including their investments and other money making avenues while you don't even have enough to open up an account because you're living paycheck to paycheck.

- As they wear their fine clothes and their spouse is dressed to kill, their children are arrayed in the latest apparel, yet you can't remember the last time you went on a shopping spree because you don't have it like that.

I do believe in the prosperity of God's servants *"For the scripture saith, Thou shalt not muzzle the ox that treadeth out the corn. And, the labourer is worthy of his reward. Even so hath the Lord ordained that they which preach the gospel should live of the gospel." 1 Timothy 5:18, 1 Corinthians 9:14* But for God sakes if the leaders are prosperous shouldn't they seek the Lord to find out how to get the people prosperous seeing that the word abounds with scriptures accentuating how God wants his people to prosper?

- *"He that spared not his own Son, but delivered him up for us all, how shall he not freely give us all things? Romans 8:32*

- *"I am come that they might have life, and that they might have it more abundantly." St. John 10:10b*

- *For God giveth to a man that is good in his sight wi-*

sdom, and knowledge, and joy: but to the sinner he giveth travail, to gather and to heap up, that he may give to him that is good before God." Ecclesiastes 2:26

- "Moreover the profit of the earth is for all: the king himself is served by the field." Ecclesiastes 5:9

- "That I may cause those that love me to inherit substance; and I will fill their treasures." Proverbs 8:21

- "If they obey and serve him, they shall spend their days in prosperity and their years in pleasures." Job 36:11

You have a right to all the good things in life; you're an heir of God and a joint heir with Jesus Christ, wealth and riches belong in your possession and God wants you to have it. (See our book: Discover Wealth Hidden In Your Salary) So let us hear the conclusion of the whole matter of wealth and riches in your house, "Every man (or woman) to whom God hath given riches and wealth, and hath given him power to eat thereof, and to take his portion, and to rejoice in his labour; this is the gift of God. For he shall not much remember the days of his life; because God answereth him (her) in the joy of his heart." Ecclesiastes 5:19

## 25
## Ten Ways that Attract Money

*"And he said unto them that stood by, Take from him the pound, and give it to him that hath ten pounds. (And they said unto him, Lord, he hath then pounds.) For I say unto you, That every one which hath shall be given; and from him that hath not, even that he hath shall be taken away from him." Luke 19:24-26*

Money is the number one medium of exchange and therefore the majority of our lives are wrapped up in the aspect of money one way or another. Therefore, we use money on a consistent basis and the majority of the time when you leave your house you will spend money in some aspect. You cannot get away from the use of money in your daily life so therefore it seems logical that our desire should be to have more money in our lives than less money. You may use money on a daily basis in one of the prescribed manners:

- **You may have to go to the service station to put gas in your car.**
- **You may have to go to the grocery store to buy food.**
- **You may have to pay some bill.**
- **You may have to stop by the store to pick up something.**
- **You may purchase something over the Internet that you like.**
- **You may stop by the store to get you a latte.**

- You may need to send something off to someone.
- You may buy breakfast on your way to work or maybe lunch at work.
- Something unexpected may come up that will cost you money.
- And then there are the kids that will need something for school.

My point is that you may spend money daily on something so it is better to have money than not to have money. And the more money you have the better off your life will be because money answers all things. In this chapter we will talk about 10 ways that will attract money to you as sure as the night follows the day. These ways have been used by many to attract money into their lives to help them live a more financially stable life and protect them from the certainties and uncertainties of life.

## WAY # 1

## BY HAVING MONEY IN YOUR POSSESSION

Money begets money, when you have money in your possession more money will come to you. When you don't have money then money is repelled from you, for some reason money doesn't like to stay in the possession of those that don't have it. When you don't use your money to make more money then money (symbolically speaking) take wings and fly away from you. According to the scriptures we see this in action in the parable of the unwise servant, *"And he said unto them that stood by,* **(Take from him the pound, and give it to him that hath ten pounds.)** *And they said unto him, Lord, he hath ten pounds For I say unto you,* **That unto everyone which hath shall be given; and from him that hath not, even that he hath shall be taken away from him."** **Luke 19:24-26** When you have money in accounts and everything is taken care of and up to date that makes you **feel good** about yourself, it makes **you feel** in control of your life and circumstances. And it's when you are **feeling** in control that money makes its way to you in abundance. When you are **feeling powerful in life** this produces an effect in your thinking and *as a man thinketh in his heart so is he. Proverbs 23:7*

It is of utmost importance that you have money, you can witness to the fact that when you have even some extra money it makes you **feel good** knowing that you have a little extra left over. How do you think you would **feel** if you had an extra $50,000 in the bank, wouldn't it make you **feel** more stable and powerful in life? Poor people and individuals living paycheck to paycheck don't **feel** powerful and in control of life they **feel** out of control and powerless. To these individuals life is whipping them and they're feeling destitute and less than adequate in their finances. Their thinking is in the realm of the negative and they just can't get ahead no matter what they do, and this produces a defeatist attitude. In the chapter on **The Intents of the Heart,** this is what we were emphasizing, your heart must be right and you have to get the feeling of success even before you become successful in reality. The moment prosperity and wealth has the ascendancy in your heart at that moment you are prosperous and wealthy. There is one thing that will clear this up and wipe away all those feelings of inadequacy and that is **money in your possession**. God has given the tool of money to answer these natural issues of life for he knows that:

- **Money will pay off those bills that are due.**
- **Money will help with the needs of life certainties and uncertainties.**
- **Money will be a defense.**
- **Money will be a hedge about you and your family.**
- **Money will enable you to contribute to the work of God in the earth.**
- **Money will enable you to feed the hungry and clothe the naked.**
- **Money will give you a sense of power and authority in the earth.**
- **Money will put you in a position that you don't have to settle for anything.**
- **Money will enable you to live in the best neighborhoods.**

- Money will enable you to drive the best automobiles.
- Money will empower you even more to say yes to life.
- Money will answer all natural things.

Individuals that are in control of their finances and not concerned with money matters are courageous for they **feel like** they are in control and not being controlled. They **feel like** they have the ability to conquer anything, they are brave, valor, strong, prowess and fearless. Therefore when they go forth to pursue their endeavors it seems as if they have the King Midas touch for they prosper in their pursuits. However, this is simply as a result of their superb way of thinking such thoughts of:

- **Excellence**
- **Brilliance**
- **Competent**
- **Qualified**
- **Prosperous**

And it all stems from two simple things, these individuals have changed their way of thinking and God has blessed these individuals to have money in their possession, and they're feeling it and it makes them feel good about themselves, life and the power to have their portion in this life. *"Every man also to whom God hath given riches and wealth, and hath given* him power to eat thereof, and to take his portion, and to rejoice in his labour; this is the gift of God. For he shall not much remember the days of his life: because God answereth him in the joy of his heart." Ecclesiastes 5:20 God wants all mankind to experience this feeling of well being, success, power, courage and victorious living but the choice is up to you. You can say yes to life and say it with the note of victory and the sound of triumph. God's greatest wish for you is "Beloved, I wish above all things that thou mayest prosper and be in health, even as thy soul prospereth." 3 John 2 Make it therefore your objective to have money in your possession and always let your money be making more money so that you can have abundance, "For unto every one that hath shall be given, and he shall have abundance." Matthew 25:29

## WAY # 2

## BE ABLE TO ACCOUNT FOR
## ALL YOUR MONEY ALWAYS

Here is a way that is repelling money from many individuals because they don't know how much money they have or where it's going. An example of this is an individual that does not take the time to balance their checkbook but they just spend without any balance or direction and find themselves bouncing checks or coming up short. Such an individual that doesn't know the state of their affairs but only haphazardly know what's going on with their finances. If we will follow the scriptures on this it says, *"Be thou diligent to know the state of thy flocks, and look well to thy herds."* Proverbs 27:23 Always know what is going on with your finances and keep your checkbook and accounts in order and up to date.

## WAY # 3

## PAY YOUR BILLS ON TIME

If you will notice the people that pay their bills on time seem to get through life with much more ease than the late payers. When you do not pay your bills on time this look bad in the eyes of your creditors and cost you more money. Also, it says to God that you're undisciplined and inattentive to money matters. When you start paying your bills on time you will begin to see that almost miraculously more money is attracted to you. It seems as if money loves to be in the possession of orderly and disciplined people but stays away from the disorderly. The scripture says, *"Withhold not good from them to whom it is due, when it is in the power of thine hand to do it. Owe no man anything but to love one another."* Proverbs 3:27, Romans 13:8a

## WAY # 4

## GIVE MONEY FREE COURSE, DON'T HOARD IT

Sometimes individuals get into the habit of hoarding money and refusing to spend it even on what they need. Not realizing that the hoarding of money cuts off the circulation that money is designed to have to flow forth freely and bless everyone in the process. Sometimes individuals will not even pay their bills with the money which they have because they want to wait for more money to come in, not realizing that once they release that money then money can take its course and come right back around to you. When you hoard money then it goes into a repelling process and stays away from you. When you give money free course it can do what it's designed to do which is:

- Be a blessing to your creditor or the store that you purchase goods.
- The store or creditor can pay their bills and their employees.
- The employees can likewise pay their creditors and purchase the goods they need.
- Which bring things right back to you the employee who wants their money at the end of their workweek so they can begin the process again. However, when money does not flow

freely then everyone is affected simply because individuals have established a broken link in the chain of attracting money. I don't think it could be better explained than with this scripture that bring home the point saying, *"There is that scattereth, and yet increaseth; and there is that withholdeth more than is meet, but it tendeth to poverty." Proverbs 11:24*

## WAY # 5

## BE A BLESSING TO OTHERS AND GIVE TO WORTHY CAUSES

When you give to help others God in return will allow more money to come to you. When you refuse to help others then money will be repelled from you and the money that could have been in your possession has taken wings and flew away. You can give to help the poor and those that are less fortunate than you are, and as you give God will make sure that more than you gave will be given back to you. God will not drop it out of the sky but he will move upon some person to give in abundance to you. The scripture says, *"Give, and it shall be given unto you; good measure, pressed down, and running over, shall men give into your bosom. For with the same measure that ye mete withal it shall be measured to you again." Luke 6:38* *"The liberal soul shall be made fat: and he that watereth shall be watered also himself." Proverbs 11:25*

## WAY # 6

## STOP WASTING MONEY

Money will not stay around for those who waste it because as a waster you're saying that money is not important. When you waste money on frivolous things you are no different than the person that is slothful in things. When you don't take the time to search and seek out bargains and simply spend money when you could have gotten the same thing at a less price you are indeed a waster and money will not be attracted to you. The scripture says, *"He also that is slothful in his work is brother to him that is a great waster." Proverbs 18:9*

## WAY # 7

## SPEAK GOOD ABOUT MONEY

Those that always have nothing good to say about money and condemn money will keep money away from them as sure as the night follows the day. When you speak badly about money then money will stay away from you simply because no one wants to be around someone that condemns and criticizes them and money for some reason is no different. When you say such things as:

- Money is filthy and crooked individuals have

all the wealth.

- I just can't seem to keep money at all.
- There is never enough to go around.
- Money is the root of all evil.
- I don't want to talk about money it seems to not like me much.
- All I do with my money is just pay bills.
- Maybe it's not meant for me to have much money.

Saying such things about money and concerning money will keep money from you all the days of your life. What you want to do is begin to say good things about money and you will find your circumstances improving and money beginning to be attracted to you like iron to a magnet. Money will seem to be magnetized to you because of your right words about money and yourself. Begin to say such things as:

- It's a blessing to have money.
- Money loves to fill my pockets.
- I have money in abundance.
- Money is good and the more I have the more good I can do.
- I like talking about money for money answers all things.
- I enjoy life with my money and I'm blessed to be a blessing.

- I am an heir of God and have a covenant right to wealth.

When you begin to speak in this manner about money then money will constantly find its way to you even if it has to come a thousand miles away. The scripture says, *"A man shall eat good by the fruit of his mouth. He that keepeth his mouth keepeth his life. Thou art snared with the words of thy mouth, thou art taken with the words of thy mouth. Death and life are in the power of the tongue: and they that love it shall eat the fruit thereof. Pleasant words are as an honeycomb, sweet to the soul, and health to the bones." Proverbs 13:2-3, 6:2, 18:21, 16:24*

## WAY # 8

## WALK WITH OTHERS THAT ARE WISE AND GOING PLACES

Money seems to be attracted to those that are in the company of others that has arrived in fulfilling their goals and plans in life. When you are in the company of others that are going places always be attentive to what they say and do for these individuals have learned the secret of attracting money. As you are around the wise you will notice that there language and mannerism is different from those that are in lack and barely making ends meet. These individuals have consciously or unconsciously stumbled upon the secret of attracting money and it's working for them. The scripture says, *"He that walketh with wise men shall be wise: but a companion of fools shall be destroyed. He that getteth wisdom loveth his own soul: he that keepeth understanding shall find good."* Proverbs 13:20, 19:8

## WAY # 9

## TAKE RESPONSIBILITY FOR YOUR OWN LIFE

Many times individuals want to blame everyone for their life situations instead of taking individual responsibility. When you blame others for your life you're saying to God that the responsibility of your future and destiny is not up to you but to others. Who wants to be around others that constantly refuse to take responsibility for their actions? Well money is no different; it seems to shun those who are slothful and irresponsible. God knows that every excuse that you can come up with someone can prove you wrong that has turned a tragedy into triumph. Excuses such as:

- A certain race is holding you back.
- Your environment is the cause of your dilemma.
- There are no opportunities available to you.
- Nobody will give you a break.

- Money is slack and therefore you can't do what you need to do.
- If my health were better then I could really do better in life.
- Maybe it's not meant for me to have success in life.

All of these are excuses and show that you're not taking responsibility for your actions, as a result life will throw you what it wants you to have and many times it's just leftovers. Begin to take responsibility and you will see how money will begin to attract itself to you in ways unknown. The scripture says, *"I went by the field of the slothful, and by the vineyard of the man void of understanding; And, lo, It was all grown over with thorns, and nettles had covered the face thereof, and the stone wall thereof was broken down. Then I saw, and considered it well: I looked upon it, and received instruction. Yet a little sleep, a little slumber, a little folding of the hands to sleep: So shall thy poverty come as one that travelleth; and thy want as an armed man."* Proverbs 24:30-34

## WAY # 10

## BE GRATEFUL FOR YOUR LIFE
## AN WHAT YOU HAVE

Many times in life individuals are not thankful and

grateful for what they have and as a result more will not be given to them. Everyone dislikes being around an ungrateful person and money is no different. God will not allow money to be attracted to you if you are not thankful for what you presently have. No matter what your circumstances may be someone will gladly exchange your circumstances for theirs because theirs are much graver than yours. You may emphasize certain things that are facts saying:

1. You don't have much money in the bank at this time, well someone don't have a bank account at all.

2. You don't like your present job; well someone doesn't even have a job.

3. Your apartment or house is too small for you or your family; well someone had to sleep outside last night.

4. Your transportation is not new and up to date; well someone doesn't have any transportation and has to catch the bus or subway daily.

5. You don't have the love of your life but you have family; well someone doesn't have the love of their life nor family.

6. You need a cell phone but don't have the money to get one; well someone is praying to simply get a home phone.

7. You haven't been able to buy you any new clothes lately; well someone just wants clothes no matter how old they are.

If you can learn to be thankful and grateful for what you have you will begin to see that God will add more to what you already have because He sees that you're thankful and content with what you have. The scripture says, *"In everything give thanks: for this is the will of God in Christ Jesus concerning you. Giving thanks always for all things unto God and the Father in the name of the Lord Jesus Christ."* 1 Thessalonians 5:18, Ephesians 5:20

# The Grateful List

*"In everything give thanks: for this is the will of God in Christ Jesus concerning you." 1 Thessalonians 5:18   , John 6:11,23*

## These Are The Things I Thank God For.

1.
2.
3.
4.
5.
6.
7.
8.
9.
10.

# The Faith List

*"NOW FAITH is the substance of things hoped for, the evidence of things not seen." Hebrews 11:1*

## These Are The Things I Believe God For.

1.
2.
3.
4.
5.
6.
7.
8.
9.
10.

## 26

# Twelve Authoritative Prayers to Bind and Blast Away — The Spirit of Poverty

*"And whatsoever you shall bind on earth shall be bound in heaven." Matthew 16:19*

Here are 12 Authoritative prayers that you can use to bind and blast away the spirit of poverty. From this day forward begin to take authority over your financial life and determine your destiny by orchestrating it in prayer. At this point go to God in prayer and confess any known sin to the Lord and repent of anything that may stand between you and God. Ask him to forgive you and cleanse you by his precious blood. Next, take about 5 minutes and begin to spend time in praises to the Lord, thanking him for who he is and what he has done for you and what he shall do for you in orchestrating the destiny of your financial life. Now, enter into this time of prayer with aggressive and bold praying. Go into Spiritual Warfare and pray these prayers repeatedly with determination and faith until you see the manifestation of your desire.

1. **I bind the spirit of poverty from coming into my life from this day forward in Jesus name.**

2. **I refuse and reject the spirit of debt and bank-**

ruptcy from coming in my life in the name of Jesus.

3. No weapon that is formed against my finances shall prosper in the name of Jesus.

4. The blood of Jesus is against every doorway of poverty that has opened up in my life in the name of Jesus.

5. I release myself from the spirit of poverty and lack in the name of Jesus.

6. Every spirit of instability in my finances I detach myself from you in the name of Jesus.

7. I break the spirit of familiarity that has caused me to attach myself to schemes, plans and things that have been wrong for me in the past in the name of Jesus.

8. Every satanic influence that has led me astray in my finances the hand of God is against you in Jesus name.

9. Every satanic deception; the fire of God is against you in Jesus name.

10. Every seducing and doubting spirit; the Lord rebukes you in Jesus name.

11. Every hidden agenda hiding in my finances come to light and be bound in Jesus name.

12. I reject and bind every hindering spirit that comes to stop my financial breakthrough and prevent my true financial destiny from coming forth in Jesus name, Amen.

# 27

# Twelve Authoritative Prayers to Loose and Attract Financial Prosperity & Wealth

*"And whatsoever ye shall loose on earth shall be loosed in heaven." Matthew 16:19*

Here are 12 Authoritative Prayers you can use to Loose and Attract Financial Prosperity and Wealth. Go into Spiritual Warfare and pray these prayers in the same manner which you prayed the prayers above and watch God attract to you financial increase, prosperity and wealth.

1. **I loose the Spirit of God to attract to me the finances that God has destined for my life in the name of Jesus.**

2. **Father, I commit my life to you and thank you for directing me toward the individual that you want to show me favor through in Jesus name.**

3. **Father, I give you praise that I'm hidden under your shadow so that poverty and lack can't locate me in Jesus name.**

4. **The blood of Jesus protects me from every demonic attack that comes against my**

finances in the name of Jesus.

5. My financial life lives now by the resurrection power of the Lord Jesus Christ.

6. The Holy Spirit of God leads me into all truth concerning financial matters in Jesus name.

7. The angel of the Lord encamps about me and brings me into financial increase, prosperity and wealth in the name of Jesus.

8. Father, I thank you for stretching forth your mighty hand to perform signs and wonders in my financial life in Jesus name.

9. My heavenly Father now attracts to me the money that God has destined for my life in the name of Jesus.

10. The anointing of God destroys every yoke and brings forth a financial breakthrough now in Jesus name.

11. Father, I thank you for your divine intervention in my finances and producing miracles in the name of Jesus.

12. Lord, thank you for releasing the spirit of attraction that attracts money to me now in the name of Jesus, Amen.

## 28
## Pay Your Vehicle

*"Go to the ant, thou sluggard; consider her ways, and be wise: Which having no guide, overseer, or ruler, Provideth her meat in the summer, and gathereth her food in the harvest." Proverbs 6:6-8*

Here is a concept on the road to financial increase that seems strange but is an idea worth it's weight in gold. I was so impressed with this idea the first time that I heard it I immediately said to myself I must put it in one of my books for my readers. I cannot personally take credit for this idea but I will give credit to whom it is due, a man by the name of Jesse McKay told me about the concept of paying your vehicle. The idea of the whole thing is that if you own a vehicle of any kind eventually you're going to have to purchase something for the upkeep of that vehicle. It matters not how new or old the vehicle is eventually the vehicle is going to require some maintenance and upkeep when such a time come the natural thing to do is either go into your account and get the money or go into your pocket to pay the expense. Well the idea of paying your vehicle accentuates that just as you pay your bills and pay yourself you omit paying the one thing that is probably the most important material thing in your possession in this day and time, your vehicle. We use our vehicle(s) in so many way you may not realize how important that piece of machinery is in your life, you may daily take it for granted but if you were without your vehicle for one week it would change your entire life. I remember on an occasion I was without my vehicle for about five days and I tell you life was not the same I found out at that time the importance of having your own vehicle and keeping it up.

## We Use Our Vehicle In Many Ways

- We use our vehicles to take us back and forth to work daily.
- We use our vehicles to run our errands back and forth.
- We use our vehicles to take us out of town when the need arise.
- We use our vehicles to take us places when emergencies arise.
- We use our vehicles to take us on vacations etc.

If you were to get into your vehicle right now ready to go to one of the destinations mentioned above and it refuses to start you would be shocked. That vehicle plays a major role in our lives and we should treat it as such. The idea of paying your vehicle is a golden nugget that I chose to insert in this book that will prepare you for whatever upkeep may arise so that you will not have to take money out of your savings or pocket to pay for it. The concept is very simple pay your vehicle just as you pay yourself, you do this by weekly putting aside a certain amount for your vehicle, the amount doesn't have to be much but it must be something that you do consistently.

You can pay your vehicle ten or twenty dollars a week whatever is comfortable for you and doesn't interfere with your other expenses. You can do one of two things with the money that you pay your vehicle with, you can put it in a location in your car that no one will ever find only you will know it or you can put it in an account that will give you a debit card to use for that account. The reason for paying your vehicle is to have the money on hand at any time you need it if an emergency arise or if you need it immediately, you need to be able to get it right away. The individual that told me about paying your vehicle related a story to me about an incident that happened once when his wife drove their vehicle out of town several hours away. His wife telephoned him to tell him that the battery had went dead and she did not have the money on her to go and buy another battery so she needed him to wire her some money immediately. He told her there is no need to send you any money for the car because the car has its own money, so he told her where to go and look in the car for the money and to get out the amount for the battery and put the rest back. Well when she went out to the car, he had about $700 that had accumulated over time in the car as a result of paying the vehicle on a continuous basis.

Readers, this concept works I use it faithfully and whenever I need anything done with my vehicle I always have the money to get it done without having to come out of my pocket or enter my savings. You will be both surprised and thrilled if you consistently pay your vehicle for when the time arise and you have something that needs to be done all you have to do is get the vehicle money to pay for the upkeep or maintenance. The beautiful thing also is that the amount that you consistently pay your vehicle will soon begin to accumulate into a considerable amount because you're not going to have to do upkeep weekly or monthly therefore the money will build up. Begin to put this concept into practice and you will be glad that you did for this is just another method of increasing your finances.

# 29
# The Power of Vision

*"Back of all great dreams, plans, achievements, accomplishments and purposes lies vision."*

*"In the beginning God created the heaven and the earth."* Genesis 1:1 The scriptures start off with a declaration of the beginning of time, the one who was in the beginning and what he did in the beginning. So it goes, *"In the beginning God created the heaven and the earth. And the earth was without form, and void; and darkness was upon the face of the deep. And the Spirit of God moved upon the face of the waters. And God said, Let there be light: and there was light. And God saw the light, that it was good: and God divided the light from the darkness. And God called the light Day, and the darkness he called Night. And the evening and the morning were the first day. And God said, Let there be a firmament in the midst of the waters, and let it divide the waters from the waters. And God made the firmament, and divided the waters which were under the firmament from the waters which were above the firmament: and it was so. And God called the firmament Heaven. And the evening and the morning were the second day. And God said, Let the waters under the heaven be gathered together unto one place, and let the dry land appear: and it was so. And God called the dry land Earth; and the gathering together of the waters called he Seas: and God saw that it was good. And God said, Let the earth bring forth grass, the herb yielding seed, and the fruit tree yielding fruit after his kind, whose*

seed is in itself, upon the earth: and it was so. And the earth brought forth grass, and herb yielding seed after his kind, and the tree yielding fruit, whose seed was in itself, after his kind: and God saw that it was good. And the evening and the morning were the third day.

And God said, Let there be lights in the firmament of the heaven to divide the day from the night; and let them be for signs, and for seasons, and for days, and years: And let them be for lights in the firmament of the heaven to give light upon the earth: and it was so. And God made two great lights; the greater light to rule the day, and the lesser light to rule the night: he made the stars also. And God set them in the firmament of the heaven to give light upon the earth, And to rule over the day and over the night, and to divide the light from the darkness: and God saw that it was good. And the evening and the morning were the fourth day.

And God said, Let the waters bring forth abundantly the moving creature that hath life, and fowl that may fly above the earth in the open firmament of heaven. And God created great whales, and every living creature that moveth, which the waters brought forth abundantly, after their kind, and every winged fowl after his kind: and God saw that it was good. And God blessed them, saying, Be fruitful, and multiply, and fill the waters in the seas, and let fowl multiply in the earth. And the evening and the morning were the fifth day. And God said, Let the earth bring forth the living creature after his kind, cattle, and creeping thing, and beast of the earth after his kind: and it was so. And God made the beast of the earth after his kind, and cattle after their kind, and every thing that creepeth *upon the earth after his kind: and God saw that it was good. And God said, Let us make man in our image, after our likeness: and let them have dominion over the fish of the sea, and over the fowl of the air, and over the cattle, and over all the earth, and over every creeping thing that creepeth upon the earth. So God created man in his own image, in the image of God created he him; male and female created he them. And God blessed them, and God said unto them, Be fruitful, and multiply, and replenish the earth, and subdue it: and have dominion over the fish of the sea, and over the fowl of the air, and over every living thing that moveth upon the earth. Genesis 1:1-28*

Before God begin his creative process he had a vision or revelation of the creative process. Everything in life except God begins in the form of a thought. Nothing happens without first a thought, an idea, a revealing, a revelation or a vision of that thing in the mind of the creator. In this case the vision or revelation of creation came from the mind of God. No one gave God vision or revelation, God gave vision to himself and decided that it was good and went forth to bring it to pass. The vision that God had in mind was a utopia, an ideal place and life which he called Eden. It was a paradise, a place of delight, enjoyment, happiness, euphoria, bliss and a place where there would be unbroken fellowship between God and man.

God had envisioned this place and who he would put there to inhabit it as well as everything that would be inclusive in it and all provisions for its upkeep and maintenance. It says, "*And the LORD God planted a garden eastward in Eden; and there he put the man whom he had formed. And out of the ground made the LORD God to grow every tree that is pleasant to the sight, and good for food; the tree of life also in the midst of the garden, and the tree of knowledge of good and evil. And a river went out of Eden to water the garden; and from thence it was parted, and became into four heads. The name of the first is Pison: that is it which compasseth the whole land of Havilah, where there is gold; And the gold of that land is good: there is bdellium and the onyx stone. And the name of the second river is Gihon: the same is it that compasseth the whole land of Ethiopia. And the name of the third river is Hiddekel: that is it which goeth toward the east of Assyria. And the fourth river is Euphrates. And the LORD God took the man, and put him into the garden of Eden to dress it and to keep it. And the LORD God commanded the man, saying, Of every tree of the garden thou mayest freely eat: But of the tree of the knowledge of good and evil, thou shalt not eat of it: for in the day that thou eatest thereof thou shalt surely die.*

*And the LORD God said, It is not good that the man should be alone; I will make him an help meet for him. And out of the ground the LORD God formed every beast of the field, and every fowl of the air; and brought them unto Adam to see what he would call them: and whatsoever Adam called every living creature, that was the name thereof. And Adam gave names to all cattle, and to the fowl of the air, and to every beast of the field; but for Adam there was not found an help meet for him. And the LORD God caused a deep sleep to fall upon Adam, and he slept:*

*and he took one of his ribs, and closed up the flesh instead thereof; And the rib, which the LORD God had taken from man, made he a woman, and brought her unto the man. And Adam said, This is now bone of my bones, and flesh of my flesh: she shall be called Woman, because she was taken out of Man. Therefore shall a man leave his father and his mother, and shall cleave unto his wife: and they shall be one flesh. And they were both naked, the man and his wife, and were not ashamed." Genesis 2:8-25*

God made mankind in his image and likeness. You were created (formed) by the Sovereign and Supreme creator of the universe. When he created you he had in his mind a creature very much like him. One that would inhabit this natural world yet flows with supernatural ability and power. He had in his mind a creature that he would call man endowed with god-like creativity and potential. This man would have dominion and authority over all the other creatures and he would rule and reign as a king. He would be *"fearfully and wonderfully made"* and full of marvelous works. His body alone would possess awesome energy that when seen by a high power microscope would show forth beams of light shooting forth in marvelous manifestation. His soul would possess such extraordinary mental capacity that his mind would be incomparable by the greatest computer.

Yet, the crowning glory of this awesome creature would be his indwelling spirit which came directly from the creator himself. *"And the Lord God formed man of the dust of the ground, and breathed into his nostrils the breath of life; and man became a living soul."* Genesis 2:7 This spirit of man is where God would dwell and abide making this man endowed with the omnipotent, omniscience and omnipresent God and all that God is will be at his disposal. God made this man greater than any fairy tale story that man can fathom, even greater than the legendary story of Aladdin's Lamp. Even though Adam committed treason and turned all rights over to Satan, all that Adam lost in the garden Jesus the last Adam regained it all back at cavalry. You are more than meet the eye; you just don't know it yet. Within you are power and potential and you have had it alone; but what was missing and made you live as a servant instead of a king is your lack of vision. Because you have no vision or revelation in areas of your life you have perished and will continue to perish until you get vision. For *'Where there is no vision, the people perish (cast of restraint, run wild and stumble all over themselves)."* Proverbs 29:18 *Message, New Living Translation, New International Readers Version*

The areas in your life where there is confusion and chaos whether it's in your finances, relationship, marriage, life, business, ministry, career, mind etc. is because you don't have vision for those areas. You must be like your father and creator God who had vision and through faith, plan and action *"Calleth those things which be not as though they were, through faith we understand that the worlds were framed by the word of God, so that things which are seen were not made of things which do appear." Romans 4:17b, Hebrews 11:3* Now it's your turn to have a beginning in the areas of your life where things are running wild and you're stumbling all over yourself. It begins with vision and where there is vision there is prosperity and success in life.

### Without Vision You Perish

*"Where there is no vision, the people perish." Proverbs 29:18a*

Many times individuals don't understand why they're not succeeding in areas of their life. They may be doing everything they know is right or they may be at a point in their life where they have much confusion and chaos. It's doesn't matter where you are in life at this moment, whether you're in prison, between jobs or have no job, in a relationship or married, living paycheck to paycheck, sickness is ravaging your body or you're spiritually low. You can change your life and become a part of the winner's circle. You may be wondering why you:

- Don't have a breakthrough in your finances?
- Aren't succeeding in your business?
- Can't find a stable career?
- Have been handed a lemon for life?

One of the main reasons that people are downtrodden and failing in life is because they have failed to have vision. If you fail to have vision then you fail. When the scripture says, *"Where there is no vision,* (meaning where there is no revelation, divine guidance from God, word or message from God) *the people perish." Proverbs 29:18a* Multitudes are perishing today because of a lack of vision yet God has freely given mankind vision but he refuses to accept the vision that God gives. As a result mankind is being destroyed in practically every area of their life.

- Without vision you don't see what God is trying to show you.
- Without vision you don't hear what God is trying to telling you.
- Without vision you're stumbling all over the place.
- Without vision you have no restraint.
- Without vision things are running wild in your life.
- Without vision you have nothing to pursue.
- Without vision your life is out of control.
- Without vision you're naked in life.

However, God never meant for mankind to live a life without vision. In the beginning of creation God gave Adam vision of what to do and what not to do. Adam had a revelation, divine guidance from God, a word and message from God. *"And the LORD God* *took the man, and put him into the garden of Eden to dress it and to keep it. And the LORD God commanded the man, saying (**vision, revelation, divine guidance, a word and message from God**), Of every tree of the garden thou mayest freely eat: But of the tree of the knowledge of good and evil, thou shalt not eat of it: for in the day that thou eatest thereof thou shalt surely die.* *Be fruitful, and multiply, and replenish the earth, and subdue it: and have dominion over the fish of the sea, and over the fowl of the air, and over every living thing that moveth upon the earth. And God said, Behold I have given you every herb bearing seed, which is upon the face of all the earth, and every tree, in the which is the fruit of a tree yielding seed: to you it shall be for meat." Genesis 2:15-17, 1:28-29*

Likewise God has given you vision you just don't know that he has and that vision, that revelation, that divine guidance and word or message from God is written for you in the Holy Bible. The Bible contains the mind of God and it's the only comprehensive revelation of God to man. In the Bible you will find the state of man, the way of salvation, the doom of unbelievers, and the happiness of believers. The Bible tells you how to manage your finances, how to choose a husband/wife, how to win in life, how to succeed in business, how to find a career, how to have a consistent walk with God, how to acquire your healing, how to have peace of mind, how to get the material things of life, how to have friends, how to succeed in ministry and how to have a happy and successful marriage.

However, mankind has gotten away from the vision of God and has turned to other beliefs and words to their detriment. Yet, the word of God says, *"For the time will come when they will not endure sound doctrine; but after their own lusts shall they heap to themselves teachers, having itching ears; And shall turn away their ears from the truth, and shall be turned unto fables."* 2 Timothy 4:3-4 If you want clear vision then you must turn to the scriptures, for *"All scripture is given by inspiration of God, and is profitable for doctrine, for reproof, for correction, for instruction in righteousness: That the man of God may be perfect, thoroughly furnished unto all good works."* 2 Timothy 3: 16-17

## The Power of Vision

*"Now unto him that is able to do exceeding abundantly above all that we ask or think, according to the **power** that worketh in us."* Ephesians 3:20

When God gave Adam vision it enabled him to walk in dominion and authority, it empowered him to walk as a king. He had *"dominion over the fish of the sea, and over the fowl of the air, and over the cattle, and over all the earth, and over every creeping thing that creepeth upon the earth."* Genesis 1:26 He was able to reign as a king because of vision **(the revelation, the divine guidance, the word and message from God)** that he received from the creator. As long as Adam walked with vision, that vision empowered him with awesome ability. When Adam disobeyed God he lost his vision and the power back of that vision. So it goes, *"And the LORD God called unto Adam, and said unto him, Where art thou? And he said, I heard thy voice in the garden, and I was afraid (the power is gone), because I was naked; and I hid myself. (Without vision you have shame, fear, guilt and misdirection) And he said, Who told thee that thou wast naked? Hast thou eaten of the tree, whereof I commanded thee that thou shouldest not eat? And the man said, The woman thou gavest to be with me, she gave me of the tree, and I did eat. And the LORD God said unto the woman,* **What is this that thou hast done?"** *Genesis 3:8-13a*

When you have vision you have power, dominion, authority and awesome ability. You reign in life through Jesus Christ, *"For if by one man's offence death reigned by one; much more they which receive abundance of grace and of the gift of righteousness shall reign in life by one, Jesus Christ. Therefore as by the offence of one judgment came upon all men to condemnation; even so by the righteousness of one the free gift came upon all men unto justification of life. For as by one man's disobedience many were made sinners, so by the obedience of one shall many be made righteous. Moreover the law entered, that the offence might abound. But where sin abounded, grace did much more abound: That as sin hath reigned unto death, even so might grace reign through righteousness unto eternal life by Jesus Christ our Lord."* Romans 5:17-21

## The Potential Within A Vision

*"Potential is present but not visible or active power. Its power that lies dormant or inactive, yet within that inactive power lies the ability to make things happen and bring things to pass."*

*"And God said, Let the earth bring forth grass, the herb yielding seed, and the fruit tree yielding fruit after his kind, **WHOSE SEED IS IN ITSELF**, upon the earth: and it was so." Genesis 1:11* Within an apple is the potential to make a forest of apple trees the potential is already within the apple to do it. An individual can take the seeds of the apple and cast them aside thereby potentially forfeiting an entire forest of apple trees from coming up, or they can plant the seeds from the apple and start an orchard. The orchard lies hidden within the apple but the seed is what will bring the orchard forth. The apple is the main object but the seed is the potential, the water and soil helps the seed to come forth and make it capable of producing an apple tree. Yet, God is the one that gives the increase and causes it to flourish.

An apple without seeds cannot produce more apple trees because the potential to do it is gone. Without potential nothing happens yet with potential comes possibilities, potential is latent power or power under the surface that can be manifested to come forth into that which you want to see happen. That which you desire to see happen comes from that which you already have.

- **Potential make things feasible, performable, achievable, accessible and obtainable.**

- **Potential has within it the ability to bring things to pass.**

## Miracles vs. Prosperity

Throughout the Christian world, many saints are waiting on God to do some miraculous financial miracle on their behalf. God truly is a miracle working God and he performs miraculous miracles both physical and financial but God doesn't want his people to live in a state of waiting on miracles. God wants you to always have financial increase and prosperity because if he has to continuously perform a miracle in your behalf you're a person that's always in debt and living paycheck to paycheck. You're living in a state of financial chaos and confusion imprisoned by the finances you posses that suppose to be an asset to your life but instead it has become a liability.

## Use What You Already Have

God is waiting on the church to allow him to use what they already have. One Sunday while on my way to a teaching engagement the Spirit of the Lord spoke to me and said, **"The blessing of the people, are in the hands of the people**." For many years, ministers have been trying to get people to give what they don't have. Even to the point of telling individuals to get the finances to give even if they have to borrow it from someone. This isn't the way of God but the way of man, God is simply trying to get his people to use what they already have in their possession. When Jesus performed the miracle of turning the water into wine, he used what the people already had in their possession.

At the marriage in Cana of Galilee Jesus mother told him they have no wine, so the story goes, *"And the third day there was a marriage in Cana of Galilee; and the mother of Jesus was there: And both Jesus was called, and his disciples, to the marriage. And when they wanted wine, the mother of Jesus saith unto him, They have no wine. Jesus saith unto her, Woman, what have I to do with thee? Mine hour is not yet come. His mother saith unto the servants, Whatsoever he saith unto you, do it. And there were set there six waterpots of stone, after the manner of the purifying of the Jews, containing two or three firkins apiece. Jesus saith unto them, Fill the waterpots with water. And they filled them unto the brim. And he saith unto them, Draw out now, and bear unto the governor of the feast. And they bare it. When the ruler of the feast had tasted the water that was made wine, and knew not whence it was:( but the servant which drew the water knew;) the governor of the feast called the bridegroom, And saith unto him, Every man at the beginning doth set forth good wine; and when men have well drunk, then that which is worse: but thou hast kept the good wine until now. This beginning of miracles did Jesus in Cana of Galilee, and manifested his glory; and his disciples believed on him. John 2:1-11*

Here we see Jesus using what the people already had to perform this miracle he didn't tell the people to borrow any water he used the water that they already had in their possession and performed a miracle. The main object here was the water it was water that was turned into wine, likewise God has placed within your salary all the financial increase you need to lay claim on your wealth.

Another Biblical story that illustrates this truth is Elijah and the widow. Here we have a case of a man of God in need but has a word from the Lord. Also, we have the case of a woman in need that has in her possession everything to sustain her when she puts it in the hand of God. Famine was in the land the prophet of God was instructed by God to go to the woman to be sustained. The widow woman was gathering sticks and he called her to fetch him some water in a vessel. As she was going he said, bring me a morsel of bread in thine hand. The woman stated *"I have a handful (**that's more than enough when you trust it to God**) of meal in a barrel and a little oil in a cruse: and me and my son, will eat it and die."*

The prophet of God is now ready to tell her **what you have in your possession is more than enough in the hand of God**. *"For thus saith the LORD God of*

*Israel, The barrel of meal shall not waste, neither shall the cruse of oil fail, until the day that the LORD sendeth rain upon the earth. And she, and he and her house, did eat many days."* 1 Kings 17:1-16

The widow woman trusted what she already had in the hand of God and it was enough to produce more than she ever imagined. And what shall I more say? For the time would fail me to tell of the **"fish and loaves Jesus used, the story of Elisha and the woman who oil was multiplied, the drought of fish that was caught by the disciples, the coin in the fishes mouth, the widow that gave two mites etc.** James 6:5-13, 2 Kings 4:1-7, Luke 5:1-9, Matthew 17:24-27, Mark 12:41-44, Luke 2:1-4

God wants to use what you already have in your possession to show you how it can produce financial increase, prosperity and wealth. God's greatest wish for your success is stated in Jeremiah 29:11, *"For I know the thoughts that I think toward you, saith the LORD, thoughts of peace (**safety, wellness, happiness, friendliness, abundance, health, plenty, wholeness and prosperity**), and not of evil (**bad, adversity, affliction, calamity, sorrow and trouble**), to give you and expected end (**a hope, a future and success**)."* Yet, we see in the life of many Christians more financial calamity and adversity than financial wellness and prosperity. If financial prosperity is God's greatest wish for mankind, then for God to say such a thing without giving man the necessary tools for increase and prosperity is both unsound and unreasonable.

Within this book, you possess the tools necessary to produce the financial increase, prosperity, abundance and wealth that you so deeply long for. What is it that you financially desire? Is it to have $100's, $1,000's, $10,000's, $100,000's, $1,000,000's or more? The potential to do it is already within your salary. Your salary is the starting point and the main object that can cause it to happen. Within your salary lie financial increase, prosperity and wealth dormant and inactive, yet within those inactive finances live the ability to make things happen and bring things to pass. Within those inactive finances lives all your financial dreams and financial expectation.

The first step to accomplishing your financial dreams is **realizing** that the financial increase and prosperity you desire you can have it. It must become a reality to you and a truth conceived in your spirit that your situation shall unquestionably change from what it is to what you desire it to be; the realization of this truth has to make such an impression in your spirit and mind that you totally accept it as fact and truth.

Next, you must **believe** that what you set out to achieve financially will certainly come to pass, it shall surely happen. You must then expect this with confidence and become fully persuaded in your mind that nothing and no one can stop it from happening, for *"If God be for you, who can be against you." Romans 4:17, Hebrews 11*

Last, you must put forth the necessary **effort** or

**work** to bring it to pass, to bring it from an idea or thought to a manifested tangible reality before your very eyes. James 2:20-26 Financial increase and prosperity belongs to you dear child of God, it's your inherited right, your family right, your holy right and your born-again right. All that God has belongs to you for you are *"heirs of God and joint-heirs with Christ." Romans 8:17*

## 30
## Your Purpose Is Your Money

*"Then the word of the LORD came unto me, saying, Before I formed thee in the belly I knew thee; and before thou camest forth out of the womb I sanctified thee, and I ordained thee a prophet unto the nations." Jeremiah 1:4-5*

Man was born for greatness he exist in order that he may become more than meets the eye, he is created in God's image and is therefore capable of becoming an individual destined to bring about a change in the life of others. Every individual has been gifted by God and assigned a purpose to fulfill in the earth. God has placed every individual's destiny in their hands and according to the decisions we make we help to orchestrate that destiny. When we make the right decisions in life, it empowers us to do the impossible. Right decisions produce right thinking, wrong decisions produce wrong thinking, a man's thinking shows forth his thoughts a man's thoughts bring forth his actions and a man's actions creates his destiny. One of the greatest needs of mankind today is to come to a realization of their sense of destiny and the original intent of God in allowing them to dwell on planet earth.

- **No one came into this world by accident, chance or even mistakenly but every individual was destined to arrive on earth** according to the calendar date of God. Ephesians 1:4-9

- No one arrived here empty without purpose, without intent, without a reason and an objective already placed in him or her by God.

- But every person arrived here pregnant with a purpose from God designed for the uplifting of mankind.

- Every person arrived here with something to accomplish, something to impart, something to leave behind.

- God put purpose in every individual while they were still in their mother's womb. Jeremiah 1:4-5

- Everyone's objective should be to discover purpose in life and since you're still here it's a great indication that either you have not yet found your purpose or haven't yet completed your task. However, it's sad that some have departed without finding their purpose yet this was never the will of God. John 17:4, 19:30, 2 Timothy 4:7-8

When an individual discover their purpose it will bring joy, success, prosperity, direction, value, and focus to their own life and to every person they encounter. A sad but true statement is that the riches place in the world is not the oil well in Texas neither is it a combination of all the banks and loan companies combined. The riches place in the world is the local cemeteries in our own towns and cities because:

1. **Many individuals have departed taking with them that song that was never recorded.**

2. **That invention that was never invented.**

3. **That series of messages that was never preached or taught.**

4. **That business plan that was never developed etc.**

All these things could have brought success, joy, and prosperity to those individuals and countless others if they would have simply found their purpose.

- **Your purpose is the reason for the creation of your existence.**
- **Your purpose is the master motivator for your own life.**
- **Your purpose is who you are.**

- **Your purpose is why you are.**
- **Your purpose was the original intent in the mind of God when he allowed you to come to planet earth.**
- **Your purpose is you.**

Many individuals are trying to find themselves, many have been told to love their neighbor as themselves, but the reason people can't find themselves or love their neighbor as themselves, is because they're trying to be who they're not. Individuals are working in a career that's not in accordance with their purpose but they need the money to meet life's obligations. They're not doing what they were born to do but something totally contrary to their life's purpose and they're miserable and unfilled people. When you're not operating in your purpose you're like a fish out of water you may not die naturally within several minutes but daily you're dying to the purpose that God has placed within you. When you go through life with an unfulfilled purpose you abandon your dreams, your ambitions for a better life, you die to your potential and begin to settle for a life of mediocrity, contentment and despair. You're alive yes but you're actually dead while you're living because you have cast aside your life's purpose.

However, you don't have to remain in that state you can be fulfilled, you can achieve, you can be you and discover the hidden riches in a purpose directed life. You can come back from that dead state that you're in. Once you become you you'll find it easy to love your neighbor because you now love yourself, you have now discovered who and what God intended you to be. Every person is born with a purpose the reason you do certain things is because that thing is your gift and purpose operating within you. That gift can be used by God to supply all your financial and material needs and make you prosperous beyond your wildest dreams. There are seven gifts that God has given to mankind; these gifts are charisma or motivational gifts designed to help mankind succeed in life. A list of these seven gifts is found in the Bible in Romans 12:4-8. When an individual find their purpose and discover their gift it gives them something to live for something to look forward to, it empowers them to go further and brings meaning and reason to their life.

- **Purpose is the driving force in the life of the lifeless.**

- **Purpose is the power that will strengthen the weak and aimless.**

- **Purpose is the authority that gives an individual the permission to succeed in life.**

- **Purpose is the influence that gives you the confidence to go boldly after your life's aim.**

- **Purpose is the expert in an individual that makes them skilled and gives them the ability to become specialist in their chosen field.**

Its purpose that will create the change and bring forth the financial increase that individuals are seeking in life because purpose causes you to function properly and it aligns you with the creator's intention. When the individual whose purpose is to be a Physician discovers their reason for being is to become a practitioner to help the sick become well, then earth's purpose is aligned slightly and one more individual is united with the creator's intention. When the individual whose purpose is to Teach discovers that their reason for being is to educate, instruct and train others in their chosen field then the earth's purpose is aligned slightly and one more individual is united with the creator's intention.

When the individual whose purpose is to Pastor discovers that their reason for being is to shepherd the people of God and help perfect them and edify the body of Christ then the earth's purpose is aligned slightly and one more individual is united with the creator's intention. When the individual whose purpose is to be a Mechanic discovers that their reason for being is to help individuals by assisting them with their automobile problems thereby easing some of life's troubles then the earth's purpose is aligned slightly and one more individual is united with the creator's intention.

- And what shall I more say, for the time would fail me to tell of the Police officer, Fisherman, Evangelist, Nurse, Lawyer, Secretary, Businessman, Prophet, Caretaker, Gospel teacher, Machine Operator, Reporter, Actress, Apostle, Actor, Singer, Administrator, President, Inventor, Writer, Speaker etc. who all combined makes the world function as God intended.

These individuals by discovering their purpose help align the earth's purpose, produce financial prosperity for their own life and unite the individual with the creator's intention. When each person aligns themselves with their purpose what a world we will portray a world of individuals portraying strength, ability, prosperity, reason, drive, principle, aim, use, confidence, influence, power and right. Purpose is what we need in the earth it gives each individual the authority to freely go forth and become that which they were born to be. Since God has blessed me to discover my purpose and gifts in life, it has brought me so much fulfillment, prosperity and satisfaction.

Life has become more meaningful and rewarding I look forward to waking up every morning to have another opportunity to operate in my purpose. It has changed my life and given me something to accomplish, something to fulfill, something to look forward to. My greatest part of the day besides drawing near to God is doing that which I was created to do. Daily I arise with great anticipation, expectation, eagerness and hope. My purpose has given me something to live for and a reason to be alive. Before discovering my purpose life had no real meaning because you seem to just exist and my only aim was to survive and stay alive, I had no daily agenda to fulfill and no goals to pursue.

Now I realize that I'm not just living for myself my life has an aim and reason for being, my purpose is not just to survive and stay alive, no, but to fulfill the reason for the creation of my existence. As I do this my life is influencing others in a positive way, for every life is connected in some way with the lives of others and has been destined by God to bring about a change in somebody else's life. If you fail to discover your purpose, it's more than just your life at stake, but the lives of others whose path you were supposed to cross that would have imparted to them something that would have sparked their purpose and influenced their life.

When an individual discovers their purpose, it's a love letter from God telling them all the wonderful things he has imparted in them and the marvelous things he has given them. It's a love letter telling you how much God loves you and that he has not abandoned you but has equipped you and outfitted you, so that you can prosper and be operational in the earth. The discovery of your purpose is the answer to life's problems and situations that face so many on a daily basis it's the answer to many financial, secular, marital, mental and social problems. Purpose gives you vision and order for *"without a vision people perish"* without vision an individual has no goal to work toward no objective to fulfill and as a result, individuals cast off restraint and do anything. But purpose brings restraint, control and discipline it gives one meaning and drive it enables one to live a prosperous and fulfilled life. There are awesome hidden riches in a purpose directed life, search your own heart for that pull that you have in a certain direction more than any other. That direction will be the occupation that you will find the most fulfillment, prosperity and satisfaction in, that occupation is your life's purpose, that thing speaks to you night and day it constantly hovers over you saying **"this is the way, walk therein."** The power of purpose has within it the ability to change the world, to align the earth's purpose and assist the creator God in his great work of enabling mankind to walk in the dominion, prosperity and authority for which he was created.

# 31
# Your Mind Is Your Money

*"Finally, brethren, whatsoever things are true, whatsoever things are honest, whatsoever things are just, whatsoever things are pure, whatsoever things are lovely, whatsoever things are of good report; if there be any virtue, and if there be any praise, think on these things." Philippians 4:8*

Your mind is your organ of thought, your thought creates your actions and your actions determine your destiny. Your mind is one of the most powerful things you possess it can turn a good situation bad or a bad situation good it's all in how you think about it. If you want wealth, you must learn to think like wealthy people think and not like poor people or paycheck living people think. You must change your mind from what it is to what you desire it to be, in doing so you also change your outlook on your situation.

When you have a change of mind the thoughts which you think change the mental image that dominate your thought life and then you begin to think according to that which you imagine. Your mind is your money and the more you train your mind to think like prosperous people the more prosperous you will become. Your mind will not automatically think prosperity consciousness but it will automatically think poverty consciousness. Your mind has to be cultivated like a garden, you must take personal responsibility to tend this garden and keep it free of all weeds and tares that will spring up to trouble it and thereby trouble your whole life. In a garden weeds seem to grow without any assistance, the weeds and tares of your mind represent the negative satanic thoughts designed to replace your positive spiritual thoughts and in return create negative circumstances and situations. If you want riches and wealth you must understand that such things don't begin in your bank account but in your mind and spirit. No one can be truly rich in mind and spirit and be poor financially.

The reason that so many are struggling financially even though they have the awesome Spirit of God dwelling in them is because they have failed to renew their mind. People are walking around with the rich spirit of God and a poor mind yet until the mind becomes rich as the spirit is rich you will never see prosperity and abundance in this life time. Until you come to the realization that what's holding you back from receiving the inheritance that rightly belongs to you is your poor mentality a mind which you've either refuse to develop or have not come into the knowledge of how to develop it. Your mind is a part of your soul which is defined as the place where your emotions, intellect and will resides, in 3 John 2 it says *"Beloved, I wish above all things that thou mayest prosper and be in health, even as thy soul prospereth."* In other words, the prosperity of your life and the goodness of health all are determined by the prosperity of your soul. If your soul and mind isn't prosperous, neither will your finances, life or health be prosperous. You must make it your personal mission to make your soul prosperous for everything hinges on what you do here.

1. **You can be saved and filled with the spirit, and yet live and die in poverty and lack if you don't learn to prosper your soul.**

2. **You can attend church every Sunday and Bible study during the week and yet live and die in poverty and lack if you don't prosper your soul.**

3. **You can spend hours in prayer lying before the Lord and yet live and die in poverty if you don't prosper your soul.**

4. **You can read the Bible every day and attend many conferences but until you learn to prosper your soul concerning finances, you can still live and die in poverty.**

Everything in every area of your life hinges on what you do with your soul if you refuse to renew your mind and do nothing with your soul then you will not receive that which God desires you to have but that which life just throw your way. You must get this truth in your spirit that your mind is your money and nothing else you do compensates for a lack in this area. God has stipulated a truth in his word that is infallible and will work for anyone, there's no getting around it and there's no making up for it this truth stands as a monument and guide. That truth is *"For as he (man) thinketh in his heart so is he."* Proverbs 23:7 You will not receive that which you think you rightly deserve or that which you think you have worked for but you will receive that which you constantly think about whether good or bad. Nothing takes the place of this, nothing supersedes this nothing makes up for this neither can you buy your way out of this because the simple truth is **we become what we think about**. Seeing therefore that your mind is your money you must begin at once to mind the things of the Spirit (increase, prosperity, wealth, abundance, plenty) and not the things of the flesh (poverty, lack, failure, paycheck living) for what you mind you will receive. *"For they that are after the flesh do mind the things of the flesh; but they that are after the Spirit the things of the Spirit."* Romans 8:5-6

- **Mind plenty instead of poverty.**
- **Mind wealth instead of lack.**
- **Mind abundance instead of barely making ends meet.**
- **Mind opulence instead of paycheck living.**
- **Mind success instead of failure.**
- **Mind health instead of sickness.**
- **Mind I can instead of I can't.**

- Mind positive, spiritual thoughts instead of negative thought.
- Mind I am the lender instead of the borrower.
- Mind I am the head instead of the tail.
- Mind I am above only instead of beneath.

As you begin to think in this manner, you will find yourself attracting money and many financial and material blessing to you as easily as a magnet attracts iron. You have to think like prosperous people in order to be prosperous, money and financial prosperity isn't just for the rich but for those individuals who are willing to think differently and act differently.

## THE BUM ON THE STREET AND THE RICH MAN ON WALL STREET

The only difference between the bum on the street and the rich man on Wall Street are the thoughts that dominating their thinking. The attitude of one is totally different from the attitude of the other. The bum on the street, have dominating thoughts of poverty, lack, and begging for their daily drink and food. The dominating thoughts of his mind have produced the events of his life. Even if once in a while he has thoughts of plenty those thoughts are soon evaporated and suppressed by the negative thoughts of lack and limitations. Thoughts of plenty have no voice in his mind because of the dominating thoughts of poverty and barely making ends meet. The bum with this state of mind will never arise from his position until he change the dominating thoughts of his thinking, *"For as he (mankind) thinketh in his heart, so is he." Proverbs 23:7* As he continues to think so he continues to be.

The rich man on Wall Street however has dominating thoughts of plenty, wealth, riches and abundance. The dominating thoughts of his mind have in return produced the events of his life. Even if once in a while he has negative thoughts of lack and loss, those thoughts are soon evaporated and suppressed by the thoughts of plenty, abundance, wealth and riches. Thoughts of lack has no voice in his mind because of the dominating thoughts of plenty and abundance. The rich man with this state of mind will never (with all things being equal) fall from his state of prosperity unless he changes the dominating thoughts of his mind. Yet, if each of the examples above would simply change to the dominating thoughts or attitude of the other over time the circumstance of each person would likewise change from one to the other. The bum would then become the rich man on Wall Street and the rich man on Wall Street would become the bum by simply changing the dominating thoughts of their mind. The heart of it all is in the matter of thoughts. Seeing that your mind is your money, you must therefore begin to focus and mind only the thinking way mentioned above for in doing this you shall become that which you are focused upon and think about. When contrary thoughts and imaginations arise you must, *"Cast down imagination, and every high thing that exalteth itself against the knowledge of God, and bringing into captivity every thought to the obedience of Christ; And having a readiness to revenge all disobedience, when your obedience is fulfilled."* 2 Corinthians 10:5

Your mind is your money and God has made it so that it can deliver to you anything that your heart desires when your thoughts are in line with the word of God whose greatest wish is *"Beloved, I wish above all things that thou mayest prosper and be in health, even as thy soul prospereth."* 3 John 2 Your thoughts in return create your circumstances, lifestyle and images. The bum does not become a bum overnight for quite awhile he had bum thoughts (poverty, lack etc.) dominating his mind and eventually these thoughts created his circumstances. The rich man does not become rich overnight (and there's no such thing as overnight riches), for quite awhile he had rich thoughts (plenty, abundance, wealth) dominating his mind and eventually these thoughts created his circumstances. All mankind will eventually become that which they secretly think about. The dominating thoughts of their mind that's hidden form others attract to them the environment and circumstances which their thoughts secretly long for, whether good or bad. The dominating thoughts of your mind over time forms a picture or image and eventually this image manifest in your life for all to see whether it's good (money, increase, prosperity and wealth) or bad (poverty, lack, barely making ends meet and paycheck living).

What I want you to understand and get in your spirit is that the thoughts that consistently dominate your mind will produce an image in your mind and this image in return creates your lifestyle. So let us hear the conclusion of the whole matter of your mind is your money. *"Finally, brethren, whatsoever things are true, whatsoever things are honest, whatsoever things are just, whatsoever things are pure, whatsoever things are lovely, whatsoever things are of good report; if there be any virtue, and if there be any praise, think on these things."* Philippians 4:8

## 32
# Your Mouth Is Your Money

*"Thou art snared with the words of thy mouth, thou are taken with the words of thy mouth." Proverbs 6:2*

The one thing that defeats more people than anything else and is more powerful than any force on earth even the power of prayer is the power of your words. Mankind everywhere are being defeated on a daily basis by the words of their mouth, the words which you speak will either put you over in life or hold you in bondage. Jesus was so concerned with the words which mankind speaks that he put a great emphasis on our speaking of idle words. He stated *"But I say unto you, that every idle word that men shall speak, they shall give account thereof in the day of judgment. For by thy words thou shalt be justified, and by they words thou shalt be condemned." Matthew 12:36* The idle words that Jesus was referring to were not the words that may come out of ones mouth as they sit around talking about certain things or events. The idle words which Jesus was referring to were words that one allows to come out of their mouth that are negative and in disagreement with God.

- *Words that are non-productive for your life.*
- *Words that doesn't produce for you.*
- *Words that doesn't magnify God nor does anything for you or anyone else.*

- *Words that bring forth death instead of life to your situation and circumstances.*

Many are held captive by their own words they are speaking words of death instead of words of life they are speaking words of the enemy more than words of God. The absence of God's word in your mouth will rob you of faith in the ability of God to produce in your behalf. When negative words come out of your mouth you have become your own worst enemy, when positive, spiritual and faith filled worlds proceed from your lips you have become your greatest asset. You can speak God's words and they will work for you and change your circumstances and situations. You are no stronger in the Lord than you are in your spirit and the words that you speak either build up or tear down your spirit man. The words you speak with consistency will become a creative force that releases the power of God within you to work on your behalf.

## HOW TO CONTROL YOUR
## LIFE AND CIRCUMSTANCES

In the book of James it states; *"If any man offend not in word, the same is a perfect man, and able to bridle the whole body."* James 3:2 This passage of Scripture is stating a most powerful declaration for life and purpose it simply states that if you can control your word(s) you can control your whole life. *"Death and*

*Life are in the power of the tongue: and they that loveth it shall eat the fruit thereof."* Proverbs 18;21 Whether you realize it or not you're where you are as a result of the words that you have spoken over your life and the thoughts that dominates your thinking. You are now reaping the fruit of your own words and the fruit that you've reaped are what you love to dwell with for it's what you have spoken out of your mouth. If you're not satisfied with your fruit then simply change your words and the fruit of your life will change in accordance. The scriptures states, *"Thou art snared with the words of thy mouth, thou are taken with the words of thy mouth".* Proverbs 6:2 Simply put, you have trapped yourself with the words of your own mouth.

Start today and break loose by beginning to affirm that which will produce for you in all areas of your life. Get rid of the negative words get them out of your spirit, mind and vocabulary. No need to struggle any longer financially, materially, spiritual, mental or in any area where death instead of life now reigns. Begin this day to speak spiritual faith filled words that's full of life, speak them with power and authority and watch your situation and all your circumstances change before your very eyes. You can work financial and material miracles through Christ in your life and also the lives of others by teaching them to speak words that will produce life instead of death. St. John 6:63 It has been estimated that the individual which will speak spiritual, prosperous and positive words in their situations and over their life will speed up the results of that which they're affirming to come into their life by as much as **80%** (*wow*). When you speak spiritual, prosperous and positive affirmations a tremendous force is set loose upon the invisible that definitely affects the visible, molding it into tangible results and bringing it into the external realm of reality for you. Words can either create or destroy bring forth life or death, success or failure, abundance or poverty, health or sickness, peace or confusion and harmony or division. Man governs his life and destiny by the words that he speaks or fails to speak.

## GOD USED WORDS TO CREATE

Jesus spoke about the power of words when he spoke to the disciples and challenged them saying, *"Have faith in God"(which interpreted means to have the faith of God)*. God's words were a created force that produced results as he spoke them. In the book of Hebrews it says; *"Through faith we understand that the worlds were framed by the word of God, so that things which are seen were not made of things which do appear."* *Hebrews 11:3* Also in the book of Genesis 1 God said words to bring to pass that which he wanted to see happen. Now it's your turn to create the spiritual, financial, physical, material, mental, social, secular and business world that God desires for you to have. Prosperity in every area of your life is your covenant right, by taking the initiative to have a daily confession of the word of God and other positive affirmations this will produce faith in your heart and a manifestation of those things in your life. By doing this faithfully it will produce for you that which you desire and renew your mind and open it to receive the abundance that rightfully belongs to you that God has already given you!

## A GREAT START FOR EACH DAY

Today is a new day, another chance to begin again.

Today I make the best of it and through Christ I win.

Today is a new day, all things work together for my good, I am an heir of God and joint heir with Jesus Christ and all things work as they should.

Today is a new day, with God's help I succeed; the key to my success is persistence with that all my goals is achieved.

Today is a new day, one I have never before seen; it presents to me a new opportunity therefore I am observant and keen.

Today is a new day, I face this day with Courage and belief; I now look beyond all negatives, today I have victory.

Today is a new day, I live this day and fulfill my true intent, accomplishing my life plans I'm now all that God meant.

Today is a new day to confess my affirmations I do this consistently and see the manifestations.

## 33
## Call it Forth

If you want to see a change in your finances then you must realize that this concept of **"Calling it Forth"** is not a natural act but a spiritual act and it will seem foolish to the natural person and the carnal citizen. The reason it is a spiritual act is because it's of God and God is not natural but He is spirit. When you desire something from God that thing is already yours as a spiritual blessing but it has to be manifested in the natural. The word of God says, *"Blessed be the God and Father of our Lord Jesus Christ, who hath (that's past tense) blessed us with all spiritual blessings in heavenly places in Christ." Ephesians 1:3* The thing that you desire is a spiritual blessing in heavenly places but it's in Christ.

- The finances that you desire are in Christ.
- The prosperity that you desire is in Christ.

So therefore anything that's outside of Christ is outside of the kingdom and is not a part of the spiritual blessing in heavenly places in Christ. Citizens of the Kingdom that say they are having a hard time making ends meet:

- They don't understand that it's already done.
- They don't understand that it's easy not hard.

- They don't understand that financial prosperity is a spiritual blessing.
- They don't understand that this thing is done in heavenly places not earthly places.
- They don't understand that it's in Christ the anointed one and his anointing that destroys every yoke of hardship.

As a citizen of the Kingdom the King has given you the authority to be like him. The only way that you will get results like him is to act like him, be like him and do like him. When Jesus was teaching his disciples about faith he said to them, *"Have faith in God."* Mark 11:22 The original Greek translation of this verse means to have *"the faith of God."* Only when you have the faith of God can you do the acts of God. Jesus went on the say, *"For verily I say unto you, That whosoever shall say unto this mountain (with the faith of God – and many theologians and others believe that he was talking about a literal mountain), Be thou removed, and be thou cast into the sea; and shall not doubt in his heart, but shall believe that those things which he saith shall come to pass he shall have whatsoever he saith."* Mark 11:23

When it comes to finances; increase and prosperity falls in the category of things that you can believe for and say. However, this is not a natural belief of just a mental assent with the word of God but an inward spiritual knowing that what you believe shall come to pass without a doubt in your heart. If you can have this kind of supernatural belief then brother/sister go ahead and begin to move in the realm of the spirit and act as if what you need is already done and you will see the financial breakthrough that you desire.

The manual says, "*(As it is written, I have made thee a father of many nations,) before him whom he believed, even God, who quickeneth the dead, and calleth those things which be not as though they were.*" Romans 4:17 Now here are the translated versions of that scripture in the Phillips, the Message and the Amplified Bible translation.

- *"The whole thing, then, is a matter of faith on man's part and generosity on God's. He gives the security of his own promise to all men who can be called "children of Abraham", i.e. both those who have lived in faith by the Law, and those who have exhibited a faith like that of Abraham. To whichever group we belong, Abraham is in a real sense our father, as the scripture says: 'I have made you a father of many nations'.* **This faith is valid because of the existence of God himself**, *who can make the dead live, and speak his Word to those who are yet unborn."* **Phillips**

- *We call Abraham "father" not because he got God's attention by living like a saint, but because God made something out of Abraham when he was a nobody. Isn't that what we've always read in Scripture, God saying to Abraham, "I set you up as father of many peoples"? Abraham was first named "father"* *and then became a father because he dared to trust God to do what only God could do: raise the dead to life, with a word make something out of nothing.* **When everything was hopeless, Abraham believed anyway, deciding to live not on the basis of what he saw he couldn't do but on what God said he would do.** *And so he was made father of a multitude of peoples. God himself said to him, "You're going to have a big family, Abraham!"* **Message**

- *"As it is written, I have made you the father of many nations. [He was appointed our father] in the sight of God in Whom he believed,* **Who gives life to the dead and speaks of the nonexistent things that [He has foretold and promised] as if they [already] existed."** *Amplified*

As a child of Abraham the father of faith, you are the seed of Abraham. *"Even as Abraham believed God, and it was accounted to him for righteousness. Know ye therefore that they which are of faith, the same are the children of Abraham. So then they which be of faith are blessed with faithful Abraham. And if ye be Christ's then are ye Abraham's seed, and heirs according to the promise." Galatians 3:6-7, 9, 29* God has given his word on finances and prosperity that it is his wish above all things. 3 John 2, Deuteronomy 8:18, 28:1-14, So if God has given his word on it then why are citizens of the Kingdom having such difficulty seeing the manifestation of financial increase and prosperity into their life. One of the reasons is because the citizens of the Kingdom are perishing for a lack of knowledge and they have not been taught how to bring the manifestation forth. Hosea 4:6 Here are some key elements that must be in place for the manifestation to happen.

1. **There must be a word from the Lord.** (We have that word as stated above according to the word God has given about finances.)

2. **You must believe the word of the Lord.** (But shall believe that those things. Mark 11:23b)

3. **You must say that which you believe not just believe it but it must be a spoken word out of your mouth.** (*That whosoever shall say unto this mountain and shall believe that those things which he saith shall come to pass; he shall have whatsoever he saith. Mark 11:a,c*)

Therefore, if you want to see the manifestation of a financial breakthrough in your finances then you must begin to not only believe but call it forth. Even though presently it isn't a manifested form before your eyes at the moment you must begin to:

- *Speak his Word to those finances which are yet unseen* (**or to those who have yet manifested** *before your eyes. Calling those things that be not as though they were.) Phillips*

- *When everything was hopeless, Abraham believed anyway, deciding to live not on the basis of what he saw he couldn't do but on what God said he would do. And so he was made father of a multitude of peoples. (Likewise you must not look at what you see – no finances – living paycheck to paycheck – barely making ends meet – lack – but you must live on the basis of God's word – beloved, I wish above all things that thou mayest prosper. Then you will see the manifestation of those finances – increase – breakthrough – prosperity and abundance.)*

- *Who gives life to the dead and speaks of the nonexistent things that [He has foretold and promised] as if they [already] existed." Amplified (You must believe and know that your money and financial life as it exist at the moment even though it's dead or dying you must believe and know that as you call it forth God is speaking of your non-existent money and financial life that he has promised in his word as if it already existed.*

When Abram was getting old in age he and his wife tried to help God with a seed to establish his covenant. Genesis 16:1-3, They tried to do it by natural means just as most citizens try to do just natural accumulation in the hopes of finding a spiritual breakthrough. The promise that God made to Abram was fulfilled but not by natural means but it was a supernatural act; Abraham was an hundred years old and Sarah was 90. To read more about the promise of God to Abram concerning a son read Genesis 12-18, 21.

- So if you're willing to believe God for a financial breakthrough you must do as God and call it forth knowing that it's the father's good pleasure for you to have money and increase financially. No matter how long you may have been struggling God can turn this thing around in your favor by supernatural means because: *of the existence of God himself, who can make the dead live, and speak his Word to those who are yet unborn."* **Phillips** *When everything was hopeless, Abraham believed anyway, deciding to live not on the basis of what he saw he couldn't do but on what God said he would do.* **Message** *In the sight of God in Whom he believed, Who gives life to the dead and speaks of the nonexistent things that [He has foretold and promised] as if they [already] existed."* **Amplified**

## Call It Forth

*Father God, thank you for your eternal word that shall not pass away. On the basis of what you said you would do and who you are I thank you for my financial breakthrough now. I believe that my finances have come forth in the realm of the spirit and shall be manifested in the natural before my eyes. Today I call into existence _____(say the amount) to come forth that you have ordained for me to enjoy from the foundations of the world through your omniscience wisdom, omnipotent power and omnipresence spirit. I thank you that it is revealed now and I accept and receive it and according to your word which never fails to produce results.* **For you said, "What things soever ye desire (I desire a financial breakthrough miracle), when ye pray, believe that ye receive them, and ye shall have them." Mark 11:24** *So shall it be and so it is in Jesus Name. Amen.*

Continue to call it forth until you see the manifestation of your finances in physical form before your eyes. For God is faithful that promised.

## 34
## Time Is Money

*"Because to every purpose there is time and judgment, therefore the misery of man is great upon him."Ecclesiastes 8:6*

We've all heard the saying that time is money and such a statement is unequivocally true, according to how you use your time will determine your financial status in life. We've heard many things concerning time management and the importance of using your time wisely but for some reason we still waste an abundance of time. We all have the same amount of time allotted to us on a daily basis, meaning 24 hours in a given day. Those hours can be broken down in segments of three as follows:

- **In one 8-hour period we will spend that time sleeping.**
- **In another 8-hour period we will spend that time working.**
- **The last 8-hour is to be used at our own discretion.**

The first two 8-hour periods are set hours and we all conform to those set standards, even if we steal an hour and two from sleep eventually we will have to get back to the routine. Therefore our focus will not be on the first two 8-hours but on the last 8-hour period. These last 8-hours will either make you or break you financially, and sad to say they are breaking most individuals. I never really gave much thought to what I did with those last 8-hours because I've always been conscious and used my time wisely. However, an incident occurred that helped me to see the value of time and how most individuals are simply wasting their time doing things that will not help them arrive at their financial destiny. The incident that I am about to relay to you occurred at a time when dissatisfaction had gotten a hold of me. As I came to a point in my life I begin to ponder about my success in life and it came to me that I had not achieved my goals in spite of all I had done to work toward them.

At this time I was upset with myself and with God for not blessing me to be further than I was in life. I did not feel like it was fair for me to have worked this hard and still not be where I wanted to be financially. I had written nine books up to this point and still hadn't seen the financial success that others had seen with one book written. Others seem to have achieved financial status and were going on about their lives, but here I was still far from my financial goals and plans. So I decided that in this unfairness I'm not going to do anything else that will promote prosperity and financial stability in my own life or the lives of others. At this point I decided that:

- I did not want any more ideas about wealth and prosperity.

- I was not going to write anything else about the subject.
- I did not want any more directions about the subject.
- I was not going to promote and market my materials anymore.
- I was not going to put out any of my inventions on the market.
- I would just live a simple life and I didn't want any more revelations about the subject.
- I wanted nothing but to be left alone.

However, at this time God in his mercy still showered me with more revelation knowledge concerning financial matters. I was not looking for anything; I just wanted to be left alone. God showed me during this ordeal one of the reasons that individuals are not alone further financially. During this time I refused to do the things I would normally do that filled my day, such as:

- **Spending time writing books.**
- **Working on my computer in one phase or another.**
- **Reading my collection of books to become knowledgeable in the field of finances.**
- **Working on some invention or game that I would eventually put out.**
- **Putting out flyer's, brochures etc.**

- Doing some marketing on the Internet or surfing the net for information.
- Or simply spending time in meditation, affirmation or prayer.

As I refused to do my normal things that fill up my day I begin to notice that I had an incredible amount of time on my hands. Here I was with all this time and nothing constructive to do with it. The only thing that I found myself doing was watching an abundance of television. Then it dawned on me, the majority of individuals in the world are not making the most of their time. They have no goals, desires or objective that they're pursuing. They are doing exactly what I was doing in this 8-hour time period, absolutely nothing that was bringing them closer to their financial goals and dreams in life. If you have nothing that you're pursuing and no goals to work toward then you are filling up your 8 discretionary hours by doing things such as:

- Watching an abundance of television.
- On the internet on social sites.
- Talking extensively on the telephone.
- Sleeping your hours away.
- Just simply wasting time.
- Or just going out visiting people.

What you have to understand is that those 8 discretionary hours are the only hours you have to plan and make your future financially stable and successful. If you do nothing during these 8-hours then nothing from nothing leaves nothing. You cannot do non-essential things for 8-hours a day and then expect to have financial increase, prosperity and wealth in your life. You cannot expect to sit on the couch these 8 hours and do nothing and your finances will increase. You cannot expect to talk on the phone these 8 hours and your finances will increase. You must make advancement toward your financial future. Time is money, and if you're wasting it then you're wasting money and if you waste money then money will not be attracted to you but repelled. You must begin to use some of those 8-hours to build your financial portfolio and you can do that by doing some or all of the following things.

1. **Begin to follow the finanatomy concept to the letter.**
2. **Read books that will help you to work toward you financial goals.**
3. **Attend seminars or workshops that will educate you concerning financial increase, prosperity and wealth.**
4. **Listen to tapes, CD's, DVD's or cassettes that will inform you in the way of financial success.**
5. **Go on the Internet and search out information about how to do what you want to do in order to get you where you want to be.**

6. Spend some time in meditation, prayer and affirmations.
7. Work in a business part time to increase your finances.
8. Take out time to plan or orchestrate your future steps for financial success.

You must begin to do something and do it now because time is money. You will not get more time nor can you retrieve wasted time. We all have 24 hours and 8 of those hours are to be used at your own discretion. From this day forward begin to use some of them in a more constructive, positive and profitable manner.

## How to Reorganize Your Time and Life

I have come to the conclusion after much reading, studying and talking with people that individuals have a problem being disciplined to do what they know they need to do. Every New Year's Day multitudes of individuals begin their new year with what is called a new year's resolution. Many of these individuals are sincere in their endeavor to fulfill this resolution, but sad to say the majority fails to attain their goals. The reason for the failure is the inability of the individual to consistently do what they know they need to do without fail until they see the manifestation of their desire become a reality in their life. There are many things which people endeavor to do but fail in their attempt, such as:

- **Losing a certain amount of weight.**
- **Trying to stop smoking.**
- **To have a certain amount of money.**
- **Having a daily Bible reading time.**
- **Having a daily consistent prayer life.**
- **Exercising on a daily basis.**
- **To finish a certain work or project, etc.**

Every time you fail to do what you set out to do it creates a defeatist attitude if you're not careful and before long you will find yourself not finishing or completing anything that you aren't (in a matter of speaking) forced to do or what your life doesn't depend on. If you are tired of living this undisciplined life and you're ready to go forth and make the most of your time and life then you must take your life by force. Time is money and if you continue to waste it and be unproductive with your time then you will continue to spiral down the road to financial suicide or slowly eradicate your financial life through financial Russian roulette. But fear not, we have the answer to get you on tract to a disciplined and productive life from this day forward. One thing that is hindering you is a spirit of slothfulness that is derived from the spirit of laziness. These spirits in turn make you slack and wasteful. You must bind those spirits so that you can be delivered from its hold on your life. The word of God gives us various scriptures that emphasize how these spirits hinders the life of individuals in many aspects

- *"The hand of the diligent shall bear rule: but the slothful shall be under tribute." Proverbs 12:24*

- *"He becometh poor that dealeth with a slack hand: but the hand of the diligent maketh rich." Proverbs 10:4*

- *"The soul of the sluggard desireth, and hath nothing: but the soul of the diligent shall be made fat." Proverbs 13:4*

- *"Slothfulness casteth into a deep sleep; and an idle soul shall suffer hunger." Proverbs 19:15*

- *"Go to the ant, thou sluggard; consider her ways, and be wise." Proverbs 6:6*

Let's pray this prayer right now so that the spirit of laziness and slothfulness can be broken over your life. Pray it with boldness and authority.

*Father, I thank you that for this purpose your Son was manifested that he might destroy the works of the devil. In the name of Jesus I command you spirit of laziness and slothfulness to be broken over my life now. I rebuke you in the name of Jesus; the blood of Jesus is against you now. I break you from the root and every other spirit that is attached to you I command you to be gone in the name of Jesus. The fire of God is against you and I frustrate your every verdict against me in the name of Jesus. I bind and cast out every hindering spirit that has caused me to procrastinate and be slothful in my endeavors in the past in the name of Jesus. I command you foul spirits to leave me now for I am free for those that the Son set free are free indeed. I now loose the liberty of God upon my life and the Presence of God upon me for where the Presence of the Lord is there is Liberty, fullness of joy and pleasures forever more. I take control of my life and my time now in the name of Jesus, and I use it to be productive, creative, and a mighty force for good in my life and the lives of others. I am free, I am free, I am free in the name of Jesus. Amen*

## ONE HOUR TO CHANGE YOUR LIFE

Now that you've done the spiritual to free yourself the next step I have put together is a strategy that can help you get from where you are to where you want to be. In my endeavors I also needed a systematic method to give me that extra boost at times. What has worked for me in simplicity I am confident will work for you also if you are willing to pay the price in time and effort to make in happen. The most important thing in forming a spirit of consistency is to first get your mind renewed so that your thinking can be in line with the desires of your heart. Many times we desire to do something but our heart (spirit) has not accepted the idea and hasn't conceived it as a matter of fact where it agrees without conscious decision to make it happen. Therefore, we must get this idea into our spirit so that it can be real to our spirit man and inspire us to do what we need to do. One way to do this is through meditation and repetition of the word of God. The scripture says, *"This book of the law shall not depart out of thy mouth; but thou shalt meditate therein day and night, that thou mayest observe to do according to all that is written therein: for then thou shalt make thy way prosperous, and then thou shalt have good success." Joshua 1:8*

However, I have discovered that to tell someone to set aside times for meditation and a confession of the word doesn't always work, because the individual will not discipline themselves to set aside that time consistently. So faced with my desire to help people and the dilemma of individuals inconsistency I still needed some way to help people do what they needed to do but somehow let it be automatically done for them without them having to think about doing it. I knew that those who were serious, if they had the inspiration and information to do what they needed to do, would do it. This is the idea that was revealed to me and it has worked like a charm with consistency and infallibly.

Just before writing this line I was inspired and informed that I needed to do a certain thing that is one of my goals to improve my financial situation. You may have never thought about this but the idea that God blessed me to come up with only takes one hour a day which can be done throughout the day and cause you to fulfill your resolution and objective in life without fail Most individuals in this day has a cell phone and I am of the belief that everything in your life should be an asset to you instead of a liability. If something is not carrying its own weight and paying for itself then it's costing you money and not putting money in your pocket. Your cell phone is a device that can help orchestrate your financial life if you understand how to make it work for you and pay huge dividends. Within your cell phone is a calendar, schedule or event planner, on that calendar, schedule or event planner you can write your daily goal or objective and then you can set a time that you would like to be reminded of your goal, objective or schedule. Your phone also has an alarm that you can set to go off at a particular time on a daily basis. Once you set this up you will discover that this is a reminder of what you need to do at that precise time and then you must go and do it. When you set up your calendar, schedule or event planner make sure to choose times that you know you can get done what you need to do uninterrupted.

The first things you want to be reminded of are things that will enable you to renew your mind and get spiritual and positive words in your spirit. What this will consist of is one hour daily of mediation and affirmations. Don't believe the lie that you don't have one hour to do this, you have the time and I will show you how to do it. Your financial life depends on doing this on a consistent basis and it will produce for you rewards untold. The systematic method that I want to break down in a methodical manner will consist of:

1. **Putting 2 "15 Minute" meditation spots on your calendar, schedule or event planner that will alarm to remind you daily.**

2. **Putting 3 "5 Minute" meditation spots on your calendar, schedule or event planner that will alarm to remind you daily.**

3. **Putting "10 Affirmation" spots on your calendar, schedule or event planner that will alarm to remind you daily.**

4. **And 2 Goals to be achieved daily or weekly.**

This is not as confusing as it sounds and I will explain exactly how this is done with clarity and understanding.

1. Let your 3 **"10 Minute"** meditation spots be worded just enough to let you know what you need to do at the time your alarm goes off. **Ex. 10 Minute Mediation: "The Lord shall increase me more and more and my money is improving every day."** Your wording should

be somewhat on this order or similar. You will put this on 3 different times on your calendar, schedule or event planner to remind you that's its meditation time. When your alarm goes off you will sit down and relax yourself and then repeat the phrase over and over for the first minute or two and then just ponder that thought allowing it to get into your spirit and renew your mind. You can also say the phrase over again in midway of the 10 minutes or the last minute or two, or both. You will begin to see results following within the first 14-30 days; some have seen results in 3-5 days and some sooner. It is preferably to do one of these in the morning before you get out of bed and also one at night while you're drifting off to sleep.

2. With your 3 **"5 Minute"** meditation spots it should be worded also just enough to let you know what to do at the time the alarm goes off. **Ex. 5 Minute Meditation: "It is God that gives me power to get wealth."** Repeat this scripture 3 times and then take out the word wealth and repeat it over and over for the remaining 5 minutes. This will have a powerful effect on your spirit and mind.

3. Last, with the 10 times you want to divide this up into 4 sections where you will set times on your calendar, schedule or event planner for

your affirmations that will go off with the alarm throughout the day.

- **Example 1: "I have $1000 in my account now."** You will set these 3 different times throughout the day for the alarm to go off in your calendar, schedule or event planner to be reminded to confess this **5-10 times when the alarm goes off.**

- **Example 2: "My business (job) is improving every day."** You will set this 2 different times throughout the day for the alarm to go off in your calendar, schedule or event planner to be reminded to confess this 5-**10 times when the alarm goes off.**

- **Example 3: "Money loves to fill my pocket."** You will set this 3 different times throughout the day for the alarm to go off in your calendar, schedule or event planner to be reminded to confess this **5-10 times when the alarm goes off. Y**ou can change any of these phrases or keep them it's up to you.

- **Example 4:** This last time you will set 2 different times throughout the day to be reminded to confess your goals that you desire to achieve. **Such as: "God I thank you for prosperity in my mutual funds, stocks, bond** etc." In this last phase you can also put here things you need to do daily to get you closer to your financial and material goals in life instead of confessing your prosperity goals. **Example: "God I thank you for my new car" or "God I thank you for my new home" etc...**

You just need to read this once or twice just to make sure you're on schedule and as a reminder of your goals in life. Here is the beauty of it all, once you have taken the time to set these times up throughout the day for the alarm to go off daily you will only have to do it **once.** From this time on your life is now on automatic and daily the alarms will go off to remind you at those specific times. When it goes off you know what to do, this renews your mind with a prosperity consciousness and get those spiritual positive thoughts in your spirit. Time is money and the more constructive you can use yours the more you will attract money to you and create for yourself a financial destiny of increase, prosperity, wealth, riches and abundance. It may take about a week for you to get the schedule set in your mind but stick with it and you will see the results.

## 35
## Prayer and Money

*"And he commanded the multitude to sit down on the grass, and took the five loaves, and the two fishes, and looking up to heaven, he blessed, and brake, and gave the loaves to his disciples, and the disciples to the multitude. And they did all eat, and were filled: and they took up of the fragments that remained twelve baskets full. And they that had eaten were about five thousand men, beside women and children." Matthew 14:19-21*

Another way to attract money and things to you is by using the power of prayer. Many have been taught that we shouldn't pray for finances and material things, but according to the scriptures just the opposite is true. In our beginning scripture we have an example of the power of prayer in action. Here we have the case where the crowd had followed Jesus and had been with him all evening, they had ended up in a desert place where there was no food. The disciples had come to Jesus to ask him to send the crowd away so that they could go to the villages and buy themselves victuals. Jesus said unto them *"give ye them to eat"* meaning you feed them, and the disciples responded saying *"we have five loaves, and two fishes,"* Jesus responded *"Bring them hither to me."* Here is an outline of what Jesus did in miraculously feeding the five thousand:

- He commanded the multitude to sit down on the grass.

- He took the five loaves and two fishes in his hand.

- He looked up to heaven in prayer.

- He blessed and gave thanks for the five loaves and two fishes.

- He broke the bread and gave to the disciples and the disciples gave to the multitude.

- And they did all eat, and were filled: and they took up of the fragments that remained twelve baskets full.

- And they that had eaten were about five thousand men, beside women and children.

What the multitude and the disciples experienced here was a creative miracle of substance. Prayer was made for the intention of multiplying what was on hands to meet a need and it happened. In other instances we see prayer in relation to substance or things and we see an increase as a result of the prayer that was made for the substance or thing.

1. The feeding of the 4000. Matthew 15:32-39, Mark 8:1-9
2. The feeding of the 5000. Mark 6:30-44, Luke 9:10-17, John 6:1-14

We behold also in other instances where substance or things were mentioned, here we have Jesus and others speaking over or about things caused increase or abundance to manifest.

1. Water turned into wine. John 2:1-11
2. Fish with coin in its mouth. Matthew 17:24-27
3. Multiplying of meal and oil. 1 Kings 17:8-16
4. Increase of widow's oil. 2 Kings 4:1-7
5. The pottage healed. 2 Kings 4:28-41
6. Bread multiplied for a 100 men. 2 Kings 4:42-44
7. Making iron to swim. 2 Kings 6:1-7

In the same manner that God moved on the behalf of the Old Testament saints, and how Jesus used his authority, he will likewise move on your behalf as you pray for money or pray over your money. I have personally seen where prayer and speaking over my money has produced miraculous results on my behalf. I recall an instance in particular where $3000 was once added to my bank account. I remember once when I was teaching a Prosperity class and one of the young ladies took the word with faith and believed it, the next day double the amount went into her account that was supposed to go in. You can pray for money if you need it just like you can pray for healing if you need it. Prayer is the one tool that God has given us to use not only in relationship and fellowship but also to ask him for what we need. It's no less spiritual to pray for money than it is to pray for your healing, a job or for God to open a door for you. Jesus opened the floodgate wide when he said,

- *"Therefore I say unto you, (money fall in the things category) soever ye desire, when ye pray, believe that ye receive them, and ye shall have them."* Mark 11:24

- *And whatsoever (meaning whatever) ye shall ask in my name, that will I do, that the Father may be glorified in the Son. If ye shall ask any thing (anything means anything, including money) in my name, I will do it."* John 14:13-14

- *"If ye abide in me, and my words abide in you, ye shall ask what ye will, and it shall be done unto you."* John 15:7

It's okay to pray for money, money is one of those things that you may desire; it's a part of the anything or what you will. When you pray for money pray with as much passion as you would if you were praying for your healing or anything else. Don't just pray and ask for it once but ask and keep on asking until you receive the money that you're praying for. Jesus said, *"Ask, and it shall be given you; see, and ye shall find; knock, and it shall be opened unto you: For every one that asketh receiveth; and he that seeketh findeth; and to him that knocketh it shall be opened. Or what man is there of you, whom if his son ask bread, will he give him a stone? Or if he ask a fish, will he give him a serpent? (The understood meaning is that what you ask for is what you will get, not something contrary to what you ask). If ye then, been evil, know how to give good gifts unto your children, how much more shall your Father which is in heaven give good things (including money) to them that ask him? And He spake a parable unto them to this end, that men ought to always to pray, and not to faint; Saying, There was in a city a judge, which feared not God, neither regarded man: And there was a widow in that city; and she came unto him, saying, Avenge me of my adversary. And he would not for a while: but afterward he said within himself, Though I fear not God, nor regard man; Yet because this widow troubleth me, I will avenge her, lest by her continual coming she weary me. And the Lord said, Hear what the unjust judge saith, And shall not God avenge his own elect, which cry (pray) day and night unto him, though he bear long with them? I tell you that he will avenge them speedily. Nevertheless when the Son of man cometh, shall he find faith (of this kind) on the earth." Luke 18:1-8*

So therefore ask and keep on asking, seek and keep on seeking, knock and keep on knocking until the money that you pray for is a manifest reality before your eyes. And when you pray for money don't pray out of lust or evil desires for money, to have money to waste and do wicked, crooked and corrupt things with. *"You ask, and receive not, because ye ask amiss, that ye may consume it upon your lusts."* James 4:3 However, if you pray for money with a sincere heart and attitude of belief so that you may have money to use in right doing, need, desire and righteousness, you will receive it as sure as the night follows the day. *Pray, pray, pray and ask your Father in heaven for the money that you need and in your persistent and prayer of importunity your Father in heaven will give you as much as you need and desire. For "Which of you shall have a friend, and shall go unto him at midnight, and say unto him, Friend, lend me three loaves; For a friend of mine in his journey is come to me, and I have nothing to set before him? And he from within shall answer and say, Trouble me not: the door is now shut, and my children are with me in bed; I cannot rise and give thee. I say unto you, Though he will not rise and give him, because he is his friend, yet because of his importunity he will rise and give him as much as he needeth." Luke 11:5-8 And so will your Father which is in heaven for you.*

## HOW TO SPEAK OVER
## YOUR MONEY FOR INCREASE

If you find that your money is low or your accounts appear empty, dark and void, begin to speak over your money the words of biblical scripture and watch your good appear. As you speak the word of God and spiritual positive decrees over your money, the Spirit of God will move upon your money and cause it to increase and become fruitful and multiply. It was not until God spoke that things begin to happen, *"And the earth was without form, and void; and darkness was upon the face of the deep. And the spirit of God moved upon the face of the waters. And God said, Let there be light: and there was light." Genesis 1:2-3* Just as the Spirit of God brought forth life out of darkness, void and chaos had to flee as the word was spoken, He will likewise bring forth increase, prosperity and abundance in your money. Here is how to speak over your money and accounts to cause increase.

1. Take your money in your hands and say *"Wealth and riches are in my house now in Jesus name."*

2. Take your bankbook and speak over it saying, *"The blessings of the Lord are upon you now in Jesus name."*

3. Take your money in your hands and say, *"God is multiplying you now and increase and prosperity is upon you."*

4. Take your bankbook in your hands and say, *"The blessing of the Lord it maketh rich and I am blessed and rich today."*

5. Take your money in your hands and say, *"God is multiplying you now just as Jesus multiplied the fish and loaves."*

6. Take your bankbook in your hands and say,

*"And we know that all things work together for good to them that love God, to them who are the called according to his purpose. Thank you Father that all things are working together in my bank account now.*

7. Take your money and bankbook in hands together and say, *"Money loves to fill my pocket and accounts and they are both filled now."*

Begin to do this on a daily basis over your money and accounts and watch God produce creative and miraculous miracles in your behalf. You have to get your mind right and understand that you're a spiritual person and you have every right to operate in the spirit realm just as Jesus did. Jesus use this same principle of speaking words over substance or things to produce results of death or life saying, *"And on the morrow, when they were come from Bethany, he was hungry: And seeing a fig tree afar off having leaves, he came, if haply he might find any thing thereon: and when he came to it, he found nothing but leaves; for the time of figs was not yet. And Jesus answered and said unto it, No man eat fruit of thee hereafter for ever. And his disciples hear it. And when even was come, he went out of the city. And in the morning, as they passed by, they saw the fig tree dried up from the roots. And Peter calling to remembrance saith unto him, Master, behold, the fig tree which thou cursedst is withered away. And Jesus answering saith unto them, Have faith in God."* Mark

*11:12- 14, 19-22* And what shall I more say concerning speaking over substance and things for increase, prosperity, wealth and abundance, for the time would fail me to write about the stories concerning:

1. The story of the fish and coin. Matthew 17:24-27
2. The Hugh catch of fishes. Luke 5:4-11, John 21:1-11
3. The water that was turned into wine. John 2:1-11

*"And there are also many other things which Jesus did, the which, if they should be written everyone, I suppose that even the world itself could not contain the books that should be written. Amen.*

# 36
# The Prosperity of Fools

*"For the turning away of the simple shall slay them, and the prosperity of fools shall destroy them." Proverbs 1:32*

God in his righteousness and goodness gives all mankind the opportunity to prosper, some are wise in their opportunity and some are foolish. Some individuals that are currently living in poverty and lack if they were to suddenly become prosperous they would return to poverty within one to three years. A foolish person is one that will not hearken to instruction and doesn't realize that instructions are what they need and what will enable them to stop being foolish and become wise. The bible has a lot to say about instruction and its value when hearken to; it starts by saying, *"A wise man will hear, and will increase learning, and a man of understanding shall attain unto wise counsels." Proverbs 1:5*

Now, a wise man will give an attentive ear to learn instructions but a fool will do the exact opposite in every situation to what a wise man will do.

- *"The wise in heart will receive commandments: but a prating fool shall fall." Proverbs 10:8*
- *"The way of a fool is right in his own eyes: but he that hearkeneth unto counsel is wise." Proverbs 12:15*
- *"He that loveth pleasure shall be a poor man: he that*

*loveth wine and oil shall not be rich."* Proverbs 21:17
- *"The wise man's eyes are in his head; but the fool walketh in darkness."* Ecclesiastes 2:14a

Our objective in this chapter is to let you see how a fool become a fool and what a fool will do verses what a wise man will do, then we want to show the fool how to cease being a fool and become a wise man. The first thing I want to relay is that even though prosperity is a good thing for a fool it can be tragic and his destruction. I once read a story about an individual that lived on the street for many years as a bum yet one day he suddenly came into a windfall of cash as a result of the death of a relative. The paper ran his story and told how the former bum gave back to an individual that always looked after him on the street (this was a good thing) and then proceeded to tell the manner in which the bum was spending some of his sudden prosperity.

It went on to note that the former bum was tipping cab drivers with hundred dollar bills, bought a Rolex watch and other non-essential things contrary to a wise man. I have no doubt within one to three years this former bum will once again be on skid row or in poverty and barely making ends meet. Now here is a classic example of a fool, along with a classic example of prosperity being his destruction. This former bum took no thought that his windfall of cash would not last him forever because if he did he would not have tipped cab drivers with hundred dollar bills nor would he have went out and immediately bought a Rolex watch that cost thousands of dollars, in the end no doubt he will end up pawning that Rolex watch for cold hard cash. This former bum because he is a fool having no instructions or not hearkening to instructions that were given him probably had no immediate thoughts about acquiring knowledge about banking, saving, investment, schooling or business so that his money could work for him. He probably did not even go and immediately buy a single book about money and how to use it for increase, prosperity and wealth. We all have read about individuals that have come into prosperity and wealth and years later they are back where they were and sometime even worse off. Why would such individuals long for prosperity all their life and then suddenly receive it and blow all that money on foolishness and vanity only to end up back in the dumps?

My conclusion is God's conclusion these individuals are fools they will not hearken to any instructions about how to use that money for the benefit of God, their life, family and mankind in general. But their main focus is immediate gratification and pleasure with no serious thought of their future or the future of others. The word of God says about the fool *"The fool and the brutish person perish, and leave their wealth to others."* Psalms 49:10 Well before we point to many fingers let's make sure that no fingers are pointing back to us (at this time take and point one finger in front of you, notice how many of your other fingers are pointing back at you) because many times we likewise have been foolish when God allowed increase and prosperity to come into our hands. How many times have you received tax money, unexpected money, bonuses, expected monies, etc. and did the unwise thing instead of the wise thing and within a month or months later were right back where you were before? Well in that instant you were foolish and probably as you look back now you see how foolish you were and what you would have done differently, yet sad to say that many if another opportunity arose would make the same foolish decision with their prosperity.

**Here are the difference between the wise man and the fool with prosperity.**

- The wise person first thought would be, I need to give God his tithes.

- The foolish person first thought would be to go out and enjoy and take this opportunity to splurge a bit.

- The wise person second thought would be "I need to sit down get pencil and paper and figure out intelligently what moves I need to make." They will seek to get a vision for their finances.

- The foolish person second thought would be to pay off their bills if they have any sense at all.

- The wise person third thought would be to talk with a banker, investment manager or someone with credibility that can guide them on the road to continual prosperity and wealth so their money can work for them instead of against them.

- The foolish person third thought would be to buy a new car, clothes and furniture.

- The wise person fourth thought would be to pay myself a portion.

- The foolish person fourth thought would be to put some in the bank if they have any sense at all.

- The wise person fifth thought would be to pay off some of their bill or a substantial amount on some of their bills to cut off some of the interest.

- The foolish person fifth thought would be no concrete thoughts after their forth thought from this point on they will simply go with the flow and that's exactly what will happen their money would just flow right out of their hands and they will end up wondering how could they have been so foolish and spent all that money and now have nothing to show of equal value.

Within three to five years, the wise person would have built a good nest egg from their prosperity and living a well defined financial life of increase and abundance. Within three to five years, the foolish person will be right back where they started and maybe even worse off than they were in the beginning because of their unwise and foolish decisions. However, the good news is that the foolish person doesn't have to remain foolish they can become wise and make wise financial decisions. The scriptures tells us many ways to become wise, in the book of Proverbs we have King Solomon giving instructions to his son saying, *"My son, if thou wilt receive my words, and hide my commandments with thee; So that thou incline thine ear unto wisdom, and apply thine heart to understanding; Yea, if thou criest after knowledge, and liftest up thy voice for understanding: If thou seekest her as silver, and searchest for her as for hid treasures; Then shalt thou understand the fear of the LORD, and find the knowledge of God. For the LORD giveth wisdom: out of his mouth cometh knowledge and understanding. He layeth up sound wisdom for the* *righteous: he is a buckler to them that walk uprightly. He keepeth the paths of judgment, and preserveth the way of his saints. Then shalt thou understand righteousness, and judgment, and equity; yea, **every good path.** When wisdom entereth into thine heart, and knowledge is pleasant unto thy soul; Discretion shall preserve thee, understanding shall keep thee. Proverbs 2:1-11*

The foolish person does not have to remain in this state, wisdom is crying out to help make this person wise and equip them to become intelligent and competent financial managers of their money. In this vast world of ours there is more than enough information to inform us about whatever we need to know, the information is available in many forms. The scriptures tells us *"He that walketh with wise men shall be wise: but a companion of fools shall be destroyed."* Proverbs 13:20

1. **You walk with wise men by reading the books they've written.**

2. **You walk with wise men by listening to their instructions.**

3. **You walk with wise men by obtaining their material in whatever form you can get it.**

4. **We have libraries in practically every city teeming with an abundance of information at your disposal.**

5. We have the information super highway where you can access the Internet and find whatever information you need to become informed.

6. We have seminars that are conducted in many cities and states on a continuous basis about practically anything under the sun.

7. We have bookstores in practically every city or adjacent city for your convenience and book purchases.

You can learn how to be wise with prosperity so that your prosperity will not be your destruction but your blessing. **So let us hear the conclusion of the whole matter:** *"Understand, ye brutish among the people: and ye fools, when will ye be wise."* Psalms 94:8

*"The wise shall inherit glory: but shame shall be the promotion of fools."* Proverbs 3:35

*"Hear instructions, and be wise, and refuse it not. Blessed is the man that heareth me, watching daily at my gates, waiting at the posts of my doors. For whosoever findeth me findeth life, and shall obtain favour of the LORD. Proverbs 8:33:35*

*"Give instructions to a wise man, and he will be yet wiser: teach a just man, and he will increase in learning."* Proverbs 9:9

*"The proverbs of Solomon, A wise son maketh a glad father: but a foolish son is the heaviness of his mother."* Proverbs 10:1

*"He that troubleth his own house shall inherit the wind: and the fool shall be servant to the wise of heart."* Proverbs 11:29

*"A wise man feareth, and depareth from evil: but the fool rageth, and is confident."* Proverbs 14:16

*"The crown of the wise is their riches: but the foolishness of fools is folly."* Proverbs 14:24

*"A reproof entereth more into a wise man than an hundred stripes into a fool."* Proverbs 17:10

*"Better is a poor and wise child than an old and foolish king, who will no more be admonished."* Ecclesiastes 4:13

*"A wise man is strong; yea, a man of knowledge increaseth strength."* Proverbs 24:5

## 37
# Honour the Lord

*"Honour the LORD with thy substance, and with the firstfruits of all thine increase: So shall thy barns be filled with plenty, and thy presses shall burst out with new wine." Proverbs 3:9-10*

God wants all of you heart, soul and mind but he also wants your money. He doesn't want what you have left over after you have dispersed it abroad; he wants the first fruits of your increase. This matter of first fruits is so vitally important that if you miss it here you can hinder your entire financial life and prosperity. It may appear that the individual that's not serving the Lord is prospering even though they're not honouring God with their money. As the scriptures accentuates, *"Be not deceived; God is not mocked: for whatsoever a man soweth, that shall he also reap." Galatians 6:7* It may appear as if they're getting away with this but God's law is getting them in another way, I promise you. Nevertheless, we as God's people can't use this as an excuse because we are people that live by another set of instructions and laws and his laws while not the laws of the land in this instant are the laws of our life and in order to receive what God has we must do what he says above all else. In the matter of money, God want you to give first and foremost to his cause by bringing your tithes and offering to his house so that his work can be achieved in the earth.

God says *"Bring ye all the tithes into the storehouse, that there may be meat in mine house, and prove me now herewith, saith the LORD of hosts, if I will not open you the windows of heaven, and pour you out a blessing, that there shall not be room enough to receive it. And I will rebuke the devourer for your sakes, and he shall not destroy the fruits of your ground; neither shall your vine cast her fruit before the time in the field, saith the LORD of hosts. And all nations shall call you blessed: for ye shall be a delightsome land, saith the LORD of hosts."* Malachi 3:10-12

What I want you to understand here is there is honor and power in giving or doing this first with your money verses doing it second or third etc... It's only the first that really counts with God. By taking your money and giving God his first before you pay yourself, bills and anything else you **honour God in doing this**. There are several things that you are silently speaking in doing this.

- **You are honoring God above everything else and he will in return honor you.**

- **It lets God know that he can trust you with financial substance.**

- **It proclaims that you're looking to God as your source in life.**

- **It proclaims God as the God of your faith.**

- **It says that you're looking to him for your provision, supply and increase in life.**

When you bring to God your tithes and offerings second, third, etc. it voids out all the things above. Many individuals aren't as prosperous as they should be because they have relegated God to a lesser position than first and foremost. When God emphasizes that something must happen first he means exactly what he says, second and third will not cut it, it's first that counts in the courts of heaven.

Let's observe some examples in scriptures of first and see if we can compare Scripture with scripture to come up with a conclusion of the importance of first. Here we have the story of the impotent man saying, *"Now there is at Jerusalem by the sheep market a pool, which is called in the Hebrew tongue Bethesda, having five porches. In these lay a great multitude of impotent folk, of blind, halt, withered, waiting for the moving of the water. For an angel went down at a certain season into the pool, and troubled the water:* **whosoever then first** *(not second, third etc.) after the troubling of the water stepped in was made whole of whatsoever disease he had."* St. John 5:1-9

Also, we have the story of the tribute money saying, *"And when they were come to Capernaum, they that received tribute money came to Peter, and said, Doth not your master pay tribute? He saith, yes. And when he was come into the house, Jesus prevented him, saying, What thinkest thou , Simon? Of whom do the kings of the earth take customs or tribute? Of their own children, or of strangers? Peter saith unto him, Of strangers, Jesus saith unto him, Then are the children free. Notwithstanding, lest we should offend them, go thou to the sea, and cast an hook,* **and take up the fish that first** *(not second, third)* **cometh up**; *and when thou hast opened his mouth, thou shalt find a piece of money: that take, and give unto them for me and thee." Matthew 17:24-27*

## Other Scriptures that emphasize the Importance of first is these.

- *"Therefore if thou bring thy gift to the altar, and there rememberest that thy brother hath ought against thee; Leave there thy gift before the altar, and go thy way;* **first be reconciled to thy brother** *(not second, third etc.), and then come and offer thy gift." St. Matthew 5:23-24*

- **"But seek ye first the kingdom of God** *(not second, third etc.), and his righteousness; and all these things shall be added unto you." Matthew 6:33*

- *"Or else, how can one enter into a strong man's house, and spoil his goods,* **except he first bind the strong man** *(not second, third, etc.)? And then he will spoil his house." Matthew 12:25-29*

Here we see in many instances the importance of obedience, unless these actions were done in the manner described nothing would have happened, only the first carries power (**go back and reread the above scriptures**). In this matter of honoring the Lord first with your money if you relegate God and his cause to any other position than first it will not work, it doesn't work that way it must be God first. So when you receive monies from this day forward always honor God first by giving him his and he will always may sure that your business is taken care of. If you want to have increase, prosperity and wealth in your house and always have abundance with more than enough in your possession then be obedient to the word of God for *"If ye be willing and obedient, ye shall eat the good of the land: But if ye refuse and rebel, ye shall be devoured with the sword: for the mouth of the LORD hath spoken it."* Isaiah 1:19-20

So let us hear the conclusion of the whole matter: *"Honour the LORD with thy substance, and with the firstfruits of all thine increase: So shall thy barns be filled with plenty, and thy presses shall burst forth with new wine."* Proverbs 3:9-1

# 38
# Condition Matches Position

This is probably the most difficult chapter to write because this chapter has to have information that is applicable to show you how to get your condition to match your position. It must show you how to get from where you are to where you should be in the financial and material arena of your life. Presently you may be living in a state of poverty, lack, barely making ends meet or paycheck living. My job as the author is to show you what steps are necessary to get you from paycheck living to the cycle of need then to get you from the cycle of need to the cycle of want, from their I must show you how to reach the ultimate, the cycle of wealth.

1. Two things are important at this stage to take you from where you are to where you should be; there is nothing new under the sun so I'm not giving you any new information.

2. Any information that you learn here is either lost information, information that you've never heard before or information that you've never heard in this manner. First, you cannot go any further than what you know, you're limited by the knowledge that you have or by the knowledge that you have but aren't applying. In the book of Hosea it says, *"My people are*

*destroyed for lack of knowledge: because thou hast rejected knowledge, I will also reject thee."* Hosea 4:6 One bit of knowledge that's vital to get you from where you are to where you want to be is "you must know what you want in life, you must have a definite purpose." If you don't know what you want in life how will you ever attain it, how will you have what you don't know you want? Until you get this bit of knowledge answered, you'll never be able to go much further in life. Right now what is it that you want in life financially and materially; to just say plenty of money is too vague, it has no life in it and therefore you have no unction to go after it.

Right now, say a financial goal that you desire to have in your life that you're willing to pay the price to attain even if it makes you shame. Forget about whether you can achieve it just say it. Now that you've said it you know what you want financially in life, I have good news for you whatever financial amount you said somebody has already attained it in life. What one man or woman can do another man or woman can do. History, success magazines, books and the bible itself are filled with men and women that has already gone before you and achieved that amount in life. I'm almost one hundred percent sure, that nobody in their financial statement affirmed the amount of fifty billion dollars well even this amount has been attained by some. Therefore, your spoken statement is definitely possible and attainable with the proper knowledge.

Second, you must have a vision of what it is you want to attain in life *for "without a vision the people perish." Proverbs 29:18* A vision can be termed as a goal or an objective, having this gives you something to strive for something to work towards. With a goal or objective in mind you have something before you to work towards, without a goal or objective you have nothing to pursue or go after. Goal isn't a bad word it's just a term stating your objective or desire, however if you would like a more sophisticated term you can use **"Prosperity Target."**

That which you spoke out as a financial attainment, is your prosperity target that's what you're shooting for and the good news is that God wants you to have it. In Jeremiah it says, *"For I know the thoughts that I think toward you, saith the LORD, thoughts of peace (prosperity, wellness, health, safety, blessing, happiness and plenty), and not thoughts of evil (grief, calamity, sorrow, trouble, and affliction), to give you an expected end (a future, a hope and success)."Jeremiah 29:11*

Now that you have a prosperity target, next you must have a plan for increase. A strategy to get you there and the good news is that there's not just one strategy to get you there, there are many strategies that can get you there. A strategy is nothing more than a plan, an approach, a tactic and a line of attack, daily you have strategies that you accomplish, some have become such a part of your everyday routine that you no longer see it as a strategy.

Here is an elementary example, at one time and point you had to make a plan or method of how to do what you easily do today without effort. A simple point in case is the place that you currently live, when you first moved there you had to come up with an approach or strategy of how to easily get there without taking a longer route.

You may have tried two different ways but finally settled on a certain way as the easiest way to get there; all you did was looked at both ways and then settled on the way that you thought was best. Now, the way that you take you take it effortlessly because your strategy is already in place.

When you take a trip or vacation to a specific place, you don't just jump up and go you plan and strategize the whole trip from beginning to end. Well if you're planning everyday of your life anyway and you plan your vacations and trips why can't you plan how to attain your prosperity target? Strategizing how to reach your prosperity target is no harder than planning for your next vacation, when you know where you want to go then you begin to call around and get the appropriate information needed to get you there. Likewise, when you want to reach your prosperity target you must get the appropriate knowledge needed to show you how to get there. This knowledge is available in books, tapes, seminars etc., it's there for your learning and you must go forth after it. Your plan for increase includes all or some of these methods to get you from where you are to where you want to be. Somebody knows how to get you there for somebody has gone where you desire to be, no need to reinvent the wheel just talk to the man that invented it.

You talk to the man by reading his books, listening to his tapes, going to his seminars and then applying what you learn. As Christians, we've become so spiritual that we believe that God will tell us everything to do; this isn't so, if it were then God would not have blessed men and women with the gift of writing, the gift of teaching and given us all these modern days' inventions of learning.

Use what's out there, it's not sinful to read a book by a man that's telling you how to be financially free and he's not a Christian, this man obviously have tapped into something that has caused him to increase, prosper or become financially wealthy. Take the time to learn what this person has learned whether they are saint or sinner as long as they're telling you truth that is legal and you're able to apply it.

Throughout the scriptures, we have an abundance of word that accentuates to us the importance of learning, counsel and acquiring knowledge. As saints of God, we haven't yet learned the importance of increasing our learning; the world has learned it and applies it faithfully. The scriptures say, *"The children* of this world are in their generation wiser than the children of light." Luke 16:8

The word of God consistently tells us about learning saying,

*"A wise man will hear, and will increase learning; and a man of understanding shall attain unto wise counsels." Proverbs 1:5*

*"Yea, if thou criest after knowledge, and liftest up thy voice for understanding; If thou seekest her as silver, and searchest for her as for hid treasures; Then shalt thou understand the fear of the LORD, and find the knowledge of God." Proverbs 2:3-5*

*"Hear instructions, and be wise, and refuse it not. Blessed is the man that heareth me, watching daily at my gates, waiting at the posts of my doors. For whoso findeth me findeth life, and shall obtain favour of the LORD." Proverbs 8:33-35*

*"Give instruction to a wise man, and he will be yet wiser: teach a just man, and he will increase in learning." Proverbs 9:9*

*"Without counsel purposes are disappointed; but in the multitude of counselors they are established." Proverbs 15:22*

*"Every purpose is established by counsel: and with good advice make war." Proverbs 20:18*

The learning and instructions that you need to get you from where you are to where you want to be is written in some book somewhere, is being taught right now at some seminar, is being lectured in some classroom, has being recorded on a tape, video or CD, somebody already knows what you want to know.

God is not going to tell you everything you have to go forth and seek out knowledge, seek out the information that you need that will cause you to increase, prosper and acquire wealth. *Matthew 7:7-8* Knowledge is potential power and the more of it you have and apply the more power you have and the more you're able to do. Little knowledge equals little power, much knowledge equals much power and an abundance of knowledge equals an abundance of power.

*"Wise man lay up knowledge: but the mouth of the foolish is near destruction." Proverbs 10:14*

*"Whoso loveth instruction loveth knowledge: but he that hateth reproof is brutish." Proverbs 12:1*

*"Also, that the soul be without knowledge, it is not good." Proverbs 19:2*

From this day forward, make it your business to get the necessary knowledge that you need to help you get ahead in the game of life. Knowledge is available everywhere you turn it's dispersed abroad and waiting for you to come after it.

Do whatever you have to do to get your condition equivalent to your position, go back to school, take up a home-study course, a course on the internet, buy the necessary books, tapes, video, CD that you need, just do something and do it now. This might seem elementary to say but stop waiting around for some great move of God upon your life to tell you go better your life, common sense tells you to better your life so that you can come out of your financial sick situation.

1. Shake yourself loose from that spirit of indecision that hounds you daily to the point where you want take that class you need to further yourself.

2. Shake yourself loose from that spirit of slothfulness that slows you down from going forward to attain that which you financially desire in life

3. Shake yourself loose from that spirit of procrastination that causes you to keep putting off doing what you know you need to do to see a change in your financial life.

4. Shake yourself loose from that spirit of laziness that makes you lethargy, sluggish and idle to

the point that you have no get up and go about you to attain that which you desire.

In the name of Jesus Christ bind that spirit and command it to go from your life so that you can be about your father's business and accomplish the things he has destined for your life. From this day forward let your daily word be action for it's action that gets things done, knowledge alone will not get it, action needs to be applied to the knowledge that you learn. *"Even so faith, if it hath not works (action), is dead, being alone. Yea, a man may say, Thou hast faith, and I have works: shew me thy faith without they works, and I will shew thee my faith by my works. But wilt thou know, O vain man, that faith without works (action) is dead, being alone. For as the body without the spirit is dead, so faith without works is dead also." James 2:14-26 So let us hear the conclusion of the whole matter of getting your condition to meet your position:*

- You can go no further than what you know therefore you must acquire knowledge.

- You must know what you want in life.

- Say a financial goal that you desire to have in life aloud right now.

- You must have a vision and objective to strive

for you must have a prosperity target to shoot for.

- God's thoughts toward you, is peace not evil to give you an expected end.

- You must have a strategy, a plan, an approach, a tactic, or a line of attack to get you from where you are to where you want to be.

- You must learn from others who have gone where you desire to be.

- Read their books; listen to their tapes, videos, CD's etc.

- JUST DO SOMETHING AND DO IT NOW!

- Shake yourself loose from indecision, slothfulness, procrastination and laziness.

- Let your daily word be ACTION!

Doing these things will assist you in getting your condition equivalent to your position, not to have your condition equivalent to your position is to settle for life's crumbs when you could have had the whole cake. In life you need money to meet life situations and God has made it so that the green stuff is the medium that God has ordained to answer your natural life situations. For he said, *"money is a defense and money answereth all things."* *Ecclesiastes 7:12a, 10:19b* Now go and get your money, that portion that rightfully belongs to you as a citizen of the kingdom *"to whom God hath given riches and wealth, and hath given him power to eat thereof, and to take his portion, and to rejoice in his labour; this is the gift of God."* *Ecclesiastes 5:19*

# 39
# The Power of Praise

*"He staggered not at the promise of God through unbelief; but was strong in faith, **giving glory to God.**" Romans 4:20*

Praise is a missing spiritual weapon in the lives of the citizens of the Kingdom. As a citizen you must use this awesome weapon to get victory in your financial situation. There is power in praise, not in the praise that comes forth after a victory has been won but the praise that comes forth before the victory or while the battle is going on. I can't think of a better display of praise before victory than the story of Jehoshaphat when he was confronted by the armies that were coming after him. Within this story you will see how God wrought victory through praise, not by natural weapons but by the spiritual weapon of praise. Your victory in your finances will come also through praise!

So the story goes; *It came to pass after this also, that the children of Moab, and the children of Ammon, and with them other beside the Ammonites, came against Jehoshaphat to battle. Then there came some that told Jehoshaphat, saying, There cometh a great multitude against thee from beyond the sea on this side Syria; and, behold, they be in Hazazontamar, which is Engedi. And Jehoshaphat feared, and set himself to seek the LORD, and proclaimed a fast throughout all Judah. And Judah gathered themselves together, to ask help of the LORD: even out of all the cities of Judah they came to seek the* LORD. *And Jehoshaphat stood in the congregation of Judah and Jerusalem, in the house of the* LORD, *before the new court, And said, O* LORD *God of our fathers, art not thou God in heaven? and rulest not thou over all the kingdoms of the heathen? and in thine hand is there not power and might, so that none is able to withstand thee?*

*Art not thou our God, who didst drive out the inhabitants of this land before thy people Israel, and gavest it to the seed of Abraham thy friend for ever? And they dwelt therein, and have built thee a sanctuary therein for thy name, saying, If, when evil cometh upon us, as the sword, judgment, or pestilence, or famine, we stand before this house, and in thy presence, (for thy name is in this house,) and cry unto thee in our affliction, then thou wilt hear and help. And now, behold, the children of Ammon and Moab and mount Seir, whom thou wouldest not let Israel invade, when they came out of the land of Egypt, but they turned from them, and destroyed them not;*

*Behold, I say, how they reward us, to come to cast us out of thy possession, which thou hast given us to inherit. O our God, wilt thou not judge them? for we have no might against this great company that cometh against us; neither know we what to do: but our eyes are upon thee. And all Judah stood before the* LORD, *with their little ones, their wives, and their children. Then upon Jahaziel the son of Zechariah, the son of Benaiah, the son of Jeiel, the son of Mattaniah, a Levite of the sons of Asaph, came the Spirit of the* LORD *in the midst of the congregation;*

*And he said, Hearken ye, all Judah, and ye inhabitants of*

*Jerusalem, and thou king Jehoshaphat, Thus saith the LORD unto you, Be not afraid nor dismayed by reason of this great multitude; for the battle is not yours, but God's. To morrow go ye down against them: behold, they come up by the cliff of Ziz; and ye shall find them at the end of the brook, before the wilderness of Jeruel. Ye shall not need to fight in this battle: set yourselves, stand ye still, and see the salvation of the LORD with you, O Judah and Jerusalem: fear not, nor be dismayed; to morrow go out against them: for the LORD will be with you.* **(When you begin to praise God steps in on your behalf because you're a citizen of the Kingdom and you're acknowledging him and using the weapons of the word to gain victory. You are not just using natural means to try and manifest a spiritual thing; therefore as you acknowledge him he will direct your paths. God even told them where to find them — at the end of the brook, before the wilderness of Jeruel — he also knows where your financial miracle or supernatural provision is at this very moment.)**

*And Jehoshaphat bowed his head with his face to the ground: and all Judah and the inhabitants of Jerusalem fell before the LORD, worshipping the LORD. And the Levites, of the children of the Kohathites, and of the children of the Korhites,* ***stood up to praise the LORD God of Israel with a loud voice on high.*** *And they rose early in the morning, and went forth into the wilderness of Tekoa: and as they went forth, Jehoshaphat stood and said, Hear me, O Judah, and ye inhabitants of Jerusalem;* ***Believe in the LORD your God, so shall ye be established; believe*** *his prophets, so shall ye prosper. And when he had consulted with the people, he appointed singers unto the* LORD, *and that should* **praise** *the beauty of holiness, as they went out before the army, and to say,* **Praise the** LORD; *for his mercy endureth for ever.*

*And when they began to sing and* **to praise**, **(your financial victory is in your right now praise—don't wait until the battle is over shout now)** *the* LORD *set ambushments against the children of Ammon, Moab, and mount Seir, which were come against Judah; and they were smitten. For the children of Ammon and Moab stood up against the inhabitants of mount Seir, utterly to slay and destroy them: and when they had made an end of the inhabitants of Seir, every one helped to destroy another. And when Judah came toward the watch tower in the wilderness, they looked unto the multitude, and, behold, they were dead bodies fallen to the earth, and none escaped. And when Jehoshaphat and his people came to take away the spoil of them, they found among them in abundance both riches with the dead bodies, and precious jewels, which they stripped off for themselves, more than they could carry away: and they were three days in gathering of the spoil, it was so much.(Victory is waiting your praise) And on the fourth day they assembled themselves in the valley of Berachah; for there they blessed the* LORD: *therefore the name of the same place was called, The valley of Berachah, unto this day.*

*Then they returned, every man of Judah and Jerusalem, and Jehoshaphat in the forefront of them, to go again to Jerusalem with joy; for the* LORD *had made them to rejoice over their enemies. And they came to Jerusalem with psalteries and harps and trumpets unto the house of the LORD. And the fear of God was on all the kingdoms of those countries, when they had heard that the LORD fought against the enemies of Israel. So the realm of Jehoshaphat was quiet: for his God gave him rest round about. 2 Chronicles 20:1-30*

Likewise God is ready to give you rest in your financial life. However, your rest will only come as you operate in the spiritual realm and allow God to lead and guide you. Jehoshaphat would have never got victory with natural weapons against this army he needed supernatural help from God. In your financial situation some of you have been struggling for 5, 10, 20 + years and you still see no breakthrough on the horizon. Your breakthrough will come as you apply praise to your situation.

Your victory is in your praise, if you want to see the manifestation of God then begin now to give God praise for your financial breakthrough and miracle. Remember, when God saw the singing and praises of Jehoshaphat and Judah *"the LORD set ambushments against the children of Ammon, Moab, and mount Seir, which were come against Judah; and they were smitten. For the children of Ammon and Moab stood up against the inhabitants of mount Seir, utterly to slay and destroy them: and when they had made an end of the inhabitants of Seir, every one helped to destroy another. And when Judah came toward the watch tower in the wilderness, they looked unto the multitude, and, behold, they were dead bodies fallen to the earth, and none escaped. And when*

*Jehoshaphat and his people came to take away the spoil of them, they found among them in abundance both riches with the dead bodies, and precious jewels, which they stripped off for themselves, more than they could carry away: and they were three days in gathering of the spoil, it was so much."2 Chronicles 20:22-25* Get your praise on now and give God the glory due his name for you shall not need to fight this financial battle as the world do *for the battle is not yours, but God's. 2 Chronicles 20:15c*

# 40
# Jehovah-Jireh

*"And Abraham called the name of that place Jehovah Jireh: as it is said to this day, In the mount of the LORD it shall be seen."* Genesis 23:14

As we come to a close of this book we could not conclude it without talking about one of the compound names of God. One way to discover what God is truly like is to look at his names, as we observe the name Jehovah-Jireh it helps us to understand one of the characteristics of God. In the name Jehovah Jireh it helps us to know God as:

- The God of supernatural provision.
- The God that makes a way out of no way.
- The God that sees.
- The God that knows.
- The God that provides.

The understanding of the Name of Jehovah-Jireh is seen in the book of Genesis when God asked Abraham to *"Take now thy son, thine only son Issac, whom thou lovest, and get thee into the land of Moriah; and offer him there for a burnt offering upon one of the mountains which I will tell thee of."* Genesis 22:2 God was putting Abraham to the test but unbeknown to Abraham God had a plan already destined to provide for him.

Your walk with God is a walk of faith and when

you don't even see a way you must believe and know that the way is already made. You must be like Abraham and go forth with what you have and believe God to provide what you need. The word of God says, *"And Issac spake unto Abraham his father, and said, My father: and he said, Here am I, my son. And he said, Behold the fire and the wood: but where is the lamb for a burnt offering? And Abraham said, My son, **God will provide** himself a lamb for a burnt offering: so they went both of them together."* Genesis 22:7-8

The meaning of the name Jehovah-Jireh is:

- The Lord who provides.
- The Lord who sees.
- The Lord who will see to it.

When you are in need you want to know the one who provides and will see to it that your needs are met. Jehovah-Jireh is the one who will meet your need and he will meet it right on time. When Abraham was about to slay his son, Jehovah-Jireh stepped in right on time. *"And Abraham stretched forth his hand, and took the knife to slay his son. And the angel of the LORD called unto him out of heaven, and said, Abraham, Abraham: and he said, Here am I. And he said, Lay not thine hand upon the lad, neither do thou any thing unto him: for now I know that thou fearest God, seeing thou hast not withheld thy son, thine only son from me. And Abraham lifted up his eyes, and looked, and behold behind him a ram caught in a thicket by his horns: and*

*Abraham went and took the ram, and offered him up for a burnt offering in the stead of his son." Genesis 22:10-13*

God will meet you at the point of your need and provide for you exactly what you need. He is faithful that promised and he is the same God of yesterday, today and forever. You can trust him to come through for you just as he did for Abraham and he know how to come through for you whether you need:

- A miracle
- A supernatural intervention
- Divine provision
- Your personal Red Sea opened
- Or water turned into wine

He has promised to meet your every need and he is a God that you can trust. From this day forward take your rightful position as a citizen of the kingdom, knowing that God is faithful that promised. This is the day of abundance for the people of God; no longer will you take a back seat to the enemy, the world, circumstances or mankind. You are not a beggar you are a king and you serve the King of kings. Jehovah-Jireh is your provider and he is the omniscience, omnipotent and omnipresence God.

Lift up your head and tell the world about the God you serve. This is our day before the coming of Christ to let the world know we serve the God of

Abraham, Issac and Jacob, the God of our Lord Jesus Christ. He is the Almighty God and:

- The God of Money
- The God of Abundance
- The God of Increase
- The God of Prosperity
- The God of Wealth

*"And Abraham called the name of that place Jehovah-Jireh: as it is said to this day, In the mount of the LORD it shall be seen. And the angel of the LORD called unto Abraham out of heaven the second time, And said, By myself have I sworn, saith the LORD, for because thou hast done this thing, and hast not withheld thy son, thine only son: That in blessing I will bless thee, and in multiplying I will multiply thy seed as the stars of the heaven, and as the sand which is upon the sea shore; and thy seed shall possess the gate of his enemies. And in thy seed shall all* **the nations of the earth be blessed; (as a citizen of the kingdom you are Christ's, And if you be Christ's, then are ye Abraham's seed, and heirs according to the promise)** *because thou hast obeyed my voice." Genesis 22:14-18, Galatians 3:29*

Hallelujah it's our time and God is ready to make some of his people millionaires and billionaires for the propagating of the gospel and also so that you can enjoy life. It will not be by your own might and power but by the power of God. *"But thou shalt remember the LORD thy God: for it is he that giveth thee power to get wealth, that he may establish his covenant which he sware unto thy fathers, as it is this day. Beware that thou forget not the LORD thy God, in not keeping his commandments, and his jugements, and his statues, which I command thee this day. Lest when thou hast eaten and art full, and hast built goodly houses, and dwelt therein; And when thy herds and thy flocks multiply (thy business and thy things multiply), and thy silver and thy gold is multiplied (thy money and they accounts is multiplied), and all that thou hast is multiplied; Then thine heart be lifted up, and thou forget the LORD thy God, which brought thee forth out of the land of Egypt (the world), from the house of bondage (your former days of paycheck living, lack and barely making ends meet). Genesis 8:18, 9:11-14*

Truly money answers all things (all natural things), but the most important thing in the world is your soul. *"For what is a man profited, if he shall gain the whole world, and lose his own soul? or what shall a man give in exchange for his soul?* So in all your getting make sure that first and foremost you are always rich towards God and money will be the defence that God will use to protect you from the cares of life. For God's thoughts about money are, *"money answereth all thing and money is a defence." Ecclesiastes 10:19c, 7:12*

## 41
## Psalms for Victory Over the
## Enemy in Your Finances

### Psalms 27

*The LORD is my light and my salvation; whom shall I fear? The LORD is the strength of my life; of whom shall I be afraid?*

*When the wicked, even mine enemies and my foes, came upon me to eat up my flesh, they stumbled and fell.*

*Though and host should encamp against me, my heart shall not fear: though war should rise against me, in this will I be confident.*

*One thing have I desired of the LORD, that will I seek after; that I may dwell in the house of the LORD all the days of my life, to behold the beauty of the LORD, and to enquire in his temple.*

*For in the time of trouble he shall hide me in his pavilion: in the secret of his tabernacle shall he hide me; he shall set me upon a rock.*

*And now shall mine head be lifted up above mine enemies round about me: therefore will I offer sacrifices of joy; I will sing, yea, I will sing praises unto the LORD.*

*Hear, O LORD, when I cry with my voice: have mercy also upon me, and answer me.*

*When thou saidst, Seek ye my face; my heart said unto thee, Thy face, LORD, will I seek.*

*Hide not thy face far from me; put not thy servant away in anger: thou hast been my help; leave me not, neither forsake me, O God of my salvation.*

*When my father and my mother forsake me, then the LORD will take me up.*

*Teach me thy way, O LORD, and lead me in a plain path, because of mine enemies.*

*Deliver me not over unto the will of mine enemies: for false witnesses are risen up against me, and such as breathe out cruelty.*

*I had fainted, unless I had believed to see the goodness of the LORD in the land of the living.*

*Wait on the LORD: be of good courage, and he shall strengthen thine heart: wait, I say, on the LORD.*

## Psalms for Victory Over the Enemy in Your Finances

## Psalms 91

*He that dwelleth in the secret place of the most High shall abide under the shadow of the Almighty.*

*I will say of the LORD, He is my refuge and my fortress: my God; in him will I trust.*

*Surely he shall deliver thee from the snare of the fowler, and from the noisome pestilence.*

*He shall cover thee with his feathers, and under his wings shalt thou trust: his truth shall be thy shield and buckler.*

*Thou shalt not be afraid for the terror by night; nor for the arrow that flieth by day;*

*Nor for the pestilence that walketh in darkness; nor for the destruction that wasteth at noonday.*

*A thousand shall fall at thy side, and ten thousand at thy right hand; but it shall not come nigh thee.*

*Only with thine eyes shalt thou behold and see the reward of the wicked.*

*Because thou hast made the LORD, which is my refuge, even the most High, thy habitation;*

*There shall no evil befall thee, neither shall any plague come nigh thy dwelling.*

*For he shall give his angels charge over thee, to keep thee in all thy ways.*

*They shall bear thee up in their hands, lest thou dash thy foot against a stone.*

*Thou shalt tread upon the lion and adder: the young lion and the dragon shalt thou trample under feet.*

*Because he hath set his love upon me, therefore will I deliver him: I will set him on high, because he hath known my name.*

*He shall call upon me, and I will answer him: I will be with him in trouble; I will deliver him, and honour him.*

*With long life will I satisfy him, and shew him my salvation.*

Read and confess these Psalms daily.

# HERE IS OUR LIST OF KINGDOM BOOKS ON DATING AND MARRIAGE: AVAILABLE AND OTHERS COMING SOON

1. **Kingdom Dating 1** — *Spiritual Dating for citizens of the kingdom of God.*

2. **Kingdom Dating 2** — *Dating for citizens of the kingdom of God*

3. **Kingdom Dating 3--** *Dating a citizen of the kingdom for the purpose of marriage.*

4. **Kingdom Marriage: The Wife's Manual--** *The newlywed wife guide for citizens of the kingdom for a successful and blessed first and second year.*

5. **Kingdom Marriage: The Husband's Manual** — *The newlywed husband's guide for citizens of the kingdom for a successful and blessed first and second year.*

6. **Kingdom Marriages Getting Wealthy** — *Financial & Material Prosperity*

7. **Kingdom Marriages In Ministry** — *Co-Laborers Together In the Work of The Lord.*

8. **Kingdom Marriages Enjoying Each Other** – *Vacation Spots, Restaurants, Outings, Hotels etc...*

9. **Kingdom Marriages Living Healthy** – *God Wants You to Have Long Life and Good Health.*

10. **Kingdom Marriages Bible Study & Prayer Manuel** – *Your Spiritual Weapons to Live Victoriously.*

**Peace and Blessings Throughout Your Life!**

## Website and Email Information

www.moneyanswersallthings.org

info@moneyanswersallthings.org

**Phone: 919-283-9118**